THE FUTURE OF THE
INTERNATIONAL SYSTEM

THE FUTURE OF THE
INTERNATIONAL SYSTEM:

The United States and the
World Political Economy

THEODORE GEIGER

Boston
UNWIN HYMAN
London   Sydney   Wellington

Allen & Unwin, Inc.
8 Winchester Place, Winchester, MA 01890, USA

Published by the Academic Division of
Unwin Hyman Ltd
15/17 Broadwick Street, London W1V 1FP, UK

Allen & Unwin Australia Pty Ltd,
8 Napier Street, North Sydney, NSW 2060, Australia

Allen & Unwin (New Zealand) Ltd, in association with the
Port Nicholson Press Ltd,
60 Cambridge Terrace, Wellington, New Zealand

Library of Congress Cataloging-in-Publication Data

Geiger, Theodore, 1913–
    The future of the international system/Theodore Geiger.   p.   cm.
Bibliography: p.
Includes index.
ISBN 0–04–445094–X.   ISBN 0–04–445100–8 (pbk.)
1. International relations.   2. International economic relations.
3. United States—Foreign relations—1945–   I. Title.
JX1391.G44   1988
327—dc19   87–27080   CIP

British Library Cataloguing-in-Publication Data

Geiger, Theodore
    The future of the international system.
1. International economic relations
2. World politics
I. Title
337   HF1411
ISBN 0–04–445094–X
ISBN 0–04–445100–8 Pbk

Set in 10 on 12 Times Roman by Paston Press, Loddon, Norfolk
and printed in Great Britain by Biddles of Guildford

CONTENTS

TO:

Jessica and Laura,
Jesse, Scott and Adam,
who have improved the present
and will make the future better.

PREFACE

This book has grown out of my efforts to meet the similar needs of two different groups. The first are graduate students in the Master of Science in Foreign Service Program at the Edmund A. Walsh School of Foreign Service, Georgetown University, where I have been teaching since 1980. The second are top-level executives of multinational corporations and banks, labor unions and farm organizations who have served on the international-affairs committees of the National Planning Association (NPA), where I was formerly Director of International Studies. The requirements of the two groups are similar because, while the second comprises existing policymakers, the first consists of students training to become future policymakers in government and the private sector.

As present or prospective policymakers, both groups are or will be engaged in trying to cause something desired to happen or to prevent something undesired from happening by means of a proposed future course of action or inaction—that is, a policy. Therefore, the effectiveness of their efforts depends upon how well they understand the political, economic, other institutional, and psychocultural factors, at both national and international levels, that are likely to determine the outcomes they seek and how the operation of these factors could be influenced by their decisions and actions.

Both groups have expressed the need for a short, interdisciplinary, nontechnical analysis of the contemporary international system and its prospects that would improve their ability to grasp the major characteristics of its structure, modes of functioning, and processes of change. The existing histories of the international system provide factual accounts of the evolution of its political and economic relations, but these and the other aspects are not always adequately interrelated and the wealth of detail often obscures the essential features of the system as a whole. Although the theoretical studies focus on the structure and functional processes of the international system, they are generally too technical and too abstracted from the complexities of real-life events and policy issues to be readily useful to policymakers. Also, both the historical and the theoretical works devote little, if any, space to forecasting the development of the international system.

This book attempts to fill these gaps in the existing literature. It analyzes (1) the system of world political and economic order established during the postwar period, the quarter century after World War II; (2) the changes at national and international levels that have been transforming the system during the 1970s and 1980s and that set the limits of the possible within which policy choices could be effective; (3) the more and less likely ways in which the system could develop over the foreseeable future, the next twenty-five years or so; and (4) some of the implications for the international role of the United States.

The review in Chapters II and III of the changing nature of the international system since World War II is included for two reasons. The first is that many of the current developments in the international system cannot be adequately understood without knowledge of their historical backgrounds. The second is to counteract the widespread tendency to regard the policy prescriptions of earlier decades as still effective in coping with the problems of today and tomorrow. One of the book's most important purposes, therefore, is to encourage students and policymakers not to walk backward into a future mistakenly assumed to be like the past but rather to look forward to the quite different conditions that lie ahead.

In recent years, analysts of international affairs have stressed that changes in the relative capabilities of the nation-states comprising the international system have been eroding U.S. power and influence. Yet, policymakers and opinion leaders have generally not recognized that the decline of U.S. power and influence has in turn been having a reciprocal effect on the nature of the international system. Their implicit assumption is that the diminishing U.S. role does not substantially affect the determinative characteristics of the international system, which will continue to function much as it has been doing.

In contrast, this book presents a new approach to understanding the present and prospective nature of the international system. Just as the hegemonic role of the United States was one of the necessary conditions for the unprecedentedly high levels of economic integration and political coordination that characterized the international system (outside the Soviet hegemony) during the postwar period, so the waning power and influence of the United States in the present period are in part responsible for the system's gradually declining integration and coordination since the 1960s. In part, too, the disintegrative trends reflect certain major sociocultural changes—surveyed in Chapters IV, V, and VI—within the member nations, including the United States, whose deeply rooted nature and consequences for their external relations are overlooked or underestimated by policy-makers and opinion leaders. And because these developments at inter-national and national levels make restoration of a U.S. hegemony very improbable, the disintegrative trends in the international system are in all likelihood irreversible, as explained in Chapter VII. This prospect has important implications for some of the most perplexing issues confronting the United States, such as the future of NATO and of international trade and monetary relations—implications which run counter to present U.S. assumptions and policies and which are discussed in Chapters VIII, IX, and X.

To make the analysis of these admittedly large and complex subjects as readable as possible, the book employs a wide-focus lens to encompass what during World War II used to be called "the Big Picture." Individual aspects of this panorama will no doubt be familiar to the policymakers and opinion leaders and the students and general readers for whom the book is intended. My hope, however, is that they will gain a better understanding of the various parts by viewing all of them together in a developmental perspective from the past to the future.

For the same reason, I have written the book in the style of a cursive essay rather than that of a detailed technical text with exhaustive references to the work of other scholars. Notes have been limited to the occasional elabora-tion of a specific point in the main text, and the short annotated bibliog-raphies for each chapter (grouped in the Bibliographical Appendix) are included simply to indicate fuller explanations or variant interpretations of subjects covered and the sources of the statistical data. Primarily, the book embodies my own experiences as a longtime participant in the Washington Foreign-policy community and the information and ideas derived from recurrent field study abroad and research over many years. (Earlier publica-tions of mine that anticipated some of the key ideas in this book are noted in the Bibliographical Appendix.)

The book does, however, include a brief technical appendix. It contains definitions of the key terms in the analysis—such as *society, culture, nation-state, international system, hegemony, market* and *nonmarket economic systems, power* and *influence, integration* and *coordination*—and a short account of my conceptual approach to understanding the nature of the interrelations between the international system and its constituent nation-states.

I am very pleased to express my gratitude for the encouragement and help I received from the two groups whose interest originally stimulated me to write this book: the members of the NPA's Committee on Changing

International Realities who read and commented on the first draft, and the students in Georgetown University's MSFS Program whose appreciative reactions to the draft also revealed interpretations and statements that needed to be clarified. Others who read the draft and gave me valuable suggestions were my former colleagues at NPA, Peter Morici and Neil McMullen (now at the World Bank); my present colleague at Georgetown University, John R. McNeill; Joseph Cirincione, a former student and now a staff member of the House of Representatives Armed Services Committee; and Robert O. Keohane of Harvard University. I am grateful to Sara N. Krulwich of the NPA for providing much of the statistical data and to former students Mark A. Buening and Peter D. Gaw for research assistance. I am indebted to my son-in-law Loren F. Ghiglione for his helpful suggestions for more effective ways to present the material and to Karen S. Feinstein for her careful and perceptive editing of the revised draft. Naturally, I assume full responsibility for the views expressed in the book and for any errors of fact it may contain.

This book is one of the products of my research program at the School of Foreign Service, the costs of which have been funded in part by grants from Exxon, Chevron, the Scaife Family Charitable Trusts, Pioneer Hi-Bred International Inc., Phillips Petroleum Co., Bristol-Myers Co., Gulf Oil Corporation, and the Dover Fund. I am most grateful for the generous financial help of these donors, who are in no way responsible for the views expressed herein.

Once again, I have the happy task of acknowledging the indispensable contribution of Frances M. Geiger, my wife. Despite her own busy schedule, she read every draft, gave me many valuable suggestions for improving the substance and the writing, and tried valiantly—this time, I must admit, with somewhat less success than in the past—to infuse my perspectives on the future with her own hopeful view of what is likely to be accomplished.

THEODORE GEIGER

Edmund A. Walsh School of Foreign Service
Georgetown University
July 1987

THE FUTURE OF THE
INTERNATIONAL SYSTEM

Chapter I

MAINTAINING THE INTEGRATION OF A SYSTEM OF NATION-STATES

The existing international system is unique; never before in human history has the entire planet been organized into a system of interacting independent nation-states. This system includes some 160 nations, well over half of which have achieved their independence only since World War II. While they already have or are in process of developing the institutional and cultural form of a nation-state, the members of the system differ widely in the ways in which and the extent to which they have realized these characteristics, as well as in their formative historical experiences. These sociocultural differences and those in population size and natural-resource endowments account for the substantial disparities in the economic, political, and military capabilities of the various nation-states and the divergences in their conceptions of their external interests and of the policies required to advance or protect them.

How can such disparate independent nation-states function together as an integrated international system? This chapter explains briefly those aspects of an answer to this question that are crucial for the analysis in the succeeding chapters.

NATIONAL INDEPENDENCE AND INTERNATIONAL INTERDEPENDENCE

The network of interactions between nation-states constitutes an *international system* because each member is significantly affected by its political, economic, and other functional relationships with other members and by the

1

totality of such relationships, that is, by the nature of the system as a whole. For a nation to be "significantly affected" by its external relationships means that they are among the necessary factors that account for its internal condition and its development over time. The nature of the international system is defined by the structure of the relative positions of power and influence of its members and by the norms of behavior that shape their functional interactions. These structural and functional characteristics of the international system change over time as the members' motivations and relative capabilities change. Thus, the individual nation-states and the international system have a mutually determinative relationship because changes at each level are among the necessary causes of changes at the other level. (See the Technical Appendix for a fuller explanation of the nature of the international system and of its interactions with its constituent nation-states.)

Moreover, the international system includes much more than the interactions among national governments and between them and the international (i.e., intergovernmental) institutions. Equally important are the functional relations across national boundaries of private organizations, groups, and individuals that are carried on for economic, scientific, religious, educational, philanthropic, and other purposes, as well as the relations between them and their own and other governments and the international institutions.

The fact that the internal conditions and developmental processes of the system's members are significantly affected by their interactions with their external environment means that they are more or less interdependent and integrated with one another (see the Technical Appendix for a fuller explanation of integration). The greater the degree of interdependence of the members, the less freedom they have unilaterally to determine their own internal and external affairs. This inverse relation reflects not only the limitations on and the opportunities for action inherent in the nature of the system but also the additional constraints on the members' behavior—that is, the explicit obligations and rules—that are required to maintain a high level of integration in the system. Conversely, to the extent that the members restrict their external relationships, thereby limiting their interdependence and increasing their national freedom of action, the system has fewer and looser rules and a correspondingly lower degree of integration.

Therefore, the more integrated an international system is, the more stable and calculable are its members' interactions and vice versa. Thus, the kind and degree of integration that characterizes an international system indicate the kind and degree of order that prevails within it. At one extreme, integration could be so high that the member states would no longer exercise enough of the essentials of national sovereignty to be considered independent and their system of relationships would have the structural form of a world government or a universal empire. At the other extreme, integration could be so low that the nation-states involved would be approaching the point where they no longer would constitute a system of any kind because the relationships among them would not significantly affect their internal conditions and future development. Under present conditions, both extremes are hypothetical possibilities.

During the postwar period—roughly the twenty-five years after World War II—the international system as a whole was subdivided into two groups of countries under the respective leadership of the two superpowers, the United States and the Soviet Union, and each group became highly integrated, although in different ways. Since the end of the postwar period in the late 1960s or early 1970s, however, integration has been declining among the larger group of nations that, as will be explained in Chapter II, were willing members or inadvertent associates of the U.S.-dominated system. The rest of this chapter explains briefly certain basic concepts relating to the benefits and costs of international integration and the conditions for maintaining a high level of integration that are essential for understanding the nature of the international system in the postwar period, how its characteristics have been changing during the 1970s and 1980s, and how they are likely to continue to change over the foreseeable future.

THE BENEFITS AND COSTS OF INTERNATIONAL INTEGRATION

A highly integrated international system with a predominantly market economy, such as that constructed under U.S. leadership during the postwar period, generates both benefits and costs for its members. The major benefit of political coordination has been the high degree of external security—and in some cases also of internal political stability—enjoyed not only by nations formally allied with the United States but also by the many others whose independence has been implicitly protected by it. The benefits of cultural integration have been the opportunities for improvement in the quality of life and the advancement of knowledge made possible by exposure to different values, ideas, technologies, aesthetic expressions, life-styles, and other cultural manifestations. The benefits of economic integration have been the increases in employment and incomes resulting from the higher rates of economic growth that—all other things being equal—are stimulated by the relatively free flows of goods, services, financial resources, technologies, and managerial skills across national boundaries.

The cost of international political and defense coordination is the corresponding reduction of national freedom of action in the pursuit of foreign-policy and security goals. This loss may be significant in terms of a nation's ability to advance or protect the conceptions of its external interests that predominate among its policymakers and opinion leaders and, hence, may be an important issue in its domestic politics. Similarly, the cost of unimpeded cultural diffusion may be the weakening of the regime in power or the impairment of a society's sense of its unique identity and destiny as expressed, for example, in its religious commitment or its sense of mission.

The costs of economic integration arise essentially from two characteristics of any system of freely trading and investing market economies. The first is that, under certain supply and demand conditions, an exporting country or group of exporting countries can become a monopolistic or oligopolistic supplier of a scarce commodity. Hence, it could drastically raise prices and/or restrict shipments to dependent importing nations that would suffer losses of income if they lacked the ability to obtain offsetting gains in their own exports.

The second characteristic is more pervasive and continuous. Economists call it the *adjustment process*, and it can operate at both macro and micro levels in a national economy. At the macro level, a nation's fiscal, monetary, and other policies may cause the country's general price and demand levels to diverge so widely from those of its major trading partners and competitors as to impose serious competitive disadvantages on its producers and sometimes to generate an unmanageably large balance-of-payments deficit. The correction of these effects usually requires restrictive measures that adversely affect employment and incomes. At the micro level, a country may have to shift labor and financial resources out of particular activities that have lost competitiveness in domestic and foreign markets due to the failure of its producers to improve their productivity relative to the greater efficiency or the lower-cost factors of production (labor, natural resources, capital, technology) of the producers of other countries. The adjustment process is always more or less painful depending on the magnitude of the initial loss of employment and incomes and the length of time required for restrictive measures to bring the country's economy back into line with those of its trading partners and/or for labor and financial resources to be shifted to more competitive activities.

On the import side, the benefits of international economic integration are usually obtained in the short term in the form of the lower prices and/or higher quality of goods and services available to consumers. On the export side, however, the benefits to employment and incomes generally take much longer to be realized because they often depend upon developing new or expanding existing productive facilities and selling their output in unfamiliar foreign markets. In contrast, most costs to employment and incomes of economic integration tend to be felt as soon as a country's producers lose competitiveness in their own and foreign markets. In these circumstances, the pressures to avoid or minimize the short-term costs may prevail over those to retain or increase both the short- and the long-term benefits. The well-organized groups of adversely affected domestic producers (both management and labor) press for immediate palliatives, such as protection against imports or subsidies for noncompetitive exports, instead of undertaking the often slow, arduous, and—especially for the workers—painful remedial measures required. As such protectionist pressures grow, the inchoate mass of consumers who benefit from imports and the producers who continue to benefit from exports may sooner or later lack sufficient political influence to counteract those forces.

THE PREREQUISITES FOR INTERNATIONAL INTEGRATION

So long as the short- and long-term benefits are clearly perceived as exceeding the short-term costs, nation-states are inclined to seek or acquiesce in membership in a highly integrated international system. In other words, they have a rational interest in preserving and increasing the integration of the system. To do so, they must be willing and able to obey the rules of behavior required to maintain its economic and cultural openness and political coordination, to settle issues and disputes by compromise and concession, and to endure the costs of the adjustment process until changes in economic policies and/or shifts in human and financial resources produce the needed effects. In essence, nation-states' pursuit of their self-interests— that is, their *particularistic* behavior—has to be guided and restrained by their commitment to the *universalistic* goal of preserving the integration of the system as a whole for the benefit of all.

However, the rational interest of any member or group of members can be perceived as also being served by actions that disregard the necessary rules of conduct. Immediate benefits obtained by this kind of particularistic behavior—for example, subsidizing noncompetitive exports—although they may be smaller than anticipated long-term gains from universalistic self-restraint, are usually less uncertain—"a bird in the hand is worth two in the bush" is a rational maxim. Short-term costs can readily be minimized, for example, by avoiding or passing on to others the burden of the adjustment process through restricting imports and engaging in many other kinds of discriminatory trade and monetary policies. Economists call such particularistic actions manifestations of the *free-rider problem*. Because the behavior involved is rational, the free-rider problem is endemic in any international system that is dependent on the voluntary cooperation and self-restraint of its sovereign members.

This is not to imply that nations always make conscious decisions to become free-riders. Sometimes, they are so owing to the inertia of long-standing self-protective policies despite their growing capabilities, as in the case of Japan's retention of restrictions on imports long after it has become a substantial net exporter. Countries may also become free-riders through the accretion of new particularistic measures that gradually wear away what they continue to regard as their universalistic commitment; witness the growing protectionism of the European Community and the United States since the early 1970s. Often, the determinative considerations are complex and ambivalent and the trade-off between long- and short-term benefits and costs is not readily apparent. What counts, however, are not the intentions but the effects of the actions. Whether a nation is a free-rider depends on whether its particularistic behavior significantly erodes the economic integration or political coordination of the system either directly or by impelling others to take actions that do.

Thus, rational interest operates ambivalently. On the one hand, it supports the long-term universalistic interest of all in the maintenance of international integration. On the other hand, it impels individual countries and groups of countries to seek to realize their short-term particularistic interests and thereby either deliberately or unintentionally to erode integration. This basic ambivalence is manifested not only within each set of functional relationships but also in trade-offs between them. Nation-states may be willing to forgo economic benefits or incur economic losses as the price of freedom of action to pursue national political goals, internal or external, or to protect their senses of cultural identity, and vice versa. Such behavior is not "irrational" but reflects the greater importance attached to one set of a country's interests compared to other sets of interests by the regime in power, or by influential organizations and groups, or as the result of the more general processes of attitude formation within the society, or some combination of these factors.

In sum, the more highly integrated an international system is, the greater are the basic tensions within it between the pressures to obtain the benefits of international interdependence and the pressures to limit the costs by preserving and increasing national freedom of action.

Given these basic tensions, rational interest operates too ambivalently to be the *sufficient condition* for maintaining a high degree of political and economic integration in an international system based on the universalistic commitment, voluntary cooperation, and self-restraint of the members. Rational interest is unquestionably a necessary condition but it needs to be buttressed by another prerequisite: the presence of something with the power to constrain and the influence to persuade the members to refrain from particularistic actions that would significantly erode the degree of integration already attained by the system or prevent it from developing a greater degree of integration. In theory, this other necessary condition could be met by a supranational authority with the power to compel members to comply with the rules of behavior and to settle disputes among them. However, such a manifestation of world government does not exist and is unlikely to be created in the foreseeable future. In the postwar period, this second necessary condition was met by the existence within the system of a member state possessed of the requisite power and influence and convinced that its own interest required it to use them to maintain a high degree of international integration—in short, a *hegemonic leader*.

A hegemonic leader can rely on several means—in addition to the members' rational interest—to attain and preserve a high degree of integration within the system which it dominates. Historically, the most prevalent means have been the members' fear of the hegemon's power to compel them to act in accordance with its objectives, and their belief that it would be willing and able to use its power to force them to do so. Respected hegemons can also rely upon their prestige to persuade members to behave appropriately, among other ways by setting an example for them to follow. Finally, a hegemon can assume a disproportionate share of the costs of integration, thereby making it less burdensome for some or all of the members to endure the adjustment process and to settle their disputes by compromise and concession. The Soviet Union has depended mainly, though not exclusively, on the use of its power and influence. The United States has relied mainly, though not exclusively, on its prestige and influence and on its willingness and ability to bear a disproportionate share of the costs of integration. Indeed, no other hegemon, past or present, has employed the latter means as extensively and effectively as did the United States during the postwar period.

The main thesis of this book stated in the Preface can now be explained more clearly by applying these basic concepts. The attainment by the international system (outside the Soviet hegemony) of an unprecedentedly high level of economic integration and political coordination by the end of the postwar period was possible because *both* of the necessary conditions were present. First, the rational interest of the members in obtaining the short- and long-term benefits of economic integration and political coordination was generally perceived as greater than their rational interest in avoiding the short-term costs. Second, a hegemonic leader existed. That is, a majority of U.S. policymakers and opinion leaders were convinced that the interests of the United States would be best served by a highly integrated international system, and the United States had the power and influence to maintain the requisite rules of behavior and the willingness and ability to bear a disproportionate share of the costs.

In contrast, since the early 1970s, the balance of rational interest has been shifting in more and more nations toward obtaining the short-term benefits of particularistic actions and/or toward avoiding the short-term costs of economic integration and political coordination. At the same time, the relative power and influence of the United States have been declining, as have also its willingness and ability to bear a disproportionate share of the costs. Nor does any other nation, such as Japan, or group of nations, such as the European Community, possess the requisite power and influence and is willing and able to assume the costs that the United States has been or will in the future be relinquishing.

In consequence, international economic integration and political coordination have been gradually eroded in the present period and the system has been becoming less orderly and calculable than it was in the postwar period. These disintegrative trends are likely to continue for the foreseeable future. They reflect the interactions between the changes in the structural and functional characteristics of the international system and those in the motivations and capabilities of the different groups of member nations, including the United States. Given the deeply rooted causes of the disintegrative trends, it is not within the limits of the possible for policymakers to eliminate or reverse them. The changes at international and national levels that generate the disintegrative trends and certain of their implications for the international role and policies of the United States are explained in the chapters that follow.

Chapter II

THE INTERNATIONAL SYSTEM IN THE POSTWAR PERIOD

After World War II, there were only two nation-states motivated and able to provide hegemonic leadership: the United States and the Soviet Union. During the postwar period—the quarter century from 1945 to 1970—each superpower organized a hegemony which differed substantially from that of the other in the nature and extent of its internal integration due to the profound differences between the two hegemons' political and economic systems and psychocultural characteristics. These differences also meant that the interactions between the two hegemonies constituted a balance-of-power system, with the degree of integration between them very much less than that within them. The main focus of this chapter is on the organization and development of the more heterogeneous, loose, and more dynamic hegemony constructed by the United States during the postwar period. The organization of the Soviet hegemony and its relationships with the U.S. hegemony are then covered more briefly.

THE DEVELOPMENT OF THE U.S. HEGEMONY

Well before the end of World War II, U.S. policymakers had outlined the kind of political and economic order they believed should be established once victory was achieved. It would be a worldwide system of independent nation-states willing and able to respect one another's freedom, to settle disputes by peaceful means, and to carry on economic relations with only moderate, if any, barriers to the flow of goods, services, and financial resources between them, which would be applied equally to all members

9

(the most-favored-nation principle). Such a system, it was confidently expected, would foster the development of pluralistic democratic societies, high rates of economic growth, and rising employment and living standards in all members.

When during the immediate postwar years the Soviet Union rejected the U.S. design and advanced its own conception of a desirable political and economic order, U.S. policymakers abandoned their notion of a "one-world" system and focused their efforts on the "free world," that is, the nations outside the then rapidly forming Soviet hegemony. Hence, U.S. objectives also came to include the organization of the "free world" for "collective security" against possible internal communist subversion and external Soviet aggression. As the largest, richest and strongest nation in the system, the United States had, in the words of Adlai Stevenson, "an awesome mission: nothing less than the leadership of the free world."

Naturally, the international system constructed in accordance with these ideas was intended to serve the conceptions of U.S. political and economic interests that predominated within the United States during the postwar period, and there can be no question that it did so. Moreover, as noted below, the United States on occasion used its power to secure advantages for itself at the expense of other members. But, I also believe that, on balance, the other nations that were willing or inadvertent participants in the system obtained greater benefits and incurred lower costs than they would have from any other design for world political and economic order *that would have been within the limits of the possible in the conditions of the postwar period.* Nor is it necessary to settle the question of whether the U.S. objectives outlined above were nothing more than official rhetoric or were sincerely intended to benefit not only the United States but the other members as well. As the Bible says, "by their fruit ye shall know them." The fruit of U.S. hegemonic leadership during the postwar period was an increasingly integrated international system that was conducive in an unprecedented degree to the economic welfare and political security of the great majority of its members, as explained below.

In its fully developed form, the U.S. hegemony consisted of several groups of nation-states differentiated by the degree of their economic and political integration with the United States and with one another. The most tightly integrated, both economically and politically, was the core group comprising the nations of Western Europe, Canada, Japan, Australia, and New Zealand. They were, and continue to be, members of the Organization for Economic Cooperation and Development (OECD) and of either the North Atlantic Treaty Organization (NATO) or the Australia–New Zealand–United States Treaty (ANZUS) or, in the case of Japan, of a bilateral mutual-defense treaty with the United States. Less integrated with the United States and with one another were the Latin American nations associated with the United States in the Organization of American States (OAS) and the Rio Pact, a multilateral mutual-defense treaty. Finally, there was a large, more heterogeneous outer ring of old and new Asian and African nations, some with formal or informal defense arrangements with the United States (e.g., Israel, the Philippines, Taiwan, Thailand, and others) but all dependent on the world market economy and, hence, on the integrated economic system constructed under U.S. leadership.

Economic Integration

The kind and degree of international economic integration established during the postwar period would not have been achieved without the strong insistence of the United States on moving steadily toward that goal and the ideas it generated for doing so. Left to their own inclinations, the West European countries and other OECD nations would have reconstructed a system with a substantially lower level of integration. As they did during the interwar period, they would very probably have retained protection for noncompetitive domestic producers, acquiesced in (if they did not actively promote) monopolies and cartels, engaged in other forms of discriminatory and preferential practices, and maintained significant controls on capital flows. True, as recovery progressed, they would have abolished bilateral barter agreements, detailed licensing of imports and exports, foreign-exchange rationing, and the other expedients adopted to cope with their wartime and immediate postwar shortages of goods and monetary reserves. Nonetheless, my own experiences in the State Department and with the Marshall Plan during the postwar period convinced me that the actions of the United States were crucial in the formation of a multilateral, nondiscriminatory, increasingly competitive, and freely trading international economic system in those years.

The determinative characteristics of this integrated world market economy were defined in the treaties negotiated at the Bretton Woods Conference in 1944, in the General Agreement on Tariffs and Trade (GATT) of 1948, and in their subsequent development and revision. These treaties and agreements committed the signatories to (1) achieving and maintaining convertible currencies, (2) reducing and eventually abolishing tariffs and quantitative restrictions on imports and direct subsidies for exports, and (3) adhering to the rules required for a multilateral system of trade and payments in which all participants would observe the most-favored-nation principle and refrain from discriminatory and preferential measures. Instead of relying only on formal treaties and agreements, the United States also insisted on the establishment of international organizations to supervise their implementation, negotiate steps toward further integration, settle disputes, authorize retaliatory measures against recalcitrant members, and provide aid to help them cope with the costs of integration.

Therefore, the Bretton Woods treaties established the International Monetary Fund (IMF) to work toward and help preserve currency converti- bility and the free flow of capital, and the International Bank for Reconstruc- tion and Development (now known as the World Bank) to provide long-term capital for postwar reconstruction and economic growth. Originally, there was to be a counterpart institution in the trade field, the proposed Inter- national Trade Organization, but the U.S. Congress refused to ratify the treaty because it believed that certain provisions would endow the organiza- tion with supranational powers. To take its place, the president negotiated the GATT as an executive agreement (which hence did not require congres- sional approval). The GATT became a de facto international organization (1) to conduct periodic negotiations for the progressive lowering of trade barriers, (2) to supervise compliance with the code of fair trade practices, and (3) to determine whether members were injured by the failure of any participant to meet its obligations and what retaliatory actions they could take.

All of the core group—the members of the OECD and NATO—joined the two Bretton Woods institutions and the GATT. Most Asian, African, and Latin American nations also became members of the IMF and the World Bank but did so less from commitment to the liberal market principles of these organizations than to obtain access to the substantial resources they could provide. For this reason, too, few of them initially joined the GATT, which had no resources to dispense, although in subsequent years the number of Asian and Latin American members gradually increased.

The Asian, African, and Latin American nations that remained outside the Soviet hegemony ipso facto became participants in this integrated world market economy. They enjoyed the benefits of membership, notably access to the increasingly open markets of the OECD countries and to the resources of the international organizations, even though most of them were unwilling and, in many cases, unable to reciprocate by lowering their own trade and payments barriers and abiding by the rules of the system. Nonetheless, their attitude toward the system soon became ambivalent. On the one hand, they were eager to obtain the benefits of participation. On the other hand, they tended to regard the system as rigged against exporters of raw materials, which most of them were, and in favor of exporters of manufactured goods, which most of the OECD nations were. The gradually growing disaffection from the system first of the Latin American nations and later of the Asian and African countries will be discussed in subsequent chapters. Here I simply wish to make the point that, regardless of whether the U.S.-designed world market economy was unfair to these nations, they would have made out worse had the inclinations of the other OECD members for less integrated and more discriminatory arrangements prevailed in the reconstruction of the system.

Political and Defense Coordination

Paralleling the high degree of economic integration achieved during the postwar period was the unprecedented extent of political and military coordination in NATO—unprecedented, that is, for mutual-defense alliances in peacetime. NATO was, and continues to be, the central and most important unit in the worldwide network of defense arrangements organized by the United States. It is characterized by an integrated command structure, a common military doctrine and common strategic and tactical plans, interdependent services of supply and communications, and an effort—only partially successful—to standardize armaments and other military equipment and to allocate their production among the members. To establish such integrated military arrangements required agreement on the political objectives of NATO and coordination of critical aspects of the foreign policies of the member nations.

In contrast, the other multilateral and bilateral mutual-defense arrangements centered on the United States involved less integration and were more like the kinds of military alliances that had hitherto been customary in peacetime. (The arrangements with South Korea and South Vietnam were, of course, much more integrated because those countries were at war.)

Maintaining Integration and Coordination

During the postwar period, the United States occasionally exerted its power within the hegemony to enforce compliance with its integration and coordination designs, as well as to advance its own interests. For example, it compelled the British to abandon their preferential trade arrangements with the Commonwealth countries (the former members of the British Empire), and it muscled its way into a dominant position in the development of the Persian Gulf oil resources. The United States intervened in Guatemala in 1954 and in the Congo (now Zaire) in the mid-1960s to oust regimes that it regarded as actual or potential Soviet clients. Another example of U.S. intervention was the ill-conceived and poorly executed (and hence unsuccessful) Bay of Pigs attempt in 1961 to overthrow the regime of Fidel Castro in Cuba. During the Suez Crisis of 1956, the United States constrained the British, French, and Israelis to cease their invasion of Egypt and to withdraw. Again, in 1958, 19,000 U.S. marines were landed in Lebanon to put a stop to the first of that country's civil wars, and the internal peace they imposed before their departure lasted until the mid-1970s.

Although it did employ its power on these and other occasions, the United States relied mainly on two other means to institute and maintain economic integration and political coordination within its hegemony—in addition to the rational interest of the members in the benefits they derived therefrom.

The first was the use of its influence. During the 1940s and 1950s, as explained below, the United States occupied by far the predominant position in the world market economy. Most West European nations and Japan relied on U.S. exports of many primary products and manufactured goods essential for feeding and housing their people and rebuilding their war-shattered economies, and on large-scale U.S. aid to provide the means of payment for these and other imports. At the same time, their perception of a growing threat of Soviet expansionism and their inability to provide for their own defense made them dependent on U.S. military protection. Hence, they were inclined to go along with the U.S. design for reconstructing the international system despite any doubts they may have had about its wisdom or practicality and their fears that it might adversely affect their own interests.

The influence of the United States was strongly reinforced by the unprecedentedly high prestige it enjoyed after World War II not only as a major victor in that struggle but, more important, for historical reasons. Since its founding, the United States had projected the image of itself as (in the words of John Winthrop, the first governor of the Massachusetts Bay Colony) a "City upon a Hill, the eies of all people are uppon us." Thus, during the colonial period, it thought of itself as the moral exemplar; after the Revolution, as the sociopolitical model; and, in the 20th century, as the technoeconomic paradigm for other countries to follow. And, it was so regarded by vast numbers of people throughout the world, millions of whom came to its shores during the 19th and 20th centuries in one of history's largest voluntary migrations—indeed, one that continues to this day. After World War I and during the troubled interwar period, U.S. prestige was enhanced by the worldwide respect accorded to Presidents Woodrow Wilson and Franklin Delano Roosevelt, who were regarded as concerned for the liberty and well-being of all peoples and not simply for those of the United

States. Hence, after World War II, not only its allies and the neutral countries but also the defeated nations looked to the United States as the guarantor of a postwar settlement that would lead to peace, freedom, justice, and welfare for all.

True, there were contrary views—of Marxists and others who regarded the United States as the enemy, not the proponent, of such a world order, of intellectuals scornful of American culture, of nationalists resentful of U.S. predominance, and so on. Moreover, from the mid-1950s on, the prestige of the United States gradually declined as the complexities of world politics and economics increasingly impelled it to undertake actions that appeared to compromise its own moral principles or that frustrated the efforts of other members of the system to advance or protect their particularistic interests. Nonetheless, during the crucial formative years of the system in the 1940s and early 1950s, the prestige of the United States was so high among policymakers, opinion leaders, and the people generally in the OECD nations and many other countries that it helped to overcome any misgivings they may have had about the U.S. design for the postwar world order.

The second major means of maintaining economic integration and political coordination was U.S. willingness and ability to bear a disproportionately large share of the costs. The United States did so in three ways.

First, it provided massive economic aid both directly to many countries and indirectly as the main financial contributor to the IMF, the World Bank and, after their establishment, other international lending and grant-giving agencies. For example, during the formative years of the system in the late 1940s and early 1950s, direct U.S. economic assistance averaged 1.3 percent a year of U.S. gross national product (GNP), compared to only 0.2 percent in the 1980s. From 1945 to 1970, the United States provided in total more than $134 billion in direct economic aid and defense-support assistance, mostly in the form of grants, to 130 nations.

Second, the United States assumed by far the largest economic burden and the greatest risk of nuclear destruction in the mutual-defense arrangements. For example, U.S. military expenditures from the mid-1950s to the mid-1960s—that is, after the Korean War and before the buildup for the Vietnam War—averaged nearly 9 percent a year of U.S. GNP, while the allies with the next largest military establishments spent less than half as much of their GNPs.

The third way by which the United States bore a disproportionate share of the costs of international economic integration was by keeping its economy substantially more open than those of its trading partners and competitors and by allowing its currency to be overvalued relative to theirs. That is, as trade barriers were progressively reduced under the GATT, the United States always retained fewer and, for most goods and services, lower restrictions on imports and exports than was the case with any of the other members of the system (except free-trade Hong Kong and Singapore). The U.S. market was by far the largest on the planet: in 1950, U.S. GNP was about half of world GNP and the proportion was still more than a third in 1970; U.S. imports were nearly 16 percent of total world imports in the former year and still 14 percent in the latter. Thus, widening access on nondiscriminatory terms to the expanding U.S. market was a major factor in the steady growth of the exports of the other members of the system, which in turn was a major factor in the ability of many of them to achieve and maintain high rates of GNP growth during the postwar period. Also, their capacity to compete with U.S. products in both the U.S. market and the markets of other countries was enhanced by the gradually increasing over-valuation of the dollar, especially during the 1960s.

Just as the U.S. economy was central to the expansion of trade during the postwar period, so too was the U.S. dollar central to the operation of the gradually restored international financial system. Not only was the major portion of world trade denominated in dollars but they soon came to form the major portion of the monetary reserves that the OECD nations and other countries were slowly rebuilding during the 1950s and 1960s as their production and exports increased. Whereas in 1950 half of world monetary reserves of gold and convertible currencies was held by the United States, its portion of the total dropped to less than a third by 1960 and to a sixth by 1970. Moreover, under the Bretton Woods system, the dollar was the only currency freely convertible into gold at the request of other governments at the fixed price of $35 an ounce; in turn, the exchange rates of their currencies were fixed vis-à-vis the dollar. While other countries could change their exchange rates—and many devalued one or more times during the postwar period—the United States could not do so without changing the price of gold, an action that, it was generally believed, would destabilize the basis of the fixed exchange-rate system and stimulate infla-tion. Hence, the dollar gradually became overvalued in terms of the currencies of other OECD nations and, by the late 1960s, the United States was running a large current-account deficit that was mainly financed by the willingness of other countries to accumulate dollar assets in their monetary reserves. Thus, the U.S. dollar served as the transactions currency, the key currency, and the reserve currency of the international monetary system.

This nonreciprocal relationship between the United States and the other members of the world market economy meant, in theory, that it should be more susceptible than they to the adverse short-term effects of the adjust-ment process. However, this was not the case in reality. For one thing, productivity in many, though by no means all, U.S. industries was sufficiently higher than in those of other countries for much of the postwar period to enable these U.S. producers to retain their competitive advantage at home and abroad. Where it was not, the short-term adjustment costs had a marginal impact on the U.S. economy as a whole, although not, of course, on the noncompetitive companies and their workers. Important as merchandise trade with the United States was to the rest of the world (as noted above), U.S. imports of goods were only 3.2 percent and U.S. exports of goods were only 3.5 percent of U.S. GNP in 1950, 2.9 percent and 3.9 percent respectively in 1960,and 4.0 percent and 4.3 percent respectively in 1970.

In turn, this asymmetrical relationship between the U.S. economy and the world economy during the postwar period made the adjustment costs to the United States of its disproportionate share of the burden of maintaining the integration of the system only marginally significant in terms of the effects on U.S. employment and incomes. It was a quite bearable price to pay, along with the costs of its economic assistance and worldwide military capabilities, for the benefits that the United States, as well as the others, were deriving from the faster economic growth of an increasingly integrated world market economy and the greater security of effectively coordinated political and defense arrangements with its allies.

The Formation of Free-Trade Areas and the Integration of Financial Markets

During the postwar period, the benefits of economic integration were sought not only within the world market economy as a whole and through the liberalized economic relations among the members of the OECD but also within regional and even smaller arrangements. The idea was that these smaller groups of countries would be able to move toward free trade with one another without having to extend the same privileges to the United States and other nations with whose exports they feared that they would be unable to compete. Although this rationale violated the GATT's most-favored-nation principle and its rules against preferential trade relations, the GATT contained an exception for such arrangements provided they were for the purpose of forming a free-trade area or a customs union.

Hence, for both economic and political reasons, the United States began under the Marshall Plan in the late 1940s to support strongly those efforts of certain innovative leaders in France, Germany, Italy, and the Low Countries to form a customs union that would be the first step toward an eventual political union of their nations. Nationalist and protectionist resistance in these countries delayed the progress of the movement for European integration, but an agreement was finally negotiated, and the European Economic Community came into existence in January 1958. At the same time, the United Kingdom, the Scandinavian countries, Switzerland, and Austria formed a more limited free-trade area of their own. Inspired by European success, interest in free-trade areas and customs unions spread to other regions during the 1960s, but negotiations to realize them in Latin America, Central America, Africa, and elsewhere were never concluded or, if they were, could not be implemented or the resulting arrangement soon collapsed.

By the end of the 1960s, the world market economy contained various groups of nations that had greater degrees of economic integration among them than characterized the system as a whole. Enlarged by the addition of the United Kingdom, Ireland, and Denmark in 1973, Greece in 1981, and Spain and Portugal in 1986, the European Community (EC), as it was eventually officially named, became the most integrated after the completion of its customs union in 1967. By then, the OECD nations and the other countries participating in the GATT had finished the sixth round of tariff-cutting negotiations (the so-called Kennedy Round), under which their remaining tariffs on most industrial products were reduced to 10 percent or less. Most of the GATT members also extended these reductions to the nonparticipating Asian, African, and Latin American countries, which thereby enjoyed nonreciprocal access to their markets. Finally, in 1971, the OECD nations adopted the General System of Preferences (GSP), under which, with certain major exceptions, they admitted exports from Asian, African, and Latin American countries on a duty-free basis, again without requiring reciprocal treatment.

The integration of financial markets started later, really only after the restoration of currency convertibility by the West European nations in January 1958, when their rising production, expanding exports, and favorable balances of payments had sufficiently replenished their monetary reserves. By the end of the 1960s, short- and long-term capital was moving freely among the OECD countries, U.S. direct foreign investment was growing substantially, European and Japanese direct foreign investment was beginning to become significant, and the Eurocurrency market—which was to have such spectacular growth during the 1970s—had emerged.

The Benefits of Economic Integration and Political Coordination

Thus, the international economic system became more and more integrated as barriers to trade and monetary flows were progressively reduced and in many cases abolished during the 1950s and 1960s. This increasing integration is indicated by the fact that world trade grew substantially faster than world GNP throughout the postwar period. During the 1950s, world trade grew at an annual average of 6.4 percent while world GNP increased at an annual average of 5.2 percent, and the corresponding annual averages for the 1960s were 9.2 percent and 5.6 percent. This meant that the members' economies were becoming more and more dependent upon foreign trade to help increase and sustain their levels of production and consumption. The average annual real rates of GNP growth enjoyed by the different groups of countries are shown in Table 1.

Table 1
Average Annual Rates of GNP Growth

	Percentages	
	1950–1959	*1960–1969*
United States	3.2	4.6
European Community	5.7	4.6
Japan	9.0	10.5
Canada	4.3	5.6
Asian developing countries	4.0	4.5
African independent countries	4.9	5.2
Latin American countries	5.0	5.5

True, there were other factors involved in these high growth rates besides the expansion of exports made possible by integration. West European and Japanese growth also benefited from the reconstruction of their war-devastated factories and farms with the newest and most productive technologies. Western Europe was able to increase its labor force first from the influx of displaced persons and refugees from Eastern Europe and later by the importation of workers from the Mediterranean, Caribbean, and African countries. Economic growth in the Asian, African, and Latin American countries also depended on the development assistance and private foreign investment provided by the OECD nations directly and through the international organizations. Nonetheless, without the expansion of export market demand made possible by the lowering of trade and payments barriers, especially by the United States and other OECD nations, the opportunities would not have been adequate to induce capital investment and the employment of additional labor on the scale required to achieve the foregoing growth rates.

Political and defense coordination, too, contributed to the high growth rates, rising employment, and improving living standards of the 1950s and 1960s. Of fundamental importance was the fact that such coordination helped the United States to preserve an international environment in which the independence of both old and new nations was reasonably assured. Thus, their national development could proceed as their internal processes of change determined, without critical interventions from outside in most, though not all, cases. In turn, the high degree of international security and calculability gave people the confidence to take advantage of the opportunities to engage in business transactions across national borders. Without such confidence in the peacefulness and orderliness of the system, it is unlikely that international trade and investment would have grown to the levels reached by the end of the period.

In sum, international economic integration, supported by political and defense coordination, was both a cause and a consequence of the unprecedented economic growth enjoyed by most of the participants in the world market economy during the postwar period. The degree of integration already achieved fostered growth and, in turn, the growth already attained gave countries the confidence and the means to participate in further integration. This positive-sum relationship between international integration and economic growth depended not only on the rational interest of the members in obtaining the resulting benefits but also on the power and influence of the United States and its willingness and ability to bear a disproportionate share of the costs involved.

POLITICAL COORDINATION AND ECONOMIC INTEGRATION IN THE SOVIET HEGEMONY

In contrast to the U.S. hegemony, political control and defense coordination were the major bonds within the Soviet hegemony and economic integration was of much less importance.

The design of world order toward which the Soviet Union was working even before the end of World War II was of an international system of socialist states with nonmarket economies and authoritarian political systems controlled by their communist parties. Among them, the Soviet Union would play the dominant role, coordinating protection against outside enemies, expanding the membership as opportunities arose and by any means that did not put its own survival at risk, and guaranteeing the supremacy within the member states of their communist parties, which would be under the tutelage of the Soviet party. Thus, the goal of the Soviet Union has not been a worldwide empire over which it would exercise direct rule, as many Americans have feared. Rather, it was and continues to be to assure the safety of the Soviet Union and to achieve the hegemonic position of world paramountcy to which its ruling elites have been convinced that its historical destiny—as the "Third Rome" under the czars and the "Socialist Fatherland" under the communists—entitled it.

In its fully developed form, the Soviet hegemony has consisted of a group of core states in Eastern Europe and Asia contiguous to the Soviet Union and a group of widely scattered states, some (such as Cuba and Vietnam and its dependencies) firmly under communist party control and others (such as Angola, Ethiopia, Mozambique, and South Yemen) in which communist rule has not yet been fully and securely established. In the early postwar years, China, Yugoslavia, and Albania were members but then seceded at different times to escape Soviet control over their internal affairs. All of the core states became members of the Soviet hegemony owing to their occupation by the Red Army during or after World War II (or after World War I in the case of Mongolia and since 1980 in the case of Afghanistan), and the others as a result of internal revolutions supported by the Soviet Union and their subsequent dependence on its continued assistance.

The principal instrument of Soviet control over the core members of the hegemony—whose loyalty and security it regards as essential to its own protection and the stability of its communist regime—has been the subordination of their communist parties to the Soviet party. This has enabled the Soviet communist party to ensure "the leading positions" of the core members' parties, that is, their unchallenged ability to direct all of the major institutional and cultural elements of their societies and to prevent the emergence of any organizations or groups that might question, let alone threaten, their right and capacity to rule. Nor has the Soviet Union hesitated to intervene by force to make certain that the core members' parties would carry out these responsibilities, as it did in Hungary in 1956, Czechoslovakia in 1968, and nearly had to do in Poland in 1981.

The more distant members of the Soviet hegemony have not been essential to the Soviet Union's own security nor readily accessible to its power either to compel their obedience or to protect them. Hence, they have had significantly greater freedom of action in their internal and external affairs than have the core states and the Soviet communist party has had to play more of an advisory than a directive role. The major means of Soviet influence over them has been their dependence on the Soviet Union and the core states to subsidize their imports, buy their exports on terms advantageous to them, and supply them with military equipment.

In addition to these direct means of political control, the Soviet Union established intergovernmental organizations for defense coordination and economic cooperation similar to and partly in response to those of the U.S. hegemony.

For defense purposes, the East European states were bound to the Soviet Union in the so-called Warsaw Pact, which provided for a common command, military doctrine and strategic and tactical plans, interdependent services of supply and communications, and much more standardization of armaments and other military equipment than in NATO. As part of these arrangements, large Soviet military forces were permanently stationed on the territories of the member states contiguous to the NATO countries—much bigger than the counterpart U.S. military forces—and their presence has also facilitated Soviet control over these countries.

For economic purposes, the Council for Mutual Economic Cooperation (COMECON) was established, charged with planning and overseeing balanced trade and payments relations among the nonmarket economies of the member states. However, it aims to achieve these goals not by lowering and removing barriers to the flows of goods, services, and financial resources as in the world market economy. Instead, its function is to ensure that only those exports and imports take place that are in accordance with the centrally directed production, investment, and consumption plans of the Soviet Union and the other members. By their nature, centrally directed nonmarket economic systems tend to be autarkic. Because their control is more assured internally than over their external relations, in which other countries are also involved, they are reluctant to become too dependent upon imports. This tendency toward self-sufficiency means that the adjustment process is nowhere near as operative in the economic relations among centrally directed nonmarket economies as among market economies, and costs are manifested much more in possible growth opportunities forgone than in actually felt losses of employment and incomes. Hence, postwar economic integration among the East European members of COMECON was quite minor, as indicated in Table 2. The economic integration of these COMECON nations with the rest of the world was even less significant. In 1960, their imports from the rest of the world were only 0.8 percent of their combined GNPs, while those of the Soviet Union were only 0.4 percent of its GNP; they were still only 1.0 percent and 0.4 percent respectively in 1965 and 1.3 percent and 0.4 percent respectively in 1970.

Thus, economic coordination rather than integration more accurately characterizes the relations among the nonmarket economies. For the six East European client states, it was the economic assistance they were obtaining from the Soviet Union, rather than the degree of their integration with it, that was important. By the 1960s, the Soviet Union was increasingly subsidizing its trade with them—as well as with the noncontinguous client states—not only by granting them low-cost export credits but also by charging them less than the world market price for some of its exports to them and paying them more than the world market price for some of its imports from them. These economic benefits helped to bind the client states more closely to the Soviet Union despite the fact that economic integration within COMECON was quite low.

Table 2
Trade between the Soviet Union and the
Six East European COMECON Members

	Imports: Percentage of Importer's GNP	
	COMECON Members[a]	Soviet Union
1960	1.4	0.4
1965	1.8	0.5
1970	2.3	0.5

a. Data for the six East European COMECON members include imports from one another as well as from the Soviet Union.

In sum, the Soviet Union has relied mainly upon its power and influence to hold its hegemony together. True, the Soviet Union has been bearing heavy costs, principally for its large military establishment and the aid provided to its client states. However, these costs have been for *the maintenance of the hegemony as a sociopolitical entity* and not for the purpose of attaining a high degree of economic integration which—unlike within the U.S. hegemony—has not been regarded as necessary or desirable.

RELATIONS BETWEEN THE HEGEMONIES

In their interactions, the two hegemonies have constituted a balance-of-power system. As explained in the Technical Appendix, the form of such a system imposes certain required capacities and actions on the two hegemons if they are to maintain the balance between them. First, each protagonist has always had to support a military establishment adequate to prevent its defeat by the other. However, unlike all previous balance-of-power systems, in which war was a recognized and often-used means of keeping the balance, the U.S.-Soviet system has been precluded from resorting to it because a nuclear war could result in mutual destruction. Second, as the protagonists of a two-party system, both superpowers' conceptions of their requirements for preserving the balance have inclined them to attach as many other nations to themselves as possible, and this tendency has been powerfully reinforced by their senses of world-transforming mission and their ideological antipathy to each other. They also have been impelled to strengthen their resulting hegemonies by institutional ties and commonly observed rules and regulations that imply substantial though varying degrees of political control or influence, defense coordination, and/or economic integration. Third, any initiative by either superpower, or any development within either hegemony that is perceived by the other superpower as likely to upset the balance, sooner or later has to be countered by an appropriate action.

The problem posed for the United States during the postwar period by these requirements was that it did not possess anywhere near the degree of political control over the members of its hegemony as did the Soviet Union. Soviet control over its core members and the dependence on Soviet support of its noncontiguous members were both great enough to assure that they would follow Soviet-approved policies toward the U.S. hegemony. In contrast, the tenuousness of U.S. political influence within its hegemony and the self-restraint imposed by its moral and political values allowed much wider freedom of action for the members to pursue independent policies toward the Soviet Union and its client states.

During the 1940s and 1950s, much of the coordination of policies and actions within the U.S. hegemony and in its external relations occurred in the central political organs of the United Nations (UN): the Security Council and the General Assembly. Indeed, until the mid-1960s, the United States could usually persuade a sufficient number of the other UN members to vote in accordance with its wishes. However, as the great decolonization process of the postwar decades brought more and more new nations into existence, this dominance was gradually eroded; by the end of the period, the United States could no longer count on majority support in the General Assembly and was constrained to use its veto in the Security Council to block proposed resolutions of which it disapproved. This change reflected the growing disaffection from the U.S.-dominated system of political and economic order of an increasing number of Asian, African, and Latin American countries and the spread of the movement for "nonalignment" among them. The reasons which impelled the formation of the nonaligned movement also inclined many of its members to "tilt" their so-called neutrality in favor of the Soviet Union, which naturally encouraged this trend.

Therefore, by the end of the postwar period, the coordination of policies and actions within the U.S. hegemony toward the Soviet hegemony was limited to the OECD countries and those nations in Asia, Africa, and Latin America that were heavily dependent on U.S. economic and political support. In other words, for many Asian, African, and even Latin American countries, their economic integration into the world market economy was not a sufficiently compelling bond to constrain them to follow U.S. leadership in determining their relations with the Soviet hegemony. Indeed, it was not sufficient to restrain them from opposing U.S. policies and actions within the U.S. hegemony itself. Thus, the U.S. hegemony became increasingly heterogeneous, diffuse, and loose in the course of the postwar period while the Soviet hegemony remained much more homogeneous and tightly controlled.

Within its hegemony during the postwar period, each superpower was seeking, with greater or lesser intensity, to bring about certain revolutionary changes. For the members of the Soviet hegemony, the revolutionary goal was the establishment, insofar as possible, of socialist societies with authoritarian political institutions, nonmarket economic systems, and closely controlled cultures. That the United States was also pursuing revolutionary changes is not generally recognized. The predominant view has always been that its aim was to maintain the status quo not only in relations with the Soviet Union but also in the institutional and cultural characteristics of the members of its hegemony. However, I regard U.S. objectives for the members of its hegemony *during the postwar period* as just as revolutionary, though in different ways, as those of the Soviet Union.

For Western Europe, the revolutionary goal of U.S. policy was the replacement of the region's system of independent nation-states by a political and economic union capable of defending itself and of helping to maintain the integration, security, and orderliness of the international system. For the new and old nations of Asia, Africa, and Latin America, the United States provided large amounts of financial and technical assistance in the expectation of fostering the transformation of their traditional institutions and cultures into modern pluralistic societies with democratic political institutions and increasingly productive market economies. Most U.S. policymakers and opinion leaders believed that, with sufficient outside assistance, these countries could make rapid progress toward these goals. As they did, they would be willing and able to bear the costs, as well as receive the benefits, of membership in an integrated international system. The domestic objectives coincided with the aspirations of many people within these countries. The issue between radical-nationalist and Marxist elites in Asian, African, and Latin American countries and the United States was not the necessity or desirability of a fundamental societal transformation but the specific form it should take, the groups that should lead it, the means for realizing it, and the implications for these nations' external political and economic affiliations.

In the event, neither the goal of European union nor the goal of sociocultural transformation in Asia, Africa, and Latin America was realized—nor could these objectives be met with the means and within the time available. Still, enough progress was made in both respects to help bring about fundamental changes in the international system that increasingly manifested themselves during the 1970s and 1980s and confronted the United States with more intractable problems than those it faced during the postwar period. On the one hand, the progress achieved was not great enough to relieve the United States of its hegemonic burden of assuring the security, order, and effective functioning of the international system. On the other hand, it has been sufficient (1) to erode the willingness and ability of the United States to bear a disproportionate share of the costs of economic integration and political and defense coordination, and (2) to increase the motivation and capacity of many other nations to act in accordance with their particularistic interests. The result has been the gradual loosening of the integration and coordination of the international system, as explained in the next chapter.

Chapter III

THE INTERNATIONAL SYSTEM IN TRANSITION: CHANGES IN ITS ECONOMIC AND POLITICAL STRUCTURE

The changes within the different types of nation-states and in their interactions that were to bring the postwar period to an end were already beginning to manifest themselves during the second half of the 1960s, although they did not become dominant characteristics of the international system until the second half of the 1970s. Even today, important elements of the postwar system persist. Thus, there has been a gradual transition from the postwar period to the present period, whose start, simply for convenience, I date at around 1970. I regard the current period as a transitional one because, as explained in Chapter IX, the international system does not yet have a determinate character as did the bihegemonic balance-of-power system of the postwar period.

In effect, the U.S. hegemony has been self-liquidating: the very success of the U.S.-designed postwar system largely made possible the changes that have been transforming it. For its core and associate members, the system provided a quarter century of secure, orderly, and calculable international conditions. The system was free of major wars and strongly conducive to high rates of economic growth and rising living standards, and it fostered the sense of national identity and self-confidence in both old and new nations. This favorable environment was essential in bringing about the developments in the motivations and capabilities of the members of the system that, in turn, have been changing their relative positions and the ways in which they interact.

This chapter deals broadly with the major alterations in the economic and political structure of the international system (outside the Soviet hegemony) that have become increasingly apparent since 1970.

27

THE CHANGING ECONOMIC STRUCTURE OF
THE INTERNATIONAL SYSTEM

The most important structural change has been in the economic position of the United States *relative* to other members of the system. True, the absolute indicators of U.S. economic capabilities have grown substantially during and since the postwar period. But, the corresponding economic capabilities of other nations, especially their competitiveness in foreign trade, have increased faster. Thus, they have been able to narrow the gap between their economic positions and that of the United States—a gap that helped to make possible the U.S. hegemonic role.

Other nations have owed their strengthened economic positions to the favorable interactions between internal improvements in their economic capabilities and the growing opportunities for expanding their external economic relations as barriers to international trade and payments were steadily reduced, and in many respects abolished, during the postwar period. Indeed, after the tariff reductions and other changes agreed to in the sixth round of GATT negotiations in the 1960s went fully into effect, the world market economy was closer to the free-trade ideal than at any time in its history. However, from the point of view of the national economies involved, this development had ambivalent effects. On the one hand, it continuously opened up new opportunities for trade, thereby greatly stimulating economic growth and rising employment and incomes. On the other hand, it meant that the world market economy was becoming increasingly competitive, with comparative advantages shifting more rapidly between national economies as their relative factor costs changed and technological innovations were disseminated much faster than in the postwar period. Thus, as explained in Chapter I, the more integrated the world market economy has become, the more the participants have been experiencing the adverse short-term effects of the adjustment process on employment and incomes even as they have been reaping the short- and long-term benefits of the gains from trade. At the same time, as will be explained in later chapters, the changes occurring within nations, especially within the OECD countries, have made them less and less willing and able to endure the unfavorable short-term impact of the adjustment process and all the more eager to maintain and expand their exports.

Changes in World Market Shares

One major consequence of shifting economic positions has been that the asymmetry between the U.S. economy and the world economy has steadily become less marked and less significant. Whereas in 1950 U.S. GNP was half of world GNP, its proportion declined to roughly a third by 1970 and a quarter by 1980. As late as the second half of the 1960s, annual U.S. direct private foreign investment averaged more than 65 percent of the world total but, by the first half of the 1980s, it had fallen to 25 percent. In 1970, the U.S. share of the total world stock of private direct foreign investment was more than two-thirds but, in the course of the 1980s, it was reduced to less than half.

The changes in the U.S. shares of total world exports have been equally dramatic, as is clear from Table 3. By 1980, both Japan and West Germany

Table 3
U.S. Share of Total World Exports

	Percentage of Total World Exports	Percentage of World Exports of Manufactures	Percentage of World Exports of Agricultural Products[a]
1950	18.3	27.3	12.7
1960	18.2	22.8	15.7
1970	15.4	18.4	17.0
1980	12.4	16.6	16.0

a. Annual averages are for the first three years of each decade.

had larger shares of world trade in manufactures than did the United States, whose share has continued to drop in consequence of further loss of competitiveness by many U.S. industries and the big overvaluation of the U.S. dollar during the first half of the 1980s. While the U.S. share of world agricultural exports rose until 1980, it too declined thereafter due to the overvaluation of the dollar, the increases in the heavily subsidized agricultural exports of the EC and other producers, and the improvements in cereal production in India, China, and other Asian countries.

As the world economy became less dependent on exports from the United States, the United States became more dependent on its trade with the rest of the world, as shown in Table 4. The decline in the total percentage from 1980 to 1985 reflected the disproportionately large growth of the services sector of the U.S. economy over the period. In the goods sector of the U.S. economy, the big increase in manufactured imports more than offset the fall in manufactured exports. Although agricultural exports dropped during the first half of the 1980s for the reasons given above, U.S. dependence on exports and imports of agricultural products nevertheless remained above 50 percent.

Table 4
Total U.S. Imports and Exports

	Goods and Services[a]	Manufacturing[b]	Agriculture[c]
1950	9.3	7.8	13.8
1960	10.5	13.4	22.3
1970	12.7	21.9	43.5
1980	24.5	46.3	76.0
1985	20.5	49.3	53.8

a. As percent of U.S. GNP.
b. As percent of manufacturing GNP originating in the United States.
c. As percent of agricultural GNP originating in the United States.

An important form in which the growth of U.S. manufactured imports and exports has been manifested is the increase of trade *within* U.S. multinational corporations—that is, the two-way flows of materials, parts, and finished products between their factories in the United States and those in other countries. By the late 1970s, 35 to 40 percent of U.S. exports and imports were estimated to be occurring within U.S. firms. This change is mainly the result of two factors. First, the lowering of barriers to international trade and investment during the postwar period provided the opportunities and the competitive pressures for U.S. manufacturers to search throughout the world economy for the lowest-cost locations in which to produce goods for sale both within the countries involved and in external markets, including the United States. Second, the continuing prohibitive restrictions on many manufactured imports in most Asian, African, and Latin American countries induced U.S. producers to move to them so as to be able to sell in their domestic markets. Similarly, the need to produce within the EC in order to avoid its common external tariff and other barriers to imports and to obtain the advantages of its internal free trade in manufactures encouraged many U.S. companies to invest in Western Europe. These overseas plants often import parts and subassemblies from the parent companies in the United States and, in turn, export both parts and finished products back to them.

Thus, since the beginning of the current period, production and consumption within the U.S. economy have become increasingly dependent, both positively and negatively, on U.S. external trade relations. In consequence, *the adjustment process has ceased to be of marginal significance in terms of its impact on U.S. employment and incomes.* This is especially true for the growing number of enterprises, workers, and farmers in the U.S. economy that have to compete with imports in the domestic market and/or with the producers of other countries in the latter's market or in third-country markets.

Changes in the International Monetary System

The changes in the position of the United States in the world monetary system have been more complex. There has been a major redistribution of the shares of world monetary reserves held by the United States as compared with other countries: in 1950, U.S. monetary reserves, mostly gold, comprised half of the world total; by 1980, they were only 6 percent. Dollars have continued to be the largest portion of the currency component of the monetary reserves of other countries, but the proportion has been declining from more than 80 percent in the late 1970s to less than 70 percent in the mid-1980s. The dollar is still the currency in which most of international trade is denominated, although the shares invoiced in Japanese yen and German marks have been rising. The dollar has ceased to have a fixed value in terms of gold and, hence, to be the universal standard in terms of which the exchange rates of other currencies are fixed.

The latter development, which occurred during the early 1970s, marked the passing of the international monetary system established at the Bretton Woods Conference. Beginning with the so-called Nixon Shock of August 1971, the United States took a series of actions designed to eliminate its balance-of-payments deficit and the resulting drain of gold from its monetary reserves, which were largely due to the accelerated overvaluation of the dollar during the late 1960s. In addition to imposing a temporary surcharge to discourage imports, it first devalued the dollar by doubling the price of gold and announced that it would no longer convert dollars into gold at the request of other governments. When these measures proved ineffective, it got the members of the IMF to agree to a radical change in the world monetary system. This was the elimination (1) of a fixed rate between the dollar and gold, whose price was thereafter free to fluctuate in accordance with supply and demand, and (2) of fixed rates of exchange for other currencies in terms of dollars. Since 1973, countries have not been required to maintain fixed exchange rates, as they were under the Bretton Woods system, although some of them have voluntarily continued to link their currencies to the U.S. dollar, the French franc, or another major currency.

During the 1960s, many economists in the OECD nations were urging the adoption of such fluctuating exchange rates as a means of enabling national governments to pursue domestic economic policies of their choice without being restrained by the necessity of defending a fixed exchange rate with limited monetary reserves and external borrowing facilities. In the event, the opposite has occurred due to the growing integration of world financial markets that began in the late 1950s after the restoration of currency convertibility by the West European countries and Japan and their gradual reduction of controls on capital movements during the 1960s and 1970s. As these changes occurred, trade and monetary flows could respond more readily, through the medium of fluctuating exchange rates, to the differentials in prices and interest rates among national product and financial markets. In consequence, major inflationary and deflationary forces have been more rapidly and drastically transmitted throughout the world market economy, especially among the OECD countries, than they were under the fixed-rate Bretton Woods system. These effects have been especially marked in the case of inflationary and deflationary impulses originating in the United States; witness the rapid transmission to other countries of the so-called Great Inflation of the 1970s and the deflation of the early 1980s.

The increasing integration during the 1970s and 1980s of the financial markets of the OECD nations, as well as those of Hong Kong and Singapore, has also been made possible by technological innovations in telecommunications and the electronic presentation of financial information—and by the development of new forms of financial assets, new facilities for trading in futures, options, and indexes, and computerized programs for managing portfolio investments and speculation. Due to these changes and the virtual abolition of controls on transborder currency and capital movements, enormous amounts of funds can now be shifted by private-sector organizations between national financial markets and between the different forms of financial assets and speculative facilities. Indeed, the financial markets of North America, Western Europe, and Eastern Asia are so closely linked that investors and speculators anywhere in the system can buy and sell currencies and securities at any time of the day or night. The integration and growth of these financial markets pose major problems for the OECD governments today and for the future that are discussed in Chapters VII and VIII.

Other Major Economic Changes

The other major shifts in relative economic positions that emerged from the developments of the postwar period have been those of the members of the

EC, Japan, the newly industrializing countries (NICs) in Asia and Latin America, and the members of the Organization of Petroleum Exporting Countries (OPEC).

By the 1960s, the West European nations had fully recovered their international trade capabilities. With the enlargement of the EC during the 1970s and 1980s to include all West European countries except Norway, Sweden, Switzerland, and Austria, they have collectively become the largest exporting and importing market on the planet and, after the United States and Japan, the largest source of capital for both portfolio and direct investment.

Beginning in the early 1960s, Japan's climb to international economic preeminence was even more spectacular. Adept at borrowing and improving the newest and most efficient product and process technologies, Japanese enterprises have been stimulated and assisted by their government to undertake export drives targeted at vulnerable product markets in the United States and the EC. Japan's exports have moved progressively up the technological scale from textiles to steel to automobiles and shipbuilding to consumer electronics and, in the 1980s, to computer-controlled machine tools and other high-technology capital goods. In consequence, Japan's share of total world trade in manufactured goods rose from 5.6 percent in 1960 to 6.3 percent in 1970, 11.3 percent in 1980, and 20 percent in the mid-1980s. By the 1980s, Japan had surpassed Western Europe as the largest source of capital for external direct and portfolio investment after the United States and, by 1985, its total capital outflow exceeded that of the latter.

The so-called NICs comprise four East Asian economies—Hong Kong, Singapore, Taiwan, and South Korea—that have been "following in Japan's footsteps," as well as several Latin American nations that have succeeded in developing manufacturing industries for export, notably Brazil and Mexico. During the 1970s, the NICs concentrated their export efforts in lines of production that were labor-intensive, made standard products, and/or had static or slowly changing process technologies—and, hence, in which their abundant, readily trained, and low-cost labor forces gave them a substantial advantage over their high-wage competitors in North America, the EC and, most recently, even Japan. Over the decade of the 1970s, South Korea's manufactured exports grew at an annual average of 33 percent, Singapore's at 30 percent, Taiwan's at 28 percent, and Hong Kong's at 21 percent, while Brazil's grew at 32 percent and Mexico's at 14 percent. In the 1980s, the East Asian NICs began to produce higher-technology goods for export, and countries in South Asia (e.g., India, Malaysia, and Thailand) and Latin America (e.g., Colombia) have been moving to join their ranks, which will undoubtedly expand further in the future.

During the 1970s, the OPEC countries were able to take advantage of temporary political and economic conditions favorable to the exercise of monopoly power by an exporters' cartel to triple the real world-market price of petroleum in 1973–1974 and to double it once again in 1979–1980. These moves greatly enhanced their economic positions in the world market economy, especially those of the biggest exporters, whose multiplied foreign-exchange earnings were much too large to be spent on imports of goods and services. The resulting OPEC current-account surplus, which mounted to a peak of $106 billion in 1980, was largely invested in the financial markets of the OECD countries, partly in their governments' securities but mainly as short-term deposits in the big international U.S., European, and Japanese banks. In turn, the banks "recycled" these enormous funds as higher-interest loans to their own governments and private-sector enterprises and to governmental and private-sector borrowers in the petroleum-importing nations.

These OPEC-related developments had two important sets of effects. First, the big increases in the price of petroleum helped to intensify and prolong the worldwide "Great Inflation" that had been generated by the U.S. decision in the second half of the 1960s to finance both its new social-welfare programs and the Vietnam War by monetizing much of the resulting budgetary deficit rather than by increasing taxation or noninflationary borrowing. Second, the OPEC surplus amounted in effect to a massive transfer of real resources to OPEC countries from the petroleum-importing nations, which would have required the latter—all other things being equal—to make compensating adjustments in their domestic patterns of resource allocation. Instead, the recycling/borrowing operation enabled many of the importing nations, especially in Latin America, to continue to buy as much petroleum as they had previously, despite its higher price, while minimizing or avoiding these internal adjustments.

During the first half of the 1980s, however, the temporary conditions that had supported the cartel's monopoly power disappeared. Both the rising petroleum prices and the general inflation stimulated intensified efforts to find new sources of oil and other natural fuels and to conserve on energy use, especially in the United States, where energy costs had previously been low relative to other factor costs. Energy exploration and conservation combined in the mid-1980s to increase the supply of and reduce the demand for petroleum, leading to lower prices, At the same time, the restrictive fiscal and monetary policies adopted by many of the OECD nations (for reasons explained in the next chapter) helped to bring on the 1981–1982 recession, the most severe worldwide depression since that of the 1930s, which accelerated the fall in petroleum prices by further contracting world demand.[1]

On the one hand, these developments eliminated the OPEC surplus, and hence the recycling/borrowing operation, and enabled the oil-importing countries in Asia, Africa, and Latin America to buy cheaper petroleum. On the other hand, these nations were also confronted with shrinking demand and falling prices for their own exports while remaining saddled with the heavy burden of servicing their accumulated external debts with diminished foreign-exchange earnings. The results during the first half of the 1980s were the rescue operations headed by the IMF. Under them, the big international banks agreed to stretch out or postpone the repayments of their loans, to provide additional borrowing facilities, and even to defer or reduce the interest in some cases. In return, the debtor nations undertook to impose austerity measures on their domestic economies to assure that the resources required for the new debt-servicing schedules would be available. Nevertheless, so burdensome has the continuing indebtedness of these countries been that some began in 1986 to default on all or part of their obligations. The likely implications of this serious debt-servicing problem are discussed in later chapters.

In sum, the developments of the postwar period bequeathed to the current period three major alterations in the economic structure and functioning of the international system. The first is the change in the position of the U.S. economy relative to the world economy that has made it significantly more dependent upon the latter and, hence, more susceptible to the adverse short-term effects of the adjustment process. The second is the greatly increased importance in the world economy of the EC, Japan, and the NICs, as well as of the OPEC countries whenever supply and demand conditions give the cartel sufficient monopoly power. The third is the system of fluctuating exchange rates and highly integrated financial markets among the OECD nations that has resulted in the more rapid and drastic transmission of inflationary and deflationary pressures among them and to the other participants in the world market economy.

THE CHANGING POLITICAL STRUCTURE OF THE INTERNATIONAL SYSTEM

The changes in the political structure and functioning of the international system have been no less important than those in its economic structure, though they have been less clear-cut. Hence, their implications have been less well understood. Two major developments and their effects need to be noted: the Soviet attainment of nuclear parity with the United States by the end of the postwar period, and the increasing capacity and propensity since the late 1960s for independent political action by most members of the postwar U.S. hegemony.

Although the first of these changes—Soviet nuclear equality with the United States and the parallel expansion of Soviet naval and other conventional military capabilities—has been very evident, there has been considerable disagreement over the implications for NATO, an issue that will be discussed in later chapters. One major consequence, however, is not much disputed: this development helped to embolden the Soviet Union during the 1970s to take advantage of opportunities to extend the peripheral membership of its hegemony—as in Angola, Ethiopia, Mozambique, and South Yemen—and to add a contiguous member, Afghanistan.

The second major change is that the relative power position of the United States in the international system (outside the Soviet hegemony) has become increasingly anomalous since the end of the postwar period. The United States continues to be a superpower with the ability to overawe any nation by the overwhelming superiority of its nuclear and/or conventional military capabilities. In other words, no nation other than the Soviet Union, not even China, has as yet become willing and able to build up its military establishment to the point where it would be a match for that of the United States. However, this immense military disparity has not enabled the United States to maintain the determinative political power in the international system that it had during the postwar period. Hence, a confusing anomaly exists between the enormous absolute magnitude of U.S. military capabilities and the declining political capacity of the United States to constrain or influence the policies and actions of other nations.

On the whole, the members of NATO continue to be the most inclined of any group of nations to follow U.S. leadership. But, their willingness to do so has become very much less in the alliance's political aspect than in its military aspect. Until now, NATO has maintained the high degree of military integration it has had since the formation of the alliance. The United States has been able—though with increasing difficulty—to persuade the European members to go along with most of the military improvements it regards as essential for the protection of Western Europe. For their part, the Europeans have sooner or later acquiesced in U.S. actions to strengthen European defense because of their continued fear of the Soviet Union and their *unwillingness* to allocate to their own military establishments the resources necessary to free them from reliance on U.S. protection. Their refusal reflects unwillingness rather than inability: they could well afford the requisite allocation of resources in view of the high level of per capita income, the huge productive capacity, and the advanced technological skills they had already attained by the end of the postwar period.

It is with respect to the alliance's political coordination that U.S. influence has substantially diminished. Although their economic achievements have not been used to free the European members of NATO from dependence on U.S. military protection, these advances have helped to strengthen their resolve to resist U.S. initiatives that they perceive as contrary to their political and economic interests. As will be explained in Chapter IV, this tendency has been reinforced by the revival of the institutions of the nation-state in Western Europe during the postwar period. The resulting restoration of the Europeans' senses of national integrity and self-confidence has been an important element in the declining influence that the United States can exercise over their policies and actions.

For example, in contrast to the extensive help given by the European members of NATO during the Korean War in the early 1950s, they provided virtually no assistance to the United States during its involvement in the war in Vietnam in the late 1960s and early 1970s and many, indeed, openly opposed it. Increasingly since the end of the postwar period, West European nations have refused to support—often have voted against—the United States in the UN General Assembly and Security Council, as well as in the UN's specialized agencies and regional commissions. Many have opposed U.S. policies and actions for dealing with the Arab-Israeli conflict, the protection of the Persian Gulf despite their own much greater dependence on oil from this source than that of the United States, the prevention of Soviet-oriented regimes from coming to power in Latin America and the Caribbean, and the suppression of international terrorism. Nor has their refusal to follow U.S. leadership been limited to problems outside the NATO area. The West European nations even successfully resisted strong U.S. pressure to forgo natural-gas supplies from the Soviet Union and to refrain from selling the necessary pipeline equipment to it.

I cite these examples of important disagreements between the United States and the European members of NATO not to discuss the question of which side was right or wrong. Rather, I want to emphasize that the increasing inability of the United States to gain the allies' support for its policies means that it no longer exercises hegemonic power within the alliance. At the same time, the European members have been unwilling to agree among themselves on common policies and actions for dealing with many important international issues. Politically, therefore, NATO has become a rather loose coalition of often divergent nations.

The gradual decline in U.S. political influence over its core NATO allies has been paralleled by its waning influence over the political actions of countries in the peripheral regions of its postwar hegemony. As explained in the preceding chapter, political coordination between the United States and Latin American, Asian, and African nations was looser than within NATO even during the postwar period—except, of course, for those countries that directly depended upon U.S. assistance to cope with actual or threatened invasions or internal insurgencies. Since the late 1960s, the changes within these nations and in their relations with one another have been impelling many of them to repudiate U.S. political leadership and to constitute a "nonaligned" movement, ostensibly neutral but in reality most often inclined to support Soviet positions in the UN and its specialized agencies and to oppose U.S. policies in other international organizations.

These changes in the political power structure of the international system since the end of the postwar period have substantially lessened U.S. ability to cope with developments that its policymakers have regarded as adverse to its interests. Some significant examples may be cited. Whereas North Korea was prevented from annexing South Korea in the early 1950s, North Vietnam was able to absorb South Vietnam two decades later. The U.S. Embassy personnel held hostage by Iran in 1979–1980 were eventually released through the intercession of other Islamic countries and not by direct U.S. actions, which included a futile, ill-planned and ill-executed rescue attempt that further eroded U.S. prestige. Unlike in the Suez Crisis of 1956, the United States could not stop the Israeli invasion of Lebanon in 1982 or the war between Argentina and the United Kingdom over the Falkland Islands in 1983. In that year, too, the 1,500 U.S. marines sent to Lebanon to restore order not only were far too few to do so but also were themselves exposed to a disastrous car-bomb attack that led to their hasty withdrawal; compare this with the successful mission of the 19,000 marines sent to end the civil war in that country in 1958. Only the U.S. invasion of the tiny Caribbean island of Grenada to oust a Marxist regime accomplished its objective. The outcomes of current U.S. efforts in El Salvador and Nicaragua are still to be determined.

Again, I am not discussing here the necessity or the desirability of these U.S. efforts but simply contrasting the results with those of analogous actions during the postwar period. However, it is relevant to the point I am trying to make that some of these futile attempts at the exercise of hegemonic power failed in whole or in part because the United States was unwilling to allocate to them the levels of military power required to accomplish the intended objectives, whether well or ill advised. In turn, this self-limitation reflected those changes in attitudes and expectations, not only in the United States but also in its NATO allies and other nations, that made them unwilling to acquiesce in, let alone support, the actions of the U.S. administration, whether Democratic or Republican, in office at the time.

In sum, *the fiat of the United States no longer runs in the international political system as it did during the postwar period.* This is not to say that, in the current period, the United States is politically powerless or that its efforts to maintain peace and order in the international system are necessarily doomed to failure. Rather, the point is that the success of U.S. efforts depends in part upon clear-eyed recognition of the policy implications of the major ongoing changes since the end of the postwar period in the economic and political structure of the international system and in the position of the United States within it.

NOTE

1. In turn, the fall in petroleum prices has both encouraged increased consumption and made the highest-cost sources uneconomic, especially in the United States, which has led to a drop in output by non-OPEC producers. To reverse the decline in prices, the OPEC countries have agreed to reduce their production so as to restrict supply. To the extent to which they succeed, rising prices would again tend to limit consumption and stimulate increased production from higher-cost sources. Also, as on previous occasions when OPEC has tried to restrict the output of its members, those under the greatest pressure to maintain their foreign-exchange earnings sooner or later become free-riders, exporting all they can regardless of their commitments. This cycle is likely to characterize the world petroleum market until basic changes in supply or demand take place or political developments strengthen or weaken OPEC's monopoly power.

Chapter IV

CHANGES WITHIN THE OECD NATIONS

The nation-states comprising the contemporary international system differ widely in historical backgrounds, psychocultural characteristics, and economic and political institutions. Indeed, every national society is unique in certain significant respects and it would be impossible within the scope of this book to do justice to all of these variations. For its purposes, I divide the members of the international system into four groups: the OECD nations, including the United States; the countries of Asia and Africa; the Latin American nations; and the communist states comprised in the Soviet hegemony. The OECD nations are covered in this chapter, the others in the next two chapters.

INSTITUTIONAL CHANGES IN THE OECD NATIONS

Market economic systems, such as those of the OECD nations, and non-market economic systems, such as those of the Soviet Union and its client states, have certain institutional structures and modes of operation that distinguish each type from the other (see the definitions in the Technical Appendix). These distinguishing institutional characteristics also endow each system with certain inherent kinds of benefits and costs. The costs are perceived as deficiencies or problems whenever, and to the extent that, they become incompatible with the values and expectations of the society of which the economic system is a part. The structural deficiencies of the nonmarket economies and the efforts to cope with them are discussed in Chapter VI; here, those of the market economies are surveyed.

Modern, complex, interdependent market systems with rapidly changing technologies have inherent tendencies toward instability and inequality.

Although the competitive market operating in accordance with efficiency criteria is an unrivaled equilibrating mechanism, the momentum of the interplay of supply and demand and the divergences between the individual markets for the different kinds of goods and services and for labor and capital usually cause the system to overshoot the balancing point, resulting in greater or lesser unemployment of workers and facilities and more or less inflation or deflation—in short, the business cycle. Also, if left to itself, the system tends to distribute income unequally in accordance with relative productivity and market power. These characteristic modes of operation are not perceived as deficiencies so long as the society's elites and nonelites accept the consequences as ordained of God, or inherent in the natural order, or beyond the existing capacity of human beings to understand and overcome. They become problems once changes in institutions, values, and knowledge have endowed the society with the conviction that these consequences are unacceptable and can be substantially mitigated, if not eliminated, by deliberate decisions and actions.

The remedy usually involves incorporating nonmarket elements into the market system so as to achieve greater stability and equity. Modern market economies, like those of the OECD nations, have always contained a significant nonmarket sector: their governments. Hence, efforts to correct the inherent shortcomings of market systems usually involve a greater or lesser expansion of the responsibilities of governments. For their part, governments characteristically act in accordance with decision criteria that give high priority to assuring national security, increasing welfare and equity, improving education and advancing knowledge, and protecting their people's health and the natural environment, as well as fostering partisan and bureaucratic advantage. To achieve these and other goals, the responsibilities of governments—and hence the nonmarket sector—can be enlarged in a variety of ways, of which the most important are (1) increasing the proportion of the GNP acquired by official agencies through taxation and borrowing and reallocated for the foregoing purposes; (2) reserving additional productive activities for state-owned and -managed enterprises and/or converting more private enterprises into state enterprises through nationalization; and (3) subjecting private-sector activities to growing governmental regulation and supervision.

The expansion of their nonmarket sectors can certainly remedy in greater or lesser degree market economies' inherent deficiencies of instability and inequity. But, as their nonmarket sectors grow, market systems become susceptible to new kinds of problems, some of the most important of which are similar to those inherent in nonmarket economic systems. (Conversely, as explained in Chapter VI, nonmarket economies endeavor to cope with their inherent shortcomings of inefficiency and lack of dynamism by adopting market elements, which in turn make them susceptible to some of the problems of market economic systems.) The points at which these new transitional difficulties emerge, the specific forms they take, and their degrees of severity vary in accordance with the differences in the institutional and psychocultural characteristics of the national societies involved and the constraints on them generated by changes in their external economic and political environments.

For example, Sweden has been able to offset some of the adverse effects of the very large proportion (nearly two-thirds) of its GNP acquired by its government and reallocated largely for welfare and equity purposes because only a small part of its industrial production has been in state-owned enterprises and it has tried to regulate the activities of its private enterprises in ways that do not unduly impair their efficiency and dynamism. The French private sector has been accustomed since the 17th century to operating under a very high degree of central government direction and supervision. In contrast, the adverse effects of the growth of the nonmarket sector began to appear in the U.S. economy at a much earlier stage in the expansion of governmental responsibilities because of the long historical commitment of American society to individual freedom of enterprise and minimal government.

Beginning in the 18th century, value changes within the societies of Western Europe and North America made improvements in economic welfare, social justice, and freedom for individual fulfillment increasingly important national goals. But, it was not until after World War II that institutional changes and the advancement of knowledge made possible the high economic growth rates and the international security and calculability of the postwar period that provided the resources and conditions necessary for decisive advances toward these and other societal goals. Despite the differences in how they progressed toward these objectives, all countries in Western Europe and North America experienced a pattern of development during the postwar decades that helped to generate broadly similar problems after the period ended. The rest of this section sketches their common institutional development during the 1950s and 1960s, the difficulties that emerged in the 1970s and 1980s, and the ways in which the OECD countries have been coping with them that affect their external economic and political behavior.

Growth of the Welfare State

Beginning in the 1950s and greatly accelerating during the 1960s, most people in the OECD nations experienced rapidly rising real incomes and full employment. These benefits were fostered not only by high economic growth rates but also by the favorable demographic situation in most of the OECD countries. The great loss of life during World War II and the low birth rates of the 1930s and 1940s meant that the annual additions to the labor force during the 1950s and for much of the 1960s were small, making labor relatively scarce. The gains in living standards and economic security produced through the market process were matched by those resulting from the adoption by national governments of a widening range of policies and programs, regulations and requirements that have collectively come to be called *the welfare state*.

In Europe north of the Alps and the Pyrenees, where national welfare systems have been most highly developed, they include the provision by governmental or quasi-governmental agencies of full medical care, child-support payments (family allowances), free tuition and grants or loans for students' living expenses, subsidized housing or home ownership, unemployment and disability benefits equal to or only slightly smaller than previous wages and salaries, pensions and supplementary grants to retired persons, and other kinds of transfers in cash, goods, and services. Most of these benefits are available to all, regardless of need, as a matter of right. In addition, private companies are required to provide four to six weeks of paid holiday leave, generous sick leave, and long maternity—and even pater-nity—leave; their ability to lay off workers is narrowly restricted and, when permitted, entails substantial severance payments; and in some cases they are responsible for subsidiary pensions. Welfare benefits, and often fringe benefits, are usually indexed to inflation and, in most West European countries, to increases in real wages, which means that the costs of the welfare system are constantly rising even though no new programs or benefits are added.

In the United States, the scope and relative cost of the welfare programs are not as great as in Western Europe. However, the United States substantially exceeds the European countries in the variety and stringency of the regulatory policies it has adopted to safeguard the natural environment, protect workers' health and safety, assure the quality of food and drugs, enforce civil rights for minorities and women, and achieve other welfare and equity goals. Also, many U.S. companies—voluntarily or in agreement with the trade unions—provide fringe benefits that are the equivalents of certain forms of welfare granted by the West European governments or which they have legally required their private enterprises to supply.

The major exception among OECD nations has been Japan, where the government-administered welfare programs, excluding the national health service, have been quite modest in scope and size. Instead, families have been encouraged by various incentives to provide for their own retirement and other forms of economic security through private savings—which are among the highest relative to national income in the OECD group—and through the supplementary benefits granted to many employees by large private companies. Nonetheless, the Japanese government plays a very active role in the economy, directing companies, and the banks that finance them, to the most promising lines of production for home and export demand. Also, it organizes the contraction of declining industries, fosters and subsidizes research and development and investment so as to improve international competitiveness, and limits imports of goods and services that might compete in the domestic market.

The growth of the welfare state, especially during its most expansionary period in the 1960s and early 1970s, substantially increased the responsibilities and expenditures of national governments for administering the benefit programs and systems of regulatory and supervisory activities. Additionally in Western Europe, governments have had to manage the enterprises that were nationalized during the postwar period. Many of these state-owned enterprises have required substantial continuing or intermittent subsidies from their governments' budgets to cover their operating deficits and investment needs.

Consequences of Public-Sector Growth

This great expansion of the scope of governmental responsibilities and expenditures has had major consequences for the OECD nations.

The first and most basic comprises *the changes in the institutional structures of their societies.* As the OECD economies have grown, their public, or nonmarket, sectors have increased much more rapidly than their private, or market, sectors, leading to the "mixed" economic systems that now characterize all of the OECD nations. One way to measure this shift is by the shares of gross domestic product (GDP) that pass through the public sector. Whereas in Western Europe in 1960 the shares were in the range of 30 to 40 percent, they increased by the 1980s to the range of 50 to 65 percent, with the highest in the Scandinavian countries, where welfare systems are the most elaborate and generous. The percentages have always been smaller in the United States: even including state and local governments, the U.S. public sector's share of GDP in the 1960s averaged only 28 percent and rose to an average of 37 percent in the first half of the 1980s.

However, measurement in terms of shares of GDP underestimates the significance of the shift because, by definition, it excludes the regulatory activities of governments. This is not the case with another way of viewing the shift, which is in terms of the difference in the criteria that govern decision making in each sector. In the private sector, economic efficiency is usually the predominant, though not the sole, criterion used in decision making; in the public sector, considerations of efficiency are generally subordinated to welfare, equity, national-defense, and other sociopolitical criteria. Nonetheless, under both definitions, it is clear that the process of resource allocation has become increasingly politicized: more of it has been taking place through the political process and less through the market process.

The second set of consequences of the growing size and importance of the public sector arises from *the ways in which it acquires resources from the private sector for its own use and for redistributive purposes.* Essentially, this is by means of taxation or borrowing, each of which creates certain difficulties for the private sector.

One form of taxation that has risen substantially has been the social-security—or equivalent—taxes levied on both employers and employees, which have further increased labor costs, especially in Western Europe. Also in Western Europe, income and other direct taxes on private enterprises are generally much higher than in the United States. So, too, are personal income taxes and other taxes that affect the disposable income of families and individuals. For example, not only do income taxes begin at higher rates in Western Europe but also the marginal rates mount much more steeply even in the lower-income brackets. Thus, a worker (with family) earning the average wage in manufacturing in the North European countries usually pays half or more of his wages in social-security, income, excise, and other taxes, much of which, however, he receives back from the government in the form of welfare benefits of various kinds. Nonetheless, worker dissatisfaction over the restriction of disposable income has generated continuous upward pressure on wages in addition to that resulting from inflation. At the same time, the payment of unemployment and disability benefits and of sick leave for long periods and at rates equal or close to regular wages has tended to encourage absenteeism, malingering, and reduced work effort.

As to government acquisition of resources by borrowing, this, too, is inflationary if it is done by monetizing the budgetary deficit (that is, directly or indirectly issuing money to cover it). And, even if it is done in a noninflationary way by absorbing business and personal savings, it can raise interest rates, "crowd out" private-sector borrowing for investment and other economic purposes, and thereby contribute over time to inflation by restricting the growth of productive capacity.

The third set of consequences relates to *the increasing influence of organized business, professional, labor, farm, and other interest groups and the proliferation of organizations to represent the actual or potential bene-ficiaries of welfare programs and the supporters of equity and other regulatory measures.* The rise of these interest and single-issue groups has been not only a consequence but also a cause of the growth and diversification of govern-mental activities since the 1950s. By the mid-1970s, it produced a paradoxical situation for national governments. On the one hand, their responsibilities, legal powers, and administrative personnel were becoming bigger than ever. On the other hand, their freedom of action to discharge their responsibilities was being significantly reduced by the growing influence of the old and new interest groups and single-issue organizations.

This effect has been felt in all OECD countries and has been particularly marked in the United States, where politicians and civil servants have never been accorded the degree of respect and deference that they have traditionally enjoyed in Europe, Japan, and even Canada. Also—and again especially in the United States—the communications media have both reflected and reinforced the activism of the interest groups and single-issue organizations by giving much greater coverage to their activities and by scrutinizing much more closely the policies and behavior of government agencies. In these circumstances, policy disputes and competition for resources among interest groups and single-issue organizations can paralyze governmental decision making on particularly controversial problems.

The freedom of action of politicians and civil servants has been further restricted by the effects of the international economic developments dis-cussed below. These internal and external constraints have impelled national policymakers to resort to measures aimed at shifting the costs of the adjustment process to their trading partners and competitors. In this way, the OECD governments have been trying to preserve and, if possible, increase their remaining freedom of action at one another's expense.

The fourth consequence of the expansion of public sectors and of the activities of governments in the OECD nations has been *the change in the relationship between welfare and efficiency.* During the postwar period, the inception and early growth of national welfare systems brought about improvements in health, nutrition, housing, education, personal and family security, and other conditions of life that were major factors in increasing workers' productivity. Thus, rising welfare helped to sustain the high economic growth rates of the 1950s and 1960s, which in turn provided the resources for further improvements in welfare. However, in the course of the 1970s, this mutually supportive interaction between welfare and effi-ciency was transformed from a positive-sum to a negative-sum relationship. Continued expansion of the variety and size of welfare benefits and equity and other regulatory requirements raised the real costs of the factors of production and, through taxation and government borrowing, restricted the resources available to the private sector and the real disposable incomes of workers. In essence, too much or the wrong kinds of welfare and regulatory activities reduce both the resources required for and the incentives to innovation, investment, and productive work; the resulting decline in economic efficiency and international competitiveness sooner or later limits—and if continued would eventually reduce—the resources allocated to welfare.

By itself, the onset of negative-sum welfare/efficiency interactions need not have generated serious problems for the OECD nations—at least not for quite a while. Western societies have been willing to forgo some economic growth in the private sector and the consequent benefits to living standards in order to realize other forms of welfare and the improvements in social equity that cannot be achieved through the market process or cannot be accomplished through it quickly enough. Hence, the OECD countries could have endured for a reasonable time the gradual decline in the relative efficiency of their economies had other determinative factors remained unchanged. Certain developments in the international economic system intervened, however, to exacerbate the unfavorable effects of negative-sum welfare/efficiency interactions, especially on international competitiveness. Conversely, the difficulties generated by these external developments for the OECD countries could have been dealt with much more readily had it not been for the adverse effects of the internal changes. Thus, internal and external factors combined to confront these nations with increasingly serious and seemingly intractable problems in the second half of the 1970s and during the 1980s.

Problems Arising from the Interaction of Internal and International Developments

The external developments explained in the preceding chapter interacted with the internal developments sketched above to generate three major problems for the OECD nations.

The first was the fact that, precisely at a time when their costs were mounting and their productivity growth was lagging, producers in Western Europe and North America were encountering more intense competition in their own and other markets due to the substantial lowering of trade barriers and the rise of lower-cost producers in Japan and the NICs during the postwar period. This effect was more severe in Western Europe and Canada than in the United States because the continued U.S. preeminence in technological innovation and the slight undervaluation of the dollar after the international monetary changes of the early 1970s slowed the decline in the competitiveness of U.S. producers until the end of that decade. The loss of international competitiveness, especially in Western Europe, contributed importantly to the gradual rise of structural unemployment, that is, workers permanently displaced from noncompetitive enterprises compelled to terminate some or all of their operations.

The second major problem was the intensification of inflation as the internal inflationary pressures noted above within each OECD economy were reinforced by those generated outside it. Among the latter, the most important were (1) the transmission abroad of inflationary impulses originating in the United States during the second half of the 1960s due to the monetizing of much of the budgetary deficit resulting from the expanding welfare programs and the Vietnam War, and (2) the much more serious inflationary impulses engendered by the OPEC-induced escalation of energy prices during the 1970s.

The third major problem was generated by the enormous jump in the net foreign-exchange earnings of the so-called surplus OPEC countries, which represented a large transfer of resources to them from the petroleum-importing nations. This meant, in effect, a loss of growth by the latter that was reflected in the 1974–1975 recession, the most severe experienced until then since World War II. In addition to accepting the deflationary effects of the recession, some OECD countries adjusted to the resource transfer by continuing restrictions on domestic demand that were designed to lower imports and augment exports, thus bringing their external accounts back into balance. However, other OECD countries—as well as many nations in Latin America, Asia, and Africa—either made few or no adjustments of this kind or endeavored to offset the deflationary impact of the transfer by stimulating domestic demand so as to reduce the losses of employment and personal income. Such choices, induced in part by the domestic constraints on national policymakers, only exacerbated inflationary pressures and budgetary and balance-of-payments deficits.

The complex interactions of these internal and external factors resulted, during the second half of the 1970s, in the paradoxical phenomenon of *stagflation*—that is, low or no economic growth with high inflation—in the OECD nations. Moreover, the adverse effects of stagflation were aggravated by the demographic changes that these countries were experiencing. For, the children born during the great postwar "baby boom" of the 1950s and 1960s were by the 1970s entering the labor force in ever-increasing numbers. At the same time in Western Europe, there was little or no new job creation due to the slowness of economic growth and the disincentives in the private sector to expanding the work force, which were implicit in the

European welfare systems and the rigidities of the European trade unions. Thus, both the numbers of unemployed and the welfare cost of supporting them were rising. In addition, the advances in medical science and health care made possible by the welfare systems were improving longevity, thereby increasing the numbers of retired people and the cost of pensions and other benefits for the elderly.

Coping with the Adverse Effects

Since the mid-1970s, therefore, national policymakers have been compelled to take action to cope with a series of interrelated problems of an increasingly pressing nature: low rates of productivity and economic growth, rising structural and cyclical unemployment, high inflation, large budgetary deficits, declining international competitiveness, and in some cases large balance-of-payments deficits. At the same time, domestic pressures have constrained the OECD governments to search unilaterally for immediate palliatives for these problems, rather than to cooperate multilaterally in devising longer-term solutions. In this way, each OECD nation has been trying to avoid as much as possible of the adjustment costs entailed by the complex problems confronting it and to pass them on to its trading partners and competitors.

In domestic policy, one major consequence has been that, since the late 1970s, no new programs or significant new benefits have been added to national welfare systems.[1] Nevertheless, the cost of national welfare systems has continued to rise as a result of both the indexation of benefits and the growth in the number of unemployed and retired persons. At the same time, the great majority of people in the OECD countries remain so deeply committed to the concept of welfare as a societal obligation that it has been politically impossible to make any substantial cuts in welfare programs or benefits, especially those that are provided to all regardless of need and hence that require the largest share of welfare expenditures. The result has been that national policymakers have been forced to cope with the adverse effects of national welfare systems not by reducing their size but by changing the ways of providing benefits in an effort to make them less detrimental to the incentives to innovation, investment, and productive work in their private sectors.

Another important change in domestic policy has been the movement to return state-owned enterprises to the private sector. Known in Western Europe as "privatization," it has gone furthest in the United Kingdom and France under their centrist governments in the mid-1980s. Where enterprises remain in the public sector, efforts have been made to improve their efficiency and reduce the subsidies paid to them. These developments have offset in part the growing costs of national welfare systems.

During the 1980s, most OECD governments have been constrained by rising welfare and related expenditures to restrict other public-sector outlays in an effort to prevent their budgetary deficits from increasing and, where possible, to reduce them. Hence, despite high unemployment, OECD governments—with the major exception of the U.S. administration—have become very cautious about stimulating domestic demand by fiscal policies for fear of the adverse effects on inflation and their balances of payments. For the same reasons, most of them have been following fairly tight monetary policies as well. Thus, during the 1980s, the West European nations implicitly and Japan explicitly relied more on their exports than on domestic demand to maintain and, if possible, to increase their rates of economic growth and to prevent or slow down rises in unemployment.

This dependence on exports has made the Europeans' problem of the loss of international competitiveness all the more important. The domestic constraints have impelled them to cope with reduced competitiveness by adopting a wide variety of measures to assist the sale of their own products in their home and foreign markets and to discourage or restrict competing imports. Tariffs, import quotas, and direct export subsidies traditionally used for these purposes were largely abolished during the postwar period and are prohibited under the GATT. Nevertheless, many OECD countries have reimposed some import quotas temporarily or permanently to protect their noncompetitive industries, such as household appliances and consumer electronics in Western Europe and steel and footwear in the United States. Also, they have expanded their export-credit subsidies to promote the sale of their products abroad. In the main, however, other means were required and national policymakers soon proved equal to the task of finding or devising them.

Some appeared ready to hand as the traditional means were reduced or abolished. These are the so-called nontariff barriers (NTBs). They constitute a heterogeneous group of regulations, requirements, and programs that include government-procurement preferences; health and safety regulations; product quality standards; customs procedures; low- or no-interest loans, tax exemptions, and other kinds of subsidies to promote employment, investment, and research and development; subventions to cover the deficits of the remaining state-owned enterprises; and other measures. Many NTBs were originally adopted for domestic policy reasons not directly related to international trade. However, as tariffs and quantitative restrictions on imports receded and disappeared, they were found to have a significant effect in restricting imports or promoting exports and hence have been increasingly used for these purposes since the early 1970s. Not only the West

European nations but also the United States, Canada, and especially Japan have been using NTBs to enhance the competitive positions of their products in their own and foreign markets.

Other measures, not strictly speaking in the category of NTBs, have also been adopted to cope with declining international competitiveness. Among the earliest and most important have been the so-called voluntary export restraints and orderly marketing agreements, under which the exporting nations, notably Japan and the NICs, impose export quotas on their own producers pursuant to an informal or formal understanding with the importing nations as to the shares of the latter's markets that they can capture. Such agreements, like the reimposed import quotas noted above, have been used to help industries that are labor-intensive, make standard products in long production runs, or have stable or slowly changing technologies or, conversely, in which the importing countries' manufacturers have failed to keep up with innovations in product or process technologies and marketing strategies. The main industries in these categories have been textiles and clothing, footwear, steel, shipbuilding, motor vehicles, household appliances, consumer electronics, and machine tools.

Similar measures have been applied to international trade in agricultural products, which is generally not covered by the GATT. In their common agricultural policy, the members of the EC have a very effective instrument not only for sustaining farmers' incomes but also for limiting imports of any competing agricultural goods and subsidizing the export of their own surplus production. The United States, Canada, and Japan, too, have various devices for restricting imports of competing agricultural products and subsidizing exports of such commodities.

How the United States Has Differed from the Other OECD Nations

The United States has deviated from the other OECD countries in several important respects. The first has been its extraordinarily high rate of net job creation, totaling more than 24 million from 1970 through 1985. Although, especially during the early years, employment increased in the public sector to staff the new welfare and regulatory activities, most of the new jobs have been in the private sector, particularly in services and the new high-technology industries. This reflects the larger size and greater dynamism of the U.S. private sector compared to those of the West European nations and the flexibility of U.S. labor unions, most of which have shunned the ideological rigidities of the European trade union movement.

Second, the United States has not followed restrictive fiscal policies, as have the West European nations and Japan. Indeed, under the Reagan administration, its budgetary deficits have been by far the largest relative to GNP in its peacetime history, mainly as a result of big tax reductions combined with major increases in national-defense expenditures and the irreducibility of the main welfare costs. The effect of the deficits and tax cuts was to give the U.S. economy an enormous demand stimulus that produced high economic growth rates for several years after the 1981–1982 recession. In contrast, U.S. monetary policy was tightened from 1979 on, which—though it raised real interest rates—helped to bring down the rate of inflation and to bring on the 1981–1982 recession, an even deeper and longer one than that of 1974–1975.

Third, not only did the United States, like the other OECD nations, refrain from further significant expansion of its welfare system but also it made a deliberate effort, beginning in the late 1970s, to reduce the network of regulations and restrictions previously imposed on its private sector. However, most U.S. deregulation has been for the purpose of restoring competition in activities long under federal control—such as rail, road and air transportation, communications, and banking—rather than easing the newer regulations adopted for environmental and equity purposes.

Fourth, although the United States, too, has resorted to import quotas, voluntary export-restraint and orderly marketing agreements, NTBs, and other means of reducing imports and promoting exports, it has done so on a smaller scale relative to the size of its economy than have the other OECD nations. The U.S. economy still remains significantly more open to foreign trade than the others, as it was throughout the postwar period.

This self-restraint has been especially important in view of the seriously adverse effects on U.S. industrial and agricultural producers and their workers of the renewed overvaluation of the U.S. dollar, which in March 1985 reached a peak of 60 percent over its 1980 value, a much bigger overvaluation than that of the postwar period. The overvaluation of the dollar helped Japan, the NICs, and some other developing countries to increase substantially their exports to the United States. It even enabled the West Europeans to offset enough of their declining competitive capabilities to raise their exports to the United States. Conversely, it aggravated declining U.S. international competitiveness, further reducing the ability of U.S. exporters to sell in foreign markets and further depressing employment and income in steel, autos, textiles, and other already noncompetitive U.S. industries.

The growing overvaluation of the U.S. dollar during the first half of the 1980s was the monetary facet of a complex, self-reinforcing set of inter-actions among internal and external factors, the real facet of which was the large and increasing U.S. deficit in merchandise trade. These interactions included (1) the higher real U.S. interest rates than in Western Europe and Japan, due primarily to the tight U.S. monetary policy needed to offset its expansionary fiscal policy (that is, its big budgetary deficit); (2) the rising demand for dollars as U.S. banks and corporations repatriated short-term funds from abroad and as banks and institutional and individual savers in other countries increasingly invested in U.S.-government bonds and other U.S. securities their countries' suplus earnings from exports to the United States so as to obtain the higher real rates of return in the faster-growing U.S. economy; and (3) as these demands pushed the dollar exchange rate even higher, the consequent further decline in U.S. competitiveness and increase in the U.S. balance-of-payments deficit, which generated additional earnings by foreigners to be invested in the United States. These incentives for the inflow of foreign funds were reinforced by the comparatively greater safety for capital invested in the United States in view of the persisting economic difficulties of the West European countries and the political insecurities and economic uncertainties in other parts of the world.

Unlike in the 1960s, this new recycling operation enabled the United States to finance its huge budgetary and balance-of-payments deficits by noninflationary means despite inadequate U.S. domestic savings. By 1985, however, the domestic pressures generated by the adverse effects of the enormous influx of imports on U.S. employment and incomes and on the growth rate of the U.S. economy impelled the U.S. Treasury to try to push down the exchange rate of the dollar. Initially with the support of the Japanese and German monetary authorities, the U.S. Treasury's efforts were successful in substantially reducing the value of the dollar vis-à-vis the yen and the mark during 1986. Nonetheless, the U.S. merchandise deficit continued to rise, as did the influx of foreign funds to finance it and the persisting large budgetary deficit. The result was that in 1986, for the first time since 1913, foreign governments and investors owned more assets in the United States than American investors owned abroad. With a net foreign debt of $264 billion at the end of 1986, the United States became the world's largest debtor nation.

The Consequences of the Institutional Changes

In sum, since the postwar period, the institutional changes within the OECD nations have been interacting with one another and with the international developments to confine national policymakers increasingly within three sets of constraints. On the first side are the domestic pressures to maintain, and if possible to raise, the levels of consumption and of welfare already attained, reinforced by the vigilance and activism of competing interest groups, single-issue organizations, and the media. On the second side are the internal limitations on national economic policy imposed by the need to avoid further negative-sum welfare/efficiency interactions and renewed inflation while endeavoring to stimulate economic growth, reduce unemployment, and offset the effects of the loss of international competitiveness. On the third side are the pressures generated by the changes in the structure and functioning of the international economic system, sketched in Chapter III.

The scope for policymaking within this triangular set of constraints varies among the OECD nations depending on the characteristics of their economies and the attitudes and expectations of their people. In all countries, however, these triangular constraints have been compelling their policymakers to cope with the resulting problems by resorting to short-term particularistic palliatives rather than to more difficult and painful longer-term solutions. So far in the 1980s, the United States has enjoyed the widest latitude within these constraints, a condition that reflects not only the specific factors noted above but also lingering elements of its postwar hegemonic status. But, even U.S. policymakers, have had to act increasingly in accordance with short-term particularistic pressures. The failure during the 1980s to prevent or substantially reduce the unprecedented U.S. balance-of-payments and budgetary deficits reflected as much the limitations under which both the president and the Congress operated as it did the shortsighted policy choices of the Reagan administration.

Generational Change and Attitudes in the OECD Nations

A basic phenomenon that is not usually taken into account in the analysis of international relations is generational change. It is significant when the life experiences of people during childhood and adolescence differ sufficiently from those of their parents. Although the new generation continues within the same general cultural heritage as its predecessor, its members are inclined as adults to shift the priorities among the transmitted social and personal values, to modify behavioral norms accordingly, and to formulate different perceptions of societal and intersocietal realities and different conceptions of how to deal with them.

This has been the case between the older generation, the people born and educated before World War II who occupied the positions of power and influence in the OECD societies during the postwar period, and the younger generation, those born and educated after World War II who, since the early 1970s, have increasingly been moving into these positions. During the 1990s, the members of the younger generation will replace all of the policymakers and opinion leaders remaining from the postwar generation. This shift has already had, and will continue to have, a major impact on national attitudes and policies because the younger generation has had markedly different life experiences during its formative years from those of the older generation. This section surveys these psychocultural changes in the OECD nations and the effects on their external perceptions and behavior.

Differences in Generational Experiences and Attitudes

Each successive age cohort of the younger generation has tended to manifest attitudes and perceptions that differ a little more from those of the postwar generation and of the oldest age cohorts of its own generation. As it became more articulate and influential, the younger generation's attitudes and perceptions increasingly affected those of people in the older generation. Moreover, not all or even most people have manifested all of the characteristics attributed to their generation in the analysis below or have done so with equal intensity and determination. Each generational characterization sketched here is what Max Weber called an "ideal type," that is, the description of a class, or category, of societal phenomena that contains all of the essential elements that differentiate it from all other classes of societal phenomena but which any actual member of the category possesses only in greater or lesser degree.

The formative life experiences of the postwar generation—my generation—included the immense destructiveness and disruption of the two world wars; the seizure of power by genocidal totalitarian regimes in Russia, Germany, Italy, and Japan and their mounting threat during the 1930s to the freedom of the Western democracies; the economic hardships and insecurities of the Great Depression; and, in continental Western Europe, the shame and horrors of Nazi conquest and occupation. Moreover, it appeared to young people born or educated during the interwar period that these deep problems and catastrophes resulted from the intellectual and moral deficiencies of the prewar policymakers. While some succumbed to hopelessness, many more young people were impelled by these grave political dangers, economic hardships, and social tensions to seek solutions. These included not only the revolutionary panaceas that attracted many despairing young idealists during the 1930s but, more significantly after World War II, the construction of the postwar system of international political and economic order described in Chapter II and of the national welfare systems that it helped to make possible.

The expectations of those working toward these goals after World War II were that, in contrast to the futile expedients and appeasements of the prewar policymakers, their efforts would assure world peace and prosperity and the easing, if not the abolition, of social tensions within nations—victors, liberated and defeated alike. Their perception soon came to be that a major threat to the fulfillment of these optimistic expectations—indeed, to many the sole threat—was the refusal of the Soviet Union to participate in the kind of national and international reconstruction they envisaged and its apparently relentless effort to realize an incompatible alternative system of world order.

Naturally, the efforts of the postwar generation fell short of its goals; naturally, their expectations were unrealistic and their perceptions were inaccurate in important respects; naturally, they made mistakes and had serious failures of their own—though not so serious as those of their parents' generation. And, naturally, their very successes helped to generate new problems and tensions that they neither foresaw nor were able to prevent. Nonetheless, their decisions and actions were essential elements in bringing about the twenty-five years of unprecedented advances in economic well-being and social justice and the political and strategic security that the OECD nations enjoyed during the postwar period.

It was these new postwar conditions—so different from those experienced by the older generation during its formative years—that have been shaping the life experiences of the younger generation. In consequence, its successive age cohorts have grown up to regard their societies as having both the obligation and the capacity to realize their expectations for self-fulfillment, satisfying work, high and rising living standards, complete medical care, environmental improvement, and the other forms of welfare and equity instituted during the 1960s and 1970s. Moreover, they expect to receive these benefits without making any substantial sacrifices of income or personal freedom of action.

This attitude contrasts sharply with that formed by the youth of the older generation during their development. To cope with the hardships of the Great Depression and the exigencies of World War II, the older generation had no other choice before the advent of the welfare state than to rely upon the initiative and ingenuity of individuals and the mutual help of families, friends, and local agencies and to subordinate shorter-term personal and group interests to the longer-term needs of the society as a whole. In contrast, the younger generation tends to be more self-willed, impatient of societal restraints, and less inclined to make the concessions required for compromise and cooperation. It is more dependent on, yet more cynical about, the role of government than the older generation. It is inclined to be more troubled by the potential destructiveness of nuclear weapons and possible environmental contamination by nuclear energy than the postwar generations which regarded the former as the ultimate safeguard against nuclear war and the latter as the source of clean and abundant power.

Thus, at all levels within their societies, the members of the postwar generation tended to be more universalistic and directed to the long term in their interactions within their societies and in their effects on the behavior of their countries in the international system. The members of the younger generation have tended to be more particularistic and intent on the short term in these respects. These contrasting orientations helped to generate the institutional changes surveyed in the preceding section and, in turn, were fostered by them.

Effects on the External Perceptions and Behavior of the OECD Nations

Since the end of the postwar period, the institutional and psychocultural changes in the OECD countries have led to deep ambivalences in the ways in which their people perceive and deal with domestic and international problems. Although there are significant differences in how these ambivalences are manifested in the various OECD nations, space limitations permit brief comments only on those between the West European societies and the United States as they affect the relations between the two and their present and prospective participation in the international system.

Most members of both generations in Western Europe recognize that their economies have grown so large and wealthy that, as combined in the EC, they now account for bigger shares of world GNP and world trade than does the United States, making their influence on world economic conditions at least equal to that of the latter. Yet despite the fact that the per capita national incomes of most nations are almost as large as that of the United States, the West Europeans are unwilling to divert sufficient resources from consumption and the realization of welfare goals to provide for their own defense and acquire the power and influence to play a major independent role in the international system. They remain dependent upon U.S. nuclear and conventional forces for protection against possible Soviet aggression or Soviet pressure to conform to its policies. In these circumstances, the West Europeans, especially the members of the younger generation, are increasingly resentful of the constraints on their freedom of action resulting from their now self-imposed dependence on the United States.

In theory, this ambivalence and resentment could be resolved by further progress toward the political and economic unification of the EC, leading to the emergence of a West European federation with the will and ability to provide for its own defense and to protect and advance its international political and economic interests. In reality, however, such progress has been blocked since the late 1960s by the institutional changes surveyed in the preceding section, notably (1) the strengthening of the nation-state as the responsibilities of national governments have expanded, (2) the accompanying politicization of the process of resource allocation, and (3) the pressures to seek nationalistic palliatives for the problems generated by negative-sum welfare/efficiency interactions and adverse international economic developments. Nor do most members of the younger generation have much desire to exercise the important power and influence in the international system that would be made possible by a European federation. These factors, responsible for the long stagnation of the movement for European unification, are not likely to change significantly in the foreseeable future and, therefore, this way of relieving West European frustrations and resentments is not a realistic possibility.

During the postwar period as noted in Chapter II, most members of the older generation in Western Europe had a generally favorable attitude toward the United States due to its role in their liberation from Nazi occupation or its threat, postwar European recovery under the Marshall Plan, U.S. willingness to protect them under NATO, and the high rates of economic growth they enjoyed in the U.S.-supported world market economy.

In contrast, most members of the younger generation in Western Europe perceive the policies and actions of the United States as restricting their countries' freedom of action and often as incompatible with their national political and economic interests. This reaction has been increasingly manifested in trade issues, defense expenditures and strategy in NATO, relations with the Third World and with the Soviet Union, policies toward the Arab-Israeli conflict and the protection of the Persian Gulf, and other problems in Asia, Africa, and Latin America of concern to the West Europeans. While most members of the younger generation are not attracted to communism as such, many believe that the Soviet Union has the same conception of detente as they do—that is, that the Soviet Union has no aggressive intentions toward Western Europe and seeks only the easing of East-West tensions. Thus, many in the younger generation in Western Europe regard U.S. policies, not those of the Soviet Union, as the main threat to international stability and even of nuclear war, a fear that the sometimes inflated rhetoric and ill-advised initiatives of the Reagan administration appeared to confirm.

In the United States, the late 1960s witnessed the beginning of the gradual abatement of the activist, interventionist mode of the U.S. sense of mission that had characterized U.S. participation in the international system since World War II and even some reversion toward the traditional passive mode of simply presenting itself as a moral, sociopolitical, and technoeconomic model for other nations to follow. This shift both reflected and in turn helped to foster three mutually reinforcing attitudes. One was the increasing conviction in the late 1960s and early 1970s that achieving welfare, equity, and other social goals was so urgent in terms of social stability and moral standards that top priority had to be accorded to them. This conviction tended to focus attention and resources on domestic rather than international problems. The second was the growing opposition of the younger generation to the Vietnam War and the unsettling effects on many in the older generation already disillusioned about how and how soon that conflict could be successfully concluded. The third, prevalent during the 1970s, was the expectation that detente with the Soviet Union would so ease the tensions and dangers in the international system that the United States could safely concentrate its attention and resources on domestic concerns.

By the end of the decade, as explained in Chapter VI, the behavior of the Soviet Union had largely dissipated this expectation and led to the Reagan administration's big increases in defense expenditures. Nonetheless, the orientation of the younger generation and many members of the older generation has continued to be inward, absorbed in the pursuit of individual satisfactions and group interests, especially as the problems discussed in the preceding section impinged more and more on their daily lives. A majority remains opposed to the use of force to protect or advance U.S. interests in the international system unless the threat is perceived as direct, serious, and imminent. At the same time, however, most Americans have been irritated by the setbacks of U.S. foreign policy in the 1970s and 1980s and the steadily declining ability of the United States to persuade even its allies and remaining dependent states to support its policies for maintaining world order.

The result has been a deep ambivalence in most members of the younger generation and in many members of the older postwar generation regarding the carrying out of U.S. responsibilities in the international system. A fuller explanation of this development is reserved for the beginning of Chapter X because the issues involved relate directly to the future international role of the United States that is explored there. Suffice it to note here that this ambivalence has substantially narrowed the freedom of action of U.S. foreign–policy makers and restricted the positive inducements and negative sanctions they could use to exert influence, let alone power, in the international system.

In sum, the net effect of the institutional and psychocultural changes within the OECD nations has been greatly to intensify the tensions within and among them between preserving the benefits of international economic integration and political coordination and obtaining the benefits of national freedom of action in domestic and foreign affairs. The internal and international changes since the early 1970s have made the adjustment process more rapid and drastic for the OECD nations than it was during the postwar period. The costs of economic integration and political coordination have increased while U.S. willingness and ability to bear a disproportionate share of them have declined. And, since the other OECD nations are even less willing to assume the costs, especially those of a short-term nature that have grown the most, there has been an increasing tendency to try to pass them on to one another—to become free-riders in the system.

NOTE

1. The main exception was France in the early 1980s, when the incoming socialist administration under François Mitterrand reflated domestic demand, instituted substantial new welfare measures, and nationalized more industrial enterprises and banks. The adverse effects, however, were soon apparent in further loss of international competitiveness and mounting budgetary and balance-of-payments deficits, which compelled the adoption of restrictive fiscal and monetary policies.

Chapter V

CHANGES WITHIN THE ASIAN, AFRICAN, AND LATIN AMERICAN NATIONS

Since the early postwar period, the Asian, African, and Latin American nations have been classified together as the less developed countries (usually abbreviated as the LDCs). This practice of regarding them as a single group, the so-called Third World, is valid insofar as these nations have a sense of solidarity and common purpose and seek to act as a unit in their relations with the OECD countries and the communist states. However, any analysis of their internal processes of change and of the resulting problems and tensions that affect their international behavior must take account of the profound differences in their historical backgrounds and existing socio-cultural characteristics. Even dividing them, as in this chapter, into the separate categories of the transitional societies of Asia and Africa and the modernizing societies of Latin America does nothing more than mark their most conspicuous dissimilarity. Nevertheless, limitations of space prevent use of a more differentiated classification. As in the preceding discussion of the OECD nations, the distinguishing characteristics of each category are regarded as constituting an ideal type, with any member nation diverging from it in greater or lesser degree.

CHANGES IN THE ASIAN AND AFRICAN NATIONS

The present-day nations of Asia and Africa are descended from quite different civilizational backgrounds than are Western societies. Yet, despite the vast differences in their institutional structures, cultural characteristics, and technological levels, all Asian and African countries were originally traditional agrarian, authoritarian societies whose basic institutions, values, and behavioral norms were eroded by their traumatic encounter with Western society and culture over the past two centuries. Having achieved national independence or freedom from Western control during the decolonization movement of the postwar period, they are now in the process of forging new ways of living and working and new senses of cultural identity and national purpose out of two incompatible heritages: the surviving institutions, values, and norms of their traditional societies and those of the intruding alien Western society. This transformation into new societies is immensely difficult and slow despite the efforts of the elites in most of these countries to guide and accelerate it. Even in the best of circumstances, the duration of the transition will be measured in generations, not decades, and its various outcomes cannot yet be discerned. By its nature, the transitional process involves periods of retrogression and stagnation as well as of forward movement.

Essentially, progress involves institutional development, social reintegration, and the creation in the culture of a new dramatic design, that is, of a new sense of societal identity and meaning. These three crucial elements of the transitional process can be accomplished through slow organic societal evolution, as generally in the past, or by deliberate efforts to guide and accelerate the process in accordance with policymakers' conceptions of desirable outcomes.

Institutional Change and Its Problems

Such "planned development" was the approach chosen by the ruling elites of most newly independent nations, many of whom designated their institutional objectives by the terms "socialism" and "nationalism."

This predilection for socialism has been the economic response to three basic characteristics of these countries. The first is that, as traditional societies, their economies were largely or wholly of the nonmarket type, which made this form of production and distribution seem more familiar and conducive to the perpetuation of traditional communal values. The second is a corollary of the first: the inadequacy or lack in many countries of indigenous capabilities, motivations, and norms of behavior required for the effective operation of modern private-enterprise market systems. The third is the strong attraction of the elites to psychologically satisfying, vaguely Marxist rationales that blame "capitalist imperialism" for their countries' problems and expect the OECD nations to provide the resources for overcoming them.

Conceptions of socialism range from putting as much as possible of the nation's economic activities in the public sector to efforts to develop communal economic arrangements reminiscent of the nonmarket institutions of the traditional society. Regardless of what type of socialism has been envisaged, however, progress toward realizing it has been very slow in most countries and has not resulted in the anticipated economic growth and rising living standards. The reasons have been the inherent limitations of nonmarket economic systems under dynamic modern technoeconomic conditions (explained in Chapter VI), the low productivity and capital accumulation of these economies, and the inadequate capabilities of the elites for economic planning and control. Except for those countries that have become members of the Soviet hegemony, the Asian and African nations seeking to develop socialist economies have continued, therefore, to depend on participation in the world market system. Intensification of their problems during the 1980s has even impelled some of them to introduce more market incentives and pressures into their economies.

In contrast, those countries—such as the East and Southeast Asian NICs—that had indigenous groups already experienced in private enterprise and that have encouraged the development of predominantly market economies have generally had higher rates of growth and bigger rises in living standards than the more socialist nations. Even in these countries, however, the government tries to direct domestic economic activities and external economic relations, and indigenous and foreign-owned private enterprises are usually subjected to extensive regulation. The aim in these countries, as in the socialist ones, is to restrict, divert, or reinforce the operation of market forces, both internal and external, so as to channel resources to the kinds of institutions, income distribution, and levels of consumption that the ruling elites believe are in the best interests of their countries, as well as of themselves and their supporters. Thus, the policies of Asian and African governments are even more determinative of the actual condition and future prospects of their economies than are those of the OECD nations.

Nationalism has been the political response to two basic needs of transitional Asian and African societies. One is for universalistic values and norms to legitimate political authority and help to restrain and orient toward common goals the intense particularism of the often conflicting groups and institutions of which these societies are composed. The other is the need to differentiate the new nation from its neighbors, as well as from its former imperial rulers and the postwar hegemon, the United States.

By its nature, the transitional process generates social tensions and particularistic conflicts over political power and control of economic resources among the old and new elites, among the different traditional tribes, sects, castes, and other ethnic groups, and between them and the modern-type organizations and groups, indigenous and foreign. Not only are the modern elites participants in these conflicts but also their efforts to guide the transitional process are further impeded by their inadequate training and experience, the tensions between their traditional kinship loyalties and their responsibilities in impersonal modern-type institutions, and the psychological insecurities and social pressures that inhibit them from making concessions and abiding by compromises.

Economic growth is essential for generating the resources required for institutional development, for meeting the consumption needs of rapidly increasing populations, and for satisfying the expectations of the elites and the people for rising living standards. But, economic growth can have seriously destabilizing effects. People are attracted away from traditional rural subsistence activities before sufficient employment is available in the modern urban industrial and service sectors. Imbalances also arise between the domestic economy and the international economic system. Over-ambitious or inappropriate development policies and programs result in waste, inflation, and unemployment. Increasing dependence on foreign trade makes the domestic economy more susceptible to the adverse effects of rising import prices and of declining demand or limited access for the country's exports in other markets, especially those of the OECD nations. These severe economic difficulties exacerbate the social tensions and particularistic conflicts; in turn, the latter make the mitigation of the economic problems even harder.

The great majority of Asian and African countries have responded to these tensions and problems by adopting more or less authoritarian political institutions, to which they have anyway been predisposed both by their traditions of autocratic rule and by the authoritarian regimes of their former imperial masters. True, toward the end of their imperial rule in Asia and Africa, the United Kingdom and France attempted to endow the soon-to-be-independent nations with parliamentary-type democratic institutions. However, with a few exceptions, such as India, these institutions were short-lived because neither the elites nor the people possessed in sufficient degree the universalistic values and the self-restraining behavioral norms necessary for their effective operation.

These authoritarian regimes tend to share in the instability inherent in the transitional process. Especially in Africa, they are characterized by frequent changes in the elite group holding power through factional coups, military takeovers, assassinations, and other forcible actions, sometimes pursuant to or to forestall outbreaks of mass discontent. Military regimes are especially prominent because the armed forces not only possess the means for seizing power but also tend to be better organized, more disciplined, and more effective operationally than the other institutions of the society. Military and civilian rulers who last longest are usually those with prepotent personalities who can evoke the adulation and fear formerly accorded to powerful kings, chiefs, and conquerors in the traditional society.

The erratic forward-and-backward course of the transitional process is also manifested in other ways. Prominent among them is the reassertion of traditional elements in the face of the intruding Western culture and institutions. Because of the crucial historical role of religion in forming a society's dramatic design, these reactions most often involve deliberate efforts to emphasize or revive aspects of the traditional religion. This can impart some sense of identity and meaning to elites and nonelites afflicted with deep feelings of anomie generated by the disintegration of traditional kinship or communal bonds and by the unfamiliar, anxiety-provoking individualism enjoined by the alien Western culture. Religions with pronounced messianic characteristics are especially able to play this role, such as the Shiite sects of Islam and the nativistic cults inspired by Christianity in Africa. Religious and other indigenous cultural reassertions also help to revive a degree of self-respect in societies whose traditional institutions and cultures failed to resist the corrosive impact of the West.

Differences between Regional Subgroups

The ability of Asian and African countries to guide and accelerate the transitional process and to cope with the tensions, conflicts, and problems involved has varied widely since they became independent. Three sets of factors are responsible for these differences: (1) the characteristics inherited from the country's traditional background, (2) for how long and in what ways it was subjected to the impact of Western society, and (3) the specific forms in which and the intensity with which the tensions and conflicts of the transitional process are manifested. In terms of their sociocultural backgrounds, four major subgroups of countries can be distinguished: the East Asian nations, the South and Southeast Asian nations, the Islamic nations of West Asia and North Africa, and the sub-Saharan African nations.

The most successful have been the East Asian countries—South Korea, Taiwan, and Singapore (as well as Hong Kong, under British rule until 1997)—that are the leading newly industrializing nations. These NICs have had the advantage of being part of or influenced by the great Chinese civilizational tradition, from which they derived much of the motivation and capabilities required for entrepreneurship, the paternalistic conception of an authoritarian government's responsibilities, and the values of self-restraint and social harmony. These elements have helped them to avoid or to experience in less severe forms the problems noted above and to orient their people's pursuit of self-interest more effectively toward national goals than elsewhere in Asia and Africa. Just as Japan—with a similar socio-cultural background—was the first and is still the only non-Western society to complete the transitional process, so the East Asian NICs are likely to be the next to do so, although how and when still cannot be foreseen and the possibilities of retrogression, diversion, or stagnation cannot be discounted.

At the other extreme are the sub-Saharan African countries, whose tribal societies were still at relatively early stages of societal evolution when they were incorporated into the European empires in the late 19th century and for which the imperial rulers had done little or nothing to prepare for independence. Even the few—such as the Ivory Coast and Kenya—that have been able since independence to maintain reasonable political stability and economic growth rates could at any time suffer overt manifestations of the tensions and problems of the transitional process. For most sub-Saharan countries, the difficulties they face are compounded by inordinately high population growth rates and periodic droughts and famines. Hence, by and large, the transitional process will be longer, harder and more erratic for the sub-Saharan African nations than for the countries in the other subgroups.

Between these two extremes are the two subgroups of the South and Southeast Asian nations and the Islamic states of West Asia and North Africa. Like the East Asian countries, the nations in these two subcategories descend from long civilizational traditions. Yet their ancestral societies, however much they may have achieved in their periods of greatness, have not endowed them with sociocultural elements as conducive to easing and accelerating the transitional process as those derived from Chinese civilization. Nonetheless, Malaysia, Thailand, and India, which already have or have been moving toward market economic systems, have been doing better in recent years—in India's case despite its enormous population pressures.

Among the Islamic nations of West Asia and North Africa, those with large petroleum resources relative to population experienced high economic growth rates during the 1970s and first half of the 1980s. In contrast, others not in this category, such as Egypt, Syria, Jordan, Tunisia, and Morocco, have had little or no rise of real per capita incomes due to low rates of economic growth and high rates of population increase. They have been dependent in greater or lesser degree on aid from the OECD nations, the Soviet Union and its East European client states, and the oil-rich Arab countries. However, even in the latter, it is not necessarily the case that the transitional process will be less long, erratic, and difficult than in the others. As explained above, rapid economic growth can be very destabilizing, especially in societies, such as those of Iraq, Iran, Saudi Arabia, Kuwait, and the Gulf Emirates, whose social structures and psychocultural characteristics are still largely traditionalistic. Moreover, as an overdetermining cultural system, Islam is not conducive in important respects to the political development of Moslem societies. It gives only very conditional legitimation to their sociopolitical institutions, which always fall short of the all-encompassing way of life of the *umma*, the community of the faithful, prescribed in the Koran and the Sharia.

Effects of External Economic Dependence

Just as the Asian and African countries were propelled into their profound transformations by their involuntary involvement in the European-dominated worldwide system of the 19th and early 20th centuries, so now are their processes of societal change dependent in part on their participation in the transitional international system of the late 20th century. This dependence can take a variety of forms and can have both positive and negative effects that are determined in part by a country's capacity to realize its external opportunities and to avoid, offset, or lessen the impact of unfavorable external developments.

Between two-thirds and three-quarters of the trade (exports and imports) of Asian, African, and Latin American countries is with the OECD nations, which also provide most of their private capital inflows and most of the aid they receive directly and through the international lending institutions and other international organizations. Therefore, the economic relations of these countries with the OECD nations are among the major determinants of their economic growth rates.

However, the increasing economic difficulties of the OECD countries during the 1970s and 1980s and their particularistic efforts to cope with them, sketched in the preceding chapter, have limited the economic resources Asian, African, and Latin American nations could obtain through trade, investment, and aid. The unfavorable impact was mitigated or blocked during the 1970s by the recycling/borrowing operations described in Chapter III. But, for many of the debtor countries, this only postponed the problem. It reappeared during the 1980s in aggravated form as a series of debt-service crises that compelled them to adopt austerity measures. Thus, except for the NICs and the other Asian nations following in their footsteps, many Asian, African, and Latin American countries have been experiencing lower (in some cases no) economic growth. While rapid economic growth can be destabilizing, too low or no growth and the resulting reductions in living standards can be even more so.

Generational Change and Attitudes toward External Relations

The humiliation of their past subjection to the European imperial powers and their dissatisfaction with their continued economic dependence on the OECD nations have combined to generate deeply ambivalent—indeed, conflicted—feelings in the Asian and African countries toward the West. However, important changes have been occurring in the content and intensity of these attitudes as members of the new postindependence generation of elites have been reaching positions of power and influence in their societies.

Members of the older generation of elites—who led the struggles for independence during the interwar and immediate post–World War II years and governed the new nations during the postwar period—had a classically conflicted attitude toward the West. On the one hand, they felt strongly the sense of failure and loss of self-confidence engendered by the traditional society's futile effort to resist Western rule and sociocultural erosion, which they knew vividly from their own and their parents' life experiences. They deeply resented their treatment as cultural or racial inferiors even after many of them had acquired Western educations and life-styles. Moreover, they were embittered by their long deprivation of power and wealth, to which they believed themselves entitled, even though they were eventually successful in obtaining them. On the other hand, they were imbued with a powerful respect for Western military, political, technoeconomic, and scientific achievements, which they envisaged their countries as eventually emulating, and they aspired to attain a Western-type standard of living.

This attraction/rejection syndrome conditioned the postindependence relationships of Asian and African nations not only with their former imperial rulers but also with the United States, which loomed large as the superpower under whose hegemonic leadership the international political and economic system was being reconstructed during the postwar period. Hence, the United States primarily and the other OECD nations secondarily were regarded by the older elites as responsible for their countries' frustrations and setbacks. Nevertheless, their respect for and awe of the West, as well as the benefits involved, constrained most Asian and African nations to accept, however reluctantly, membership in the reconstructed system of world order. Nor did the fact that, in the late 1950s and the 1960s, a growing number of these countries declared themselves "nonaligned" as yet imply rejection of the system. Rather, it expressed simply the desire not to be involved in the cold-war rivalry between the United States and the Soviet Union.

By the 1970s, however, members of a new generation born or educated after the achievement of independence were beginning to attain positions of power and influence in Asian and African nations. Unlike their elders, the elites of the younger generation had little or no personal experience of Western rule and of the Western military, political, and economic capabilities that had made it possible. Rather, their perception during the 1970s was of the former European imperial rulers as much declined in military and political effectiveness and, though still economically rich and powerful, as nevertheless vulnerable due to their dependence on imported petroleum and other raw materials. They perceived the United States as weakened by its defeat in Vietnam, its domestic distractions, and its apparent inability either to arrest the expansion of Soviet influence or to prevent the OPEC countries from drastically increasing petroleum prices. No longer in as much awe of the West as their parents had been, the new generation gained greater confidence in its own abilities during the 1970s.

The attitude toward the Soviet Union of both the older and the younger generation of elites has been markedly different from their conflicted feelings toward the United States and Western Europe. Only a few countries—notably Iran, Turkey, and Afghanistan, as well as China—had been affected by Russian imperial expansion in the 19th and 20th centuries. Nor has the Soviet Union become a model to be followed, except for those Asian and African nations that have been incorporated into the Soviet hegemony. Even countries dependent on Soviet economic and military assistance and political support, such as Syria and Libya, do not pattern their own development on Soviet society. Thus, the relationship of most Asian and African nations to the Soviet Union does not have anything like the psychological depth and complexity that has characterized their relationships with their former imperial rulers and with the United States. Asian and African countries are careful not to antagonize the Soviet Union, except under such extreme provocation as its occupation of Afghanistan, and even then their criticisms are soon watered down or forgotten. These countries recognize that, as Soviet behavior toward its client states has demonstrated, the Soviet Union has the ability and the will to defend its interests by force, and that, in the exercise of its power, it is not restrained by the moral, legal, and public-opinion considerations that generally affect U.S. policymakers.

The Marxist ways of thinking of many Asian and African elites justify and reinforce the resentment engendered by their countries' continued economic dependence on the OECD nations, and incline them to accept both the Soviets' characterization of this relationship as "neoimperialism" and Soviet support for their demands for a drastic redistribution of world wealth and income, explained below. Hence, their nonalignment has been tilted toward the Soviet Union.

During the 1970s, their declining awe and respect for the United States and the other OECD nations and their own increasing self-confidence enabled the new generation of elites in Asia and Africa to express more openly and drastically their resentment against the West and their demands for major Western concessions. This basic resentment was aggravated in particular groups of countries by special grievances against the United States—for example, in the Islamic nations over U.S. support for Israel and in the black African states over U.S. refusal to apply sanctions against South Africa.

These attitudes were most conspicuously articulated in large multinational forums, such as the periodic conferences of the Nonaligned Movement and of the Group of 77 (now numbering more than 120 nations), and the meetings of the UN General Assembly, UNCTAD, UNESCO, and other UN regional and specialized agencies in which the Third World countries (including the Latin American nations) outnumber and can outvote the OECD countries. On these public occasions, the sense of solidarity and of mutual approbation—as well as the encouragement of the Soviet Union and the urging of many staff members of these international organizations—helped to strengthen the conviction of the justice of the Third World's demands and of its presumed negotiating strength.

Emboldened by the success of the OPEC nations, Third World elites demanded major Western concessions during the 1970s that were chiefly economic in nature and were expressed in the concept of a "new international economic order" (NIEO). The NIEO was designed (1) to bring about a drastic redistribution of world income in favor of the Asian, African, and Latin American nations and (2) to subject the world market economy to extensive management by national governments, among which those of the Third World would constitute a determining majority. Thus, the NIEO represented a repudiation of the kind of world market economic system constructed during the postwar period. The reaction of the OECD countr[.] was to talk and to temporize. Their basic interest in maintaining the existing system and the increasing particularism of their policies sketched in the preceding chapter constrained them to oppose the NIEO. But, they were also impelled by their moral values and economic interests to try to avoid exacerbating conflicts with the Third World. The result was a series of inconclusive "North-South dialogues."

The pressure of their needs, however, has induced many Third World countries to deal individually with OECD nations, and these bilateral relationships have usually produced much greater benefits for them than have their collective initiatives. Also, in smaller, less conspicuous negotiations—such as those between the EC members and their former subjects in Africa, the Caribbean, and the Pacific (the so-called ACP Conventions)—

Third World countries have been able to obtain substantial trade, aid, and other concessions from the OECD nations. Such bilateral and multilateral agreements have been predicated on the maintenance of the existing international economic system. Thus, the new generation of Third World elites has been prepared to work both within the international economic system and for its radical transformation.

The demands for the NIEO and the North-South dialogues continued until the onset of the severe worldwide depression of 1981–1982 and the consequent debt-service problems of many Asian, African, and Latin American countries, as well as the droughts and famines in Africa. These deeply adverse experiences have diverted the attention and energies of Third World nations to their internal difficulties. Combined with their perception of OPEC's loss of its monopoly power under the supply and demand conditions after 1985 these problems have moderated Third World countries' notions of their bargaining strength vis-à-vis the OECD nations and have muted their demands for a substantial redistribution of world income and wealth. Nonetheless, the NIEO has not been abandoned but is only in abeyance, and it, or an equivalent, is likely to be revived when conditions in Asian, African, and Latin American countries and in the OECD nations again become conducive to new Third World initiatives.

The solidarity of Asian and African countries is most evident in their collective relationships with the OECD nations and, to a much lesser extent, the Soviet Union and its hegemony. However, the peer-group conformism that buttresses their solidarity in the big UN and other multilateral forums is generally ineffective in their relationships with one another when important interests and problems are at issue. True, Asian and African nations have established various intergovernmental organizations for economic cooperation and political coordination. The most effective has been the Association of Southeast Asian Nations (ASEAN), embracing Brunei, Indonesia, Malaysia, the Philippines, Singapore, and Thailand, which share a common concern about possible Vietnamese aggression and Chinese pressure and have set modest goals for their economic cooperation. In contrast, other bodies, such as the Organization for African Unity and the various associations of Arab and Islamic states, usually adopt ambitious objectives which they are neither willing nor able to implement. Often, too, these organizations are paralyzed by conflicts of interest and ideological divisions among their members that are reinforced by traditional animosities.

In addition, ideological differences, irredentist claims, political ambitions, or desires to divert popular attention from domestic failures impel regimes in some Asian and African countries to overt or covert actions (including support for guerrilla insurgencies) against their neighbors. These motivations have been manifested in wars (for example, India/Pakistan,

Iraq/Iran, Ethiopia/Somalia) and in efforts to develop the technoeconomic means for producing nuclear weapons or to purchase them.

In sum, impelled like the older generation to foster the development of nationalism, the current generation's lesser awe of the West and greater self-assertiveness have made the constraints imposed on national freedom of action by dependence on the international system seem even more irksome than in earlier decades. The basic tensions between international interdependence and national independence are and will continue to be more acute and frustrating for most Asian and African nations than for the much wealthier OECD countries or the more autarkic communist states. The tensions and problems inherent in the transitional process and the disputes and animosities between Asian and African countries aggravate these frustrations. They also compel many of these nations to adopt policies and undertake actions that not only prevent economic and political cooperation among them but instead result in the inability to resolve disagreements, whose perpetuation is damaging to both sides and which sometimes end in war. Thus, the outlook is for continuing tensions and instability both within many Asian and African nations and in their relations with one another.

CHANGES IN THE LATIN AMERICAN NATIONS

There are undeniable similarities in the economic problems, political instabilities and international behavior of the Latin American countries and the Asian and African nations surveyed in the preceding section. Nonetheless, the historical background and the present nature of the changes occurring in the two groups of societies are fundamentally different.

Unlike Asian and African societies, Latin American societies have constituted a subcategory of Western civilization since their beginnings in the 16th century, when the indigenous New World societies were destroyed or absorbed by the invading Spaniards and Portuguese. True, descendants of the indigenous people have continued to form substantial portions of the population and to retain many of their cultural characteristics, especially in the Andean nations and Central America. These cultural traits have not been of major determinative significance, however, because the people manifesting them have always been nonelites. The distinctive characteristics of all Latin American elites, regardless of their racial or ethnic backgrounds, have consisted of European-derived institutions, values, and norms of behavior. Nor have Latin American societies been unwillingly exposed to fundamentally alien influences, as Asian and African societies were due to their subjugation by the European imperial powers. Latin American societies have always been attracted to and affected by all of the great institutional and cultural developments in Western Europe and North America. These have included the ideas of the Enlightenment and of the American and French revolutions in the 18th century, the industrial and democratic revolutions in the 19th century, and the new cultural movements—romanticism, positivism, Marxism, technocratic utopianism, and so on—and the major political and economic developments of Western societies in the 20th century.

The essence of Latin America's problems is that its societies have continued to be so heavily influenced by certain sociocultural characteristics derived from their Iberian background. This legacy has never been conducive to realizing the goals of political democracy, social justice, and economic welfare to which Latin American societies have long aspired and toward which Western Europe and North America have made such conspicuously greater progress. In the 20th century and especially since World War II, Latin America has been engaged in a very difficult and frustrating effort to catch up with Western Europe and, more important, the United States. At faster or slower rates and with varying degrees of effectiveness, Latin American societies have been seeking to *modernize* their inherited institutions, values, and behavioral norms—not to transform them fundamentally, as Asian and African societies have been struggling to do in consequence of their traumatic encounter with alien Western societies.

The Iberian Legacy

The development of the Iberian peninsula during the entire medieval period differed significantly from that of the rest of Western Europe due to its rapid conquest by the Moslems early in the 8th century and its subsequent reconquest by the Christians, a process completed only with the fall of Granada in 1492. Certain indigenous institutions, values, and behavioral norms, as modified by strong Arab/Islamic influences, were adapted to the needs of the reconquest and resettlement of the peninsula and the reconversion of its inhabitants to Christianity. These elements proved to be readily transferable to meet the requirements of the immediately ensuing conquest and conversion of the indigenous inhabitants of the New World and the settlement among them of the *conquistadores* and their followers.

These Iberian sociocultural characteristics were institutionally based in the traditional Mediterranean pattern of small towns controlling their surrounding countrysides through elite patronal families. These patronal families were linked to their nonelite dependents by personalistic ties of paternalistic obligation combined with ruthless suppression of nonelite disobedience, on the elite side, and of loyalty combined with resentment, on the nonelite side. Resting on these basic institutions were the complex vertical relationships and tensions between, on the one hand, the major functional groups and organizations (such as the Church, the military, the landowners, the merchants) intent on preserving and increasing their rights and privileges and, on the other hand, the authoritarian centralizing royal administration (the Crown). The central authorities were also expected to protect the interests of the various groups and institutions vis-à-vis one another in the absence of effective direct horizontal relationships among them. These institutions and relationships were shaped by and in turn helped to sustain a distinctive set of values and behavioral norms that impelled intense individual self-seeking, mutual suspicion and rivalry among social groups, and a punctilious sense of status honor on the part of the patronal families and elite factions and cliques.

Thus, particularism, personalism, and paternalism, as well as the superordinate bureaucratic state, were indelibly imprinted on Latin American societies during the colonial period—which lasted for more than 300 years (twice as long as that of the British colonies in North America)—and their institutional and attitudinal manifestations persisted after independence.

So ingrained have these relationships, values, and norms been that they have continued to exert a determinative influence even after the basic institutions on which they originally rested were seriously eroded or disappeared during the 20th century. Their prestige has been so great that even the new modern elites—the owners and managers of modern industrial and financial enterprises, the technocrats in government bureaucracies and state-owned corporations, the populist politicians, the lawyers and other professionals, the scientists and the intellectuals, and the technically trained military officers—have conformed to them in greater or lesser degree. Moreover, they continue to meet certain emotional and socioeconomic needs of the employed workers and the slum dwellers of Latin America's burgeoning cities.

The predominance of these inherited relationships, self-images, and behavioral norms constitutes a *sociocultural lag* that largely accounts for Latin America's slow and erratic forward-and-backward movement toward the goals of political democracy, social justice, and economic welfare. This lag is manifested in the intense, often fanatical, particularism of the various old and new groups and institutions. It impels the proliferation of factions and cliques not only within the legal political parties and other institutions but also in the radical dissident movements, and it is responsible for the recurrent breakdown of cooperative efforts among groups and individuals. It sustains the authoritarian paternalism of the technocrats and liberal reformers no less than of the landowners and industrialists and the military and the Marxist revolutionaries. It underlies the relative inefficiency of the new modern organizations in government and the economy. Finally, it fosters the persisting conviction that both the causes of and the solutions to problems come from elsewhere and not from the individuals, groups, organizations, or national societies involved.

Implanted by the ideas of the Enlightenment and the examples of the American and French Revolutions, political democracy has been a major goal in Latin America even though its realization has always been severely impeded by the effects of the sociocultural lag. Since independence, no nation has had an unbroken experience of democratic rule and, throughout the region, the frequency and duration of civilian and military dictatorships have been much greater than those of elected democratic regimes. Costa Rica since the late 1940s and Colombia and Venezuela since the late 1950s are the only countries in which the governments have been stable and administrations have been changing through reasonably free elections. Mexico has had a stable civilian government since the early 1930s, but, as its economic problems have intensified, its social tensions have increased and its elections have been more disputed. Since World War II, all of the other Latin American nations have had self-perpetuating oligarchies, military dictatorships, or repeated sequences of elected governments superseded by military regimes. During the 1970s, the trend was toward military dictatorships; in the 1980s, it has been toward elected civilian regimes. However, given the persistence of the underlying sociocultural lag, the likelihood is that such swings have not ended and many of the elected administrations will again succumb to dictatorships.

Economic Problems

Whether a dictatorship or an elected regime, all Latin American governments have been authoritarian and have followed the tradition of the centralizing royal administrations of the colonial period in controlling the domestic economy and its external economic relationships. Due largely to their rich natural-resource endowments, most Latin American economies have good growth potentials and, under favorable conditions, have been able to maintain reasonably satisfactory rates of increase. This basic productiveness is all the more impressive in view of the interacting external and internal factors that combine to inhibit economic growth and to dissipate much of the beneficial effects on per capita income and living standards.

The exogenous factor that significantly affects economic growth rates from year to year is the dependence of Latin American economies on exports of primary products, demand for which is largely determined by conditions in the OECD nations. Even those countries that have succeeded in developing manufactured goods for export, notably Brazil and to a lesser extent Mexico, sell principally to the United States and other OECD nations and hence are dependent not only on demand in the latter but also on their willingness to admit products that compete with their domestic industries.

The other factors involved are indigenous and, in theory at least, are within the control of Latin Americans themselves. The first is the still high (though recently declining) rate of population growth, which is exceeded only by that of sub-Saharan Africa. Hence, a significant portion of the increase in resources makes no contribution to per capita income, and unemployment rises when economic growth is too low to create jobs for all of the new entrants into the labor force. Second, national economic policies often have adverse effects. Public-sector expenditures usually exceed revenues by substantial amounts due to the costs of (1) ambitious infrastructure development projects, investment in the numerous state-owned enterprises, and subsidies to cover their operating deficits; (2) servicing the growing national debt, both internal and external; and (3) the waste and inefficiency in government ministries and quasi-governmental agencies, as well as in state-owned enterprises. These bureaucratic deficiencies result from overstaffing, bribery and corruption, excessive procedural formalism, and the effects of patronal-type relationships on appointments, promotions, and the assignment of responsibilities.

In consequence of persistently excessive expansionist economic policies, Latin American countries generally have the highest rates of inflation in the international economic system and a tendency toward balance-of-payments deficits. These are aggravated by overvalued exchange rates intended to keep down the local-currency prices of imported capital and consumer goods. In turn, high rates of inflation combined with fears of periodic economic recessions and recurrent political instability generate capital flight which, over time, has deprived Latin American economies of substantial amounts of resources. Finally, detailed and time-consuming government regulation of the private sector discourages indigenous investment and innovation, while restrictions on private foreign investment limit this source of additional resources and skills. As I have often been told in Latin America, "the economy grows at night while the government sleeps!"

During the 1970s, Latin America was the principal Third World recipient of the recycling/borrowing operations of U.S., European, and Japanese banks. They lent freely to Latin American governments and to state-owned and private enterprises and thus helped to sustain these countries' economic growth rates, despite the drain on most of them resulting from the big increases in the price of imported petroleum. However, in many cases, neither lenders nor borrowers did enough to assure that these financial resources were invested in projects that could earn foreign exchange directly or indirectly and thereby contribute to servicing the debt.

Thus, in the 1980s, many Latin American nations have been struggling with severe debt-servicing problems, which have compelled the imposition of unaccustomed austerity measures on their economies in order to limit imports, promote exports, and obtain additional external financing from the IMF and the foreign banks. Such policies have further increased already large unemployment and underemployment in some countries, and their effectiveness has been limited by reduced demand,in the OECD nations for Latin American goods and by the internal factors sketched above. Hence, several countries have been constrained to default on some or all of their external debt obligations. Nonetheless, as in some Asian and African countries, these difficulties have also impelled several Latin American nations to introduce more market incentives and pressures into their economies, although it is uncertain how long they will be permitted to operate by the highly directive bureaucracies characteristic of these societies. The likely future development of Latin America's debt-service problem is discussed in Chapter VII.

Attitudes toward External Relations

The external relations of Latin American nations with one another and with the United States and the other OECD countries are powerfully affected by the sociocultural lag explained above. Due to it, Latin American societies have strong senses of their national identities and are quick to take offense at real or imagined infringement of their sovereignty by one another, as well as by the United States. Thus, they are concerned to preserve at least the appearance of their national freedom of action. This concern, reinforced by the national economic interests at stake, has blocked recurrent initiatives to form free-trade areas or customs unions in Latin America, and even looser arrangements for economic cooperation have not been notably effective.

Although formally allied with the United States in the Rio Pact, Latin American nations have been active in the various Third World movements noted in the preceding section, especially those concerned with economic matters. Indeed, Venezuela was a leader in the formation of OPEC, and the ideological justification for and the content of the NIEO were originally derived from the ideas of Latin American economists associated with the

UN Economic Commission for Latin America (ECLA) in the 1950s and 1960s. These and other Third World activities reflect not only Latin Americans' sense of solidarity with Asian and African countries but also the emotional drive of their deeply ambivalent feelings toward the United States.

From the beginning, Latin American writers, artists, and philosophers have always been more drawn to European than to U.S. models. However, in the 20th century, the scientific, business, and government elites have generally looked to the United States both as the source of ideas, techniques, and resources for modernizing their societies and, as many of them want to believe, as the main obstacle to achieving that goal.

Latin Americans generally resent the asymmetrical relationship between their countries and the United States—that is, the fact that Latin America is much more dependent on the United States for its economic well-being and external security than the reverse. In essence, Latin American ambivalence toward the United States tends to parallel that embodied in the patronal relationship: the expectation of benefits from the patron and resentment at the feelings of dependency and powerlessness thereby entailed. For their part, North Americans tend to feel the patron's equivalent ambivalence: satisfaction at giving much advice and some material help and exasperation at the recipients' failure to follow the advice and to be grateful for the help.

The Prospects for Latin American Modernization

I do not believe that generational change and its psychocultural effects are anywhere near as important in Latin America as in the other groups of nation-states so far discussed. Indeed, I see little evidence of significant differences between the older and younger generations in attitudes and behavior. Although young people, especially among the elites, may rebel at the autocratic rule of their patriarchal fathers, most of them as adults become authoritarian parents in their own families and manifest the other ways of thinking and acting imposed by the sociocultural lag, regardless of the kind of work they do and the political commitments they choose to make. Those who reject these inherited relationships, values and behavioral norms often do so by emigrating to the United States or Western Europe, thereby depriving their natal societies of precisely the people who are the most motivated and the best able to hasten the modernization process and keep it on a steady course.

In sum, the basic impediments to accelerating the modernization process in Latin America have been and are likely to continue to be the institutional and behavioral elements comprising the sociocultural lag. They hold back attainment of the necessary degrees of universalistic motivation, intergroup cooperation, impersonal objective decision making, decentralized initiative, and administrative efficiency. The resulting slow and intermittent progress toward the goals of political democracy, social justice, and economic welfare builds up internal tensions that are exacerbated by the endemic high rates of inflation and unemployment. In turn, these tensions and the efforts to repress them sooner or later undermine military dictatorships no less than elected governments. Even the three nations with continuous records of stable elected governments since the early postwar period have been experiencing difficulties during the 1980s that could set back their progress.[1] For these reasons, I think it unlikely that any Latin American nation will make a decisive breakthrough toward its political, social, and economic modernization goals in the foreseeable future.

NOTE

1. Costa Rica has been victimized by its unwilling involvement in the civil wars of its neighbors and the declines in the prices of its exports. Colombia has been plagued by internal terrorism and has become increasingly dependent on its exports of drugs. Venezuela has been saddled with a large external debt, incurred when high and rising petroleum prices made it seem a good lending risk, and has been constrained to impose restrictions on its people hitherto accustomed to rising living standards.

Chapter VI

CHANGES WITHIN THE COMMUNIST NATIONS

Unlike the U.S. hegemony, the Soviet hegemony has remained intact since the end of the postwar period and is not likely to change fundamentally in the foreseeable future. The reasons for this judgment are explained in this chapter, which surveys developments within the Soviet Union and its client states, as well as in China, and in their participation in the international system.

CHANGES IN THE SOVIET UNION

After the postwar period, the Soviet Union experienced gradually deepening economic problems and other changes that reduced its average real rate of economic growth from 5.1 percent a year in the 1960s to 3.7 percent a year in the 1970s and to 2.2 percent a year during the first half of the 1980s. This trend reflected the interactions of a variety of factors, some inherent in a nonmarket command economy and others resulting from adverse internal and external developments.

Soviet Economic Difficulties

A highly centralized nonmarket economy such as that of the Soviet Union depends crucially upon the ability of the central authorities to assure that

adequate resources will be allocated to achieve the planned output, investment, and consumption goals while maintaining a balance between the
supply of and the demand for the goods and services produced. The means
for doing so include detailed quantitative targets for the output of the
producing units and the distribution of their production, administered prices
and wages, subsidies to inefficient enterprises, forced savings, tight control
of imports and exports, subsidized low prices for essential consumer goods
(notably basic foodstuffs, fuel, rent, transportation), and their rationing
when shortages become acute. Policymakers guide their decisions by criteria
that usually subordinate economic efficiency to considerations of national
security, domestic and international political objectives, and ideological
principles, such as equality of nonelite incomes.

Such a nonmarket command economy has certain inherent difficulties in
operating, especially under modern conditions of complex differentiation
and interdependence of economic activities and of rapid technological
innovation. Even with the aid of computerized information networks—
whose installation has lagged in the Soviet Union in part for internal security
reasons—the flow of orders from and reports to the central authorities is so
voluminous and slow as to reduce their capacity for efficient decision making
and implementation. These limitations often prevent correction of planners'
own mistakes as well as of deviations from the plan by specific sectors,
industries, and producing units. The resulting waste and inefficiency are
compounded by (1) the tendency of cost prices, which are changed very
infrequently, to lag behind real costs, necessitating increasing subsidies to
inefficient enterprises; (2) ineffective cost and quality controls; (3) excessive
delays in the completion of projects; (4) resistance of mid- and lower-level
party and government officials to coordinating the activities of their agencies
with those of others with which they should cooperate to fulfill the plan; (5)
indifference to consumer preferences; (6) inadequacy of research and
development and application of new technologies outside the military and
heavy-industry fields; and (7) favoritism and corruption.

Moreover, the incentives inherent in the system do not encourage—
indeed, in many ways they discourage—innovation and initiative, conservation of scarce resources, and conscientious performance of work responsibilities. In the Soviet Union, criteria for judging the performance of
enterprises were originally based on physically measured production targets,
which inclined enterprise managers to favor the heaviest products in their
range of permitted outputs. The deficiencies of this system led to its
replacement by one involving the value of an enterprise's total output
measured in roubles and calculated on a cost-plus basis. Under this system,
the more costly the inputs, the higher the value of the total output and,
hence, the better the enterprise's performance. This not only resulted in

wasteful use of resources but also deterred managers from interrupting the production process so as to introduce new products and technologies. For their part, workers' incomes have been fixed in terms of output norms, and improvements in their productivity have usually resulted in higher norms without corresponding increases in pay. Continuity of employment has been assured, and absenteeism, drunkenness on the job, and poor work performance have rarely been causes for dismissal.

In addition to these systemic difficulties, the Soviet economy has been experiencing the adverse effects of certain internal trends and external changes. Military expenditures and investment in the related heavy industries and supporting facilities have increased faster than GNP since the early 1960s, thereby diverting relatively more resources from the rest of the economy and holding back its rate of growth proportionately. Although the share of national output allocated to investment has been rising, the productivity of the capital stock as a whole has been declining since the postwar period due to its increasing age and the failure to utilize the most advanced product and process technologies outside the military and heavy-industry fields. The most severe adverse effects of these trends have been on the consumer industries and services sector, where the volume, variety, and quality of the available goods and services are much too low to provide incentives for workers to try to improve their productivity and incomes. Despite comparatively large capital investment, productivity and net usable output in the agricultural sector have lagged in consequence of inadequate incentives on the collective and state farms, outmoded production methods, poor utilization and maintenance of equipment, and major deficiencies in storage facilities and farm-to-market transportation, as well as unfavorable weather conditions in some years.

Also, in the 1980s, demographic changes have been reducing the annual increases in the labor force on which the Soviet economy has always relied as a source of growth to make up for the limitations of the investment and technology components. At the same time, labor productivity declined as work discipline was relaxed, moonlighting and black-market activities grew, and an increasing proportion of the new labor-force entrants were in the non-European republics, whose societies have had less experience of the educational and attitudinal prerequisites for industrialization than those of the Russian and other European republics. The continuing shift of economic activity to Siberia has resulted in rising costs for the economy, especially for transportation of goods over the immense distances involved and for the development of new sources of raw materials, especially energy supplies, that are increasingly located in remote, environmentally hostile regions. Finally, in the mid-1980s, the decline in world energy prices and in the exchange rate of the dollar (in which world energy trade is conducted) reduced the Soviet Union's foreign-exchange earnings precisely when it was seeking to import more technologically advanced capital goods.

Coping with Soviet Economic Problems

Mitigation of these systemic and other problems would have to involve considerable decentralization of decision making to the operating units of the economy with respect particularly to procurement of capital equipment and production inputs, determination of the goods and services to be produced, marketing of the resulting outputs, hiring and firing of workers, and distribution of after-tax profits among reinvestment, improved workers' amenities, and increased wages or bonuses. To be effective, such decentralization would have to be accompanied by the use of market-determined prices to improve cost and quality control; the evaluation of enterprises' performance by market-type criteria, such as profit; differential rewards for managers and workers in accordance with initiative, innovativeness, and work performance; and an adequate volume, variety, and quality of consumer goods and services on which to spend their increased incomes. Conversely, persistent failure to meet performance standards would have to confront enterprises with bankruptcy and managers and workers with at least temporary unemployment and its attendant personal disruptions.

Soviet efforts to cope with the nonmarket economy's inherent deficiencies and adverse trends have been severely limited by three basic constraints. One is the resistance to change within both the party and the governmental bureaucracies, where officials' fear of the loss of their individual power and benefits is widespread. The second constraint is the concern of many workers throughout the economy that they would have to work harder, longer, or under less favorable conditions. The third is the regime's fear that any substantial introduction of market elements into the nonmarket command system would permit pressures to emerge for continuing economic reforms and eventually for political changes that would undermine its control over the society as a whole. The restraints imposed by this fear are reinforced by the resistance of orthodox members of the regime to changes that would contradict their strong ideological opposition to private enterprise, competition, and inequality of workers' incomes.

For example, movement toward a more market-determined system, as sketched above, would require the operating units of the economy not only to compete for supplies of inputs and markets for outputs but also to cooperate with one another in joint initiatives for various purposes independent of the central authorities. In turn, these actions would encourage the formation of continuing associations based on common interests among enterprises, managers, technicians, and even workers. The emergent organizations and groups would sooner or later be impelled to press for further increases in their freedom of action that would progressively reduce the regime's means for maintaining surveillance and control over the society. The Soviet leadership believed that this course of development was occurring in Hungary in 1956, Czechoslovakia in 1968, and Poland in 1981. It reacted by intervening directly in Hungary and Czechoslovakia and threatening to do so in Poland to prevent their communist parties from losing their "leading positions."

For these reasons, the Soviet regime has in the past adamantly resisted all suggestions from Soviet economists for major reforms that would involve substantial decentralization of decision making and introduction of market-type pricing, incentives, and performance criteria. Instead, it usually tried to improve the system from above by more rigorous enforcement of the central authorities' orders, efforts to suppress favoritism and corruption, and tightening of work discipline combined with exhortations to work harder. From time to time, there have been experiments with delegation of limited decision making to the managers of producing units in narrowly designated fields, but these never led to significant decentralization. Such measures have left the essential features of the highly centralized nonmarket economy intact, and Nikita Khrushchev's attempt to move beyond them led to his ouster in 1964 for having "hairbrained ideas."

When he came to power in 1985, Mikhail Gorbachev recognized and articulated the need for more substantial reforms if the inherent deficiencies and adverse trends of the Soviet economy were to be mitigated. However, the measures initially implemented were very similar to those used in the past, supplemented by a substantial cut in workers' access to vodka and more rigorous suppression of favoritism and corruption. Also, greater efforts were made to obtain—commercially and clandestinely—advanced technology and related capital equipment from abroad. Equally important were the positive effects on people's attitudes and expectations of Gorbachev's vigor, determination, and candor (*glasnost*) after the immobility and secretiveness of his enfeebled predecessors.

As in the past, however, the effect of these measures was temporary and superficial. By early 1987, it was evident that the thorough "reconstruction" of the nonmarket economy sought by Gorbachev and his supporters would require more radical changes. In June 1987, Gorbachev proposed and the Central Committee of the Communist Party and the Supreme Soviet approved in broad outline an unprecedented decentralization program. Under it (1) enterprises eventually comprising perhaps 70 percent of the economy would be permitted to determine their own product output under general guidelines of the central authorities; (2) they would increasingly be free to compete in negotiating contracts with the government and directly with one another to obtain inputs and market outputs; (3) the wholesale prices at which these transactions occurred would gradually be agreed between contracting enterprises in accordance with supply and demand, again under central supervision; (4) enterprises could set their own differential wage rates within general limits and workers could be fired; (5) enterprises' performance would be measured by profits, of which they would retain a substantial portion to use as they determined for self-financing of capital replacement and expansion and improvement of managers' and workers' incomes; and (6) direct relations and joint ventures between Soviet and foreign enterprises would be allowed in certain fields. In addition, subsidies to inefficient enterprises and to keep down the retail prices of essential consumer goods would be gradually reduced, and small cooperatives and individual and family enterprises in a variety of services would be permitted. Concomitantly with these changes, the functions, powers, and size of the central control authorities would be cut back and they would henceforth focus on long-range planning and general policy guidance.

The crucial questions are the extent to which these radical measures will be implemented and the specific ways in which they will be carried out. Gorbachev and his supporters frankly admit the powerful resistances, noted above, that have to be overcome. Detailed regulations for putting into effect most of the proposed changes have to be drafted and enforced by the very party and government bureaucrats whose functions and power will thereby be substantially reduced. Their natural tendency will be to carry out their generalized supervisory powers as specifically as possible and to draft the required regulations in ways that maintain their control over as many decentralized activities as they can or that make it impractical for anyone to undertake them. As John Stuart Mill wrote in 1859, "The Czar himself is powerless against the bureaucratic body; he can send any one of them to Siberia, but he cannot govern without them, or against their will. On every decree of his they have a tacit veto, by merely refraining from carrying it into effect."[1] The ability to frustrate the intentions of even the most autocratic executive is equally possessed by the Soviet bureaucracy today—as it is by large bureaucratic organizations in the governments and private sectors of the OECD nations as well.

Moreover, to the extent that the decentralization program is carried out, the Soviet economy will become susceptible to the new transitional difficulties that have plagued the nonmarket systems of Yugoslavia, Hungary, China, and Poland as they have introduced significant market elements into their economies. The transitional problems will be discussed in the next section. Suffice it to note here that, as they emerge in the Soviet Union, they will provide motive and opportunity not only for disaffected bureaucrats to sabotage the reform program but, more important, for members of the ruling bodies of the regime ideologically opposed to radical change to assert themselves. True, Gorbachev has been replacing opponents of his reconstruction efforts with his own supporters in the top agencies of the party and the government, which enabled him to push through his program. Nonetheless, some potential rivals will remain, and they will be emboldened to rally the opportunists who always exist in such organizations and are quick to sense when an existing leader is losing credibility and to shift their allegiance. Despite his greater political skills, it is well within the limits of the possible that Gorbachev would suffer the fate of Khrushchev.

Given the transitional difficulties that will emerge and the basic institutional constraints on radical innovation in the Soviet system, it is unlikely that the reform program will be implemented as fully and as consistently as would be required to enable the Soviet economy to catch up technologically with the OECD economies and to narrow substantially the gap between its dynamism and living standards and theirs. Nor, however extensive its reconstruction might be, would the Soviet economy cease to be a predominantly nonmarket system in the foreseeable future. So long as the existing regime remains in power, it is most unlikely to permit the development on a large enough scale of a true private sector involving freedom of enterprise and market-determined prices, profits, and investments. Rather, the most probable prospect is that the Soviet economy will follow a zigzag course, oscillating between recurrent efforts toward more decentralization and market-type incentives and pressures, and a greater or lesser return to centralized command methods when problems arise and opposition intensifies. In the years to come, this forward and backward movement is likely, at the most, to produce some significant continuing improvements in Soviet economic efficiency and living standards and, at the least, to prevent further substantial deterioration in productivity and the real incomes of the Soviet people.

Generational Change and Attitudes in the Soviet Union

Thus, I do not believe that the current and prospective problems confronting the Soviet economy are so formidable that the only alternatives are drastic reform or deepening crisis. Nor do I believe that, if progress is not made in improving the system sufficiently to permit steadily rising levels of living for the great bulk of the Soviet people, the result would be growing mass disaffection that would sooner or later undermine the existing regime.

Well over half the Soviet population was born after World War II. Despite declining birthrates in the European republics, the proportion of the younger generation in the society is increasing more rapidly than in Western Europe and the United States due to lower life expectancy in the Soviet Union and absence of the millions who lost their lives during the 1930s and the wartime years. Thus, a large and growing majority of Soviet citizens has been habituated to the regime since birth, and its self-image and approved values and behavioral norms have been more deeply inculcated into the younger generation than into its predecessor. While the members of the younger generation have not become the cheerful, hardworking, selfless "new Soviet men and women" predicted by communist ideologues, they are basically loyal to the Soviet system and take pride in its accomplishments at home and abroad. This attitude is reinforced by the persistence of certain traditional Russian ways of thinking and acting: the submissiveness to authority; the devotion to "Mother Russia" (if perhaps not also in the same degree to the "Socialist Fatherland") and its world mission; the strong commitment to societal order and security bred of centuries of invasions and internal turmoil; and the related ambivalence toward the West which, since the 16th century, has been both admired for its cultural achievements and feared for its presumed immorality and hostile intentions.

For the past two centuries, mass disaffection from the ruling regime has occurred only twice, in 1905 and 1917, when the czarist government was conspicuously incompetent to prevent a disastrous defeat in a foreign war and, in 1917, the collapse of the domestic economy as well. Neither of these possibilities has a high probability of recurring. Moreover, the dissident groups of mostly intellectuals and scientists are small and have little, if any, access to the great majority of the Soviet people who, if they are aware of the dissidents' activities, tend to regard them as disrupters of the valued orderliness of Soviet society.

Traditionally, Russians strongly enough dissatisfied with their conditions of life and future prospects have been inclined toward apathy and with-drawal-type reactions, especially drunkenness, absenteeism, reduced work effort, and, at the extreme, suicide. Such behavior was increasingly mani-fested during the 1970s and early 1980s and it had adverse effects on the productiveness of the economy. Since then, the tightening of work discipline, the reduced availability of vodka, and the rise in morale inspired by Gorbachev's vigor and candor have lessened these manifestations of disaffection. But, even if they were to reappear, neither they nor the other problems of the Soviet economy are likely to become so great as to threaten an economic collapse. Prolonged failure to raise living standards or even to prevent some fall in them would not have the same effect on elite and nonelite attitudes in the Soviet Union as would be the case in most of its East

European client states, let alone in Western Europe and the United States. Nor does the Soviet regime's detailed regulation of and tight control over all the major institutions and relationships of the society arouse much sense of oppression and resentment in the Soviet people, who—except briefly in the Baltic republics during the interwar period—have never in their history lived under conditions of democratic rights, individual freedom, and self-responsibility.

Thus, the generational change now under way in the Soviet Union is not likely to modify basic attitudes and expectations substantially. Moreover, Gorbachev and his top-level associates represent the coming to power of a younger generation of leaders, better educated, more skillful, and more self-assured than their predecessors of the postwar generation. They can probably make the complex machinery of central authoritarian control work less inefficiently than it has in recent decades, and they should be able to contain the dissatisfaction of lower-level party and government bureaucrats. They are more adept at influencing nonelite attitudes than were the elites of the older generation. Like the latter, they are committed to maintaining the essential political and economic institutions of the Soviet system and the Soviet hegemony externally, but they can be expected to pursue these goals more flexibly and competently than their predecessors.

CHANGES IN THE EAST EUROPEAN CLIENT STATES

The situation is rather different in the East European members of the Soviet hegemony. With relatively smaller military expenditures than the Soviet Union, the East European economies are not as skewed toward heavy industry and armaments production and can devote relatively more resources to the output of consumer goods, especially in economically more advanced East Germany, Czechoslovakia, Hungary, and Poland. Living standards in these four countries have always been higher than in the Soviet Union or Rumania and Bulgaria. Nonetheless, even these four have been plagued by the same inherent difficulties of nonmarket command systems as has the Soviet Union, and new problems have emerged as significant market elements have actually been incorporated into their economies.

To cope with nonmarket deficiencies, Hungary took the lead—within the limits it thought the Soviet Union would permit—in decentralizing economic decision making, providing market-type incentives and pricing, and permiting the formation of cooperatives and individual enterprises. It has also introduced procedures for making inefficient enterprises liable to bankruptcy under certain conditions. In addition, some enterprises have been allowed to raise capital by issuing securities for sale to organizations and individuals, the state banking monopoly has been split into five (presumably competing) units, and West European and U.S. banks have been permitted to open some branches.

East Germany has followed a different route, reflecting its more industrialized economy and its Prussian tradition of centralized authoritarian control and popular discipline, which long predates its commitment to communism. The main East German reform has been the regrouping of many industrial organizations into larger associations to bring about more effective coordination of production, distribution, and research and development. Also, the inherent difficulties of its nonmarket command economy have been significantly eased by the substantial direct and indirect subsidies it receives from West Germany. These include large annual credits to finance imports, free access for many of its exports to the West German market and through it to the rest of the EC, and periodic ransom payments for emigrants wishing to leave East Germany.

Poland's efforts at economic reform have been much less effective than those of Hungary or East Germany. Recurrent attempts to raise consumer prices closer to real costs so as to ease the transition to market pricing have provoked popular demonstrations and riots that sometimes have led to replacement of the top communist leadership. In 1980–1981, some relaxation of central control unleashed organized workers' pressures for accelerated decentralization that would have encroached on the regime's autocratic power and hence precipitated the threat of Soviet intervention. Czechoslovakia has been paralyzed since the brutal Soviet suppression of its "Prague Spring" reforms in 1968, and both Rumania and Bulgaria have adhered in internal affairs to the Soviet model. In Hungary and East Germany, moreover, economic growth rates have been trending lower in the 1980s due to the transitional difficulties engendered by their reforms and to adverse developments in their external economic relations.

The introduction into a modern nonmarket command economy of significant decentralization, market incentives and pricing, and differential incomes related to efficiency brings with it new kinds of problems. The longer that administered prices have been in effect, the bigger the suppressed inflation their removal is likely to unleash. The greater the dependence on foreign trade, the more susceptible the economy becomes to unemployment and balance-of-payments difficulties generated by inadequate international competitiveness or falling demand in export markets. If the central authorities relax their control over individual producing units by decentralizing considerable decision making without imposing market discipline on them—that is, protecting them from bankruptcy and other adverse consequences of uneconomic actions—many would continue to need subsidies and little, if anything, would be gained in efficiency and the elimination of waste. Conversely, forcing them into bankruptcy would cause unemployment of managers and workers unaccustomed to the painful adjustments involved. The growing inequality of incomes resulting from differential wage rates and the success of cooperative and individual enterprises contradicts egalitarian communist doctrine and provokes resentment in those who do not benefit therefrom.

In essence, the introduction of significant decentralization and market elements into a nonmarket economy generates pressures either for a more thoroughgoing "marketization" that would eventually ease the transitional difficulties or for a return to tighter control by the central authorities. These contradictory pressures account in large measure for the shifts in policy from one direction to the other in Hungary since the late 1960s and would underlie similar behavior in the Soviet Union to the extent that its reform program is carried out, as noted in the previous section. The difference would be that, if left to itself, Hungary would probably resolve the contradiction by moving toward greater marketization while the Soviet Union would undoubtedly ease the transitional difficulties by recurrent recentralization.

As to changes in their external economic relations, the East Europeans' imports from one another and from the Soviet Union rose from 2.3 percent of their GNPs in 1970 to 4.4 percent in 1975, 7.4 percent in 1980, and 8.4 percent in 1984. Soviet imports from other COMECON states grew from 0.5 percent of its GNP in 1970 to 1.7 percent in 1980 and 2.2 percent in 1985. The growing integration within COMECON during the 1970s reflected in part the willingness of the Soviet Union to increase substantially its subsidization of its client states by charging them less than world market prices for more of its exports to them—especially petroleum—and paying them above world market prices for more of its imports from them. These subsidies reached a peak during the period 1974–1978, when they are estimated to have involved the forgoing of an annual average of $5.7 billion of theoretically additional earnings or savings by the Soviet Union. During the 1980s, however, the Soviet Union's own economic difficulties have impelled it to narrow the spreads between its export and import prices and those prevailing in the world market economy. In addition, the noncontiguous members of the Soviet hegemony, notably Cuba and Vietnam, are estimated currently to cost the Soviet Union around $4 billion a year in direct economic and military aid, as well as in export and import subsidies.

The East European nations also increased their trade with the rest of the world, from 1.3 percent of their GNPs in 1970 to 3.5 percent in 1975 and 5.4 percent in 1980. (So, too, did the Soviet Union as its trade with the rest of the world grew from 0.4 percent of its GNP in 1970 to 2.8 percent in 1980.) At the same time, the East European states borrowed rather heavily from Western Europe to finance imports of capital equipment to modernize their industries and improve their energy efficiency, and they also bought more consumer goods to satisfy the rising consumption expectations of their people. However, the economic difficulties of the OECD nations in the late 1970s and the 1980s have adversely affected the East European nations, contributing to the slowing of their economic growth rates and intensifying the strain of meeting their debt-service payments. Hence, their trade with the rest of the world declined as a percentage of their GNPs in the 1980s.

The economic outlook for the East European client states is, therefore, quite uncertain. On the one hand, they have become more dependent on their trade with the Soviet Union, especially for energy supplies, even as the latter reduced its subsidies to them. On the other hand, their trade with the rest of the world—particularly with Western Europe, their largest trading partner outside COMECON—has become more difficult. And, they are having to cope internally with the continuing, though lessened, deficiencies inherent in still predominantly nonmarket economies and the new problems engendered by the introduction of significant market elements. In turn, these economic difficulties are likely to have implications for the attitudes of people in the East European countries toward their regimes.

It is difficult to estimate the degree of legitimacy accorded to the communist regimes of the client states by their people, although it is certainly much less than that enjoyed by the regime in the Soviet Union. In Poland and Czechoslovakia, the removal of Soviet control and support would probably result in mass pressures to replace or basically reform the existing political and economic systems. In Hungary and East Germany, the consequence could well be that the regimes themselves would institute drastic changes in an effort to preserve their power and, in the case of East Germany, to resist pressure for reunification with West Germany. In Rumania and Bulgaria, however, the communist regimes have maintained such tight control that too little evidence on popular attitudes is available for forecasting the likely results of the removal of Soviet control.

Therefore, the four more advanced countries that have historically looked to Western Europe for their sociocultural models—and perhaps also Rumania—are likely to experience frustration of their expectations for continuing improvements in their conditions of life and resentment toward the Soviet Union as the perceived suppressor of their national freedom of action. These frustrations and resentments could generate recurrent mass pressures for reforms and persisting efforts by the regimes to test the limits of the changes that the Soviet Union would permit. Such developments would confront the Soviet Union with increasingly difficult problems of hegemonic control.

So far, however, there have not been any major modifications in the structure of the Soviet hegemony and in the relative positions of the client states vis-à-vis the hegemon. And, with the coming to power of younger and more vigorous leaders in the Soviet Union, its vigilance over the contiguous core states is unlikely to be significantly relaxed even though the limits of its tolerance of their freedom of action could be somewhat broadened. Thus, except in the unlikely event of a severe internal crisis in the Soviet Union, I do not foresee any major changes in its control over the East European client states even if increasing tensions are generated by their frustrations and nationalistic resentments.

SOVIET PARTICIPATION IN THE TRANSITIONAL INTERNATIONAL SYSTEM

During the 1960s, the intensity of the cold-war rivalry between the Soviet Union and the United States began to moderate and, in the early 1970s, this trend was generally regarded as inaugurating a new period of "detente" in superpower relationships. On the Soviet side, the change expressed the greater self-confidence engendered by its attainment of nuclear parity with the United States, the continuation of its quantitative superiority in conventional armaments, and the desire to reduce the U.S. threat to Soviet security after the scare experienced during the Cuban missile crisis in 1962. On the U.S. side, the change reflected preoccupation with the Vietnam War, the diversion of interest and attention to critical domestic political and economic issues (such as the "Great Society" programs, the civil rights movement, student unrest and New Left agitation, and the Watergate and other scandals), and the widespread yearning for a stable peaceful relationship with the Soviet Union. Yet, detente did not change fundamentally the superpower relationship, as many in North America and Western Europe during the 1970s believed that it would.

As noted in Chapter II, war has been used to maintain or restore balance in all of the balance-of-power systems that existed prior to World War II. In the postwar Soviet–U.S. system, however, both protagonists recognized that a war between them would risk inflicting unacceptable nuclear destruction on each other and would probably not result, as always in the past, either in the restoration of a balance or in the termination of the system due to the triumph of one over the other. Thus, by preserving a credible nuclear capability vis-à-vis each other, the two superpowers were *implicitly* agreeing that war between them would not be a rational means of policy in maintaining their balance-of-power relationship.

To the Soviet Union, the emergence of detente at the end of the postwar period meant that both superpowers now *explicity* agreed that war between them was not to be used as an instrument of policy. In the Soviet view, peaceful coexistence meant and continues to mean nothing more than that the superpowers would pursue their conflicting objectives in the international system by *any means of policy other than war* that each considered appropriate and effective. In this way, competition for power and influence would persist but the superpowers would try to avoid situations which could lead to direct confrontations that might constrain one or the other to resort to war.

Accepting this interpretation, President Richard Nixon and Secretary of State Henry Kissinger sought to contain the competition by involving the Soviet Union in a network of treaty obligations and inducements to moderate behavior, reinforced by the implicit deterrence of Soviet actions resulting from the U.S. rapprochement with China. In the end, their efforts were unsuccessful due in part to Soviet concern over the U.S.–China accord and the Soviet refusal to refrain from taking advantage of the opportunities that arose during the 1970s for advancing its international power and influence. In part, too, the Nixon/Kissinger policy failed not only because of the undermining of the administration's domestic support during the Watergate scandal but, more important, because of the rise to predominance of a different interpretation of the meaning of detente. In this view, peaceful coexistence meant that each superpower would henceforth respect the sphere of influence of the other and disputes between them would be settled by negotiation. This interpretation was especially prevalent in the Congress and among opinion leaders in the media, and it influenced the foreign policy of the Carter administration until its last year. Had the Soviet Union, too, accepted this interpretation of detente, it would have changed fundamentally the nature of the superpower relationship. By the late 1970s, however, the continuing increases in Soviet nuclear and conventional capabilities, the advances of Soviet influence in Africa and, finally, the Soviet invasion of Afghanistan in late 1979 made clear to many proponents of the prevailing U.S. view, including President Carter himself, that it had been in error. Accordingly in the 1980s, predominant U.S. opinion tended to accept the Soviet interpretation of peaceful coexistence.

How will the Soviet Union be likely to pursue competitive coexistence with the United States over the foreseeable future? To answer this question, we need to look again at the self-conceptions and perceptions of the Soviet regime sketched in Chapter II. A common view in North America and Western Europe—one which helped to foster the mistaken interpretation of detente during the 1970s—has been that the ruling elites of the Soviet Union no longer "believe in communism" and that their foreign policies and actions are motivated solely by nationalistic interests. To my mind, this opinion overlooks the basic relationships between the institutions of any society and its culture and how they both help to shape a society's external motivations and behavior.

The fundamental institutions of Soviet society consist of authoritarian-political and nonmarket-economic systems vigilantly controlled by central authorities through the pervasive power of the communist party. In all societies, whether traditional or modern, the distribution of power, prestige, and control over economic resources embodied in their institutions is legitimated by certain elements of their cultures. These are the values, self-images, explanatory rationales—religious or secular—and feelings by which evey society justifies to its members and to outsiders its sense of unique identity, its reason for being, its aspirations, and its claim for the loyalty and conscientious effort of its members necessary for its continued existence. Thus, the values and rationales expressed in the ideology of Soviet communism reflect the basic authoritarian institutions of Soviet society and vice versa.

The ruling elites of the Soviet Union continually strive to maintain and strengthen these basic institutions, which they regard as being not only in their own interest but also in that of Soviet society as a whole. This institutional commitment necessarily implies commitment to the legitimating cultural elements. Nor can their professed devotion to communism be for the elites only self-interested utility, that is, the ideology is to them nothing more than a cultural means for assuring the loyalty and obedience of the nonelites—to paraphrase Marx, "communism is the opiate of the people." For, if the elites' commitment to communism were purely cynical, so too would be their support for the institutions which the ideology validates. In that case, their responses to the Soviet Union's problems would be much more flexible and pragmatic than those that Gorbachev and his supporters—let alone their predecessors—have been willing and able to implement. For these reasons, I believe that the ruling elites of the Soviet Union are and will continue to be committed to the Soviet system and its legitimating ideology, both of which have been constructed under their leadership and which they have implacably defended regardless of the cost in human lives and economic resources.

Nor is it likely that the Soviet elites regard their system as inferior in its developmental potential to that of the United States or of any other nation. Whatever the system's present shortcomings, the Soviet elites are convinced—indeed, they are forever reiterating—that its further development would eventually enable it to surpass the achievements of the societies of Western Europe and North America. They maintain that the Soviet system provides a model for others to follow, although variations in details due to "national differences" might occur. Moreover, they believe that the Soviet Union, as the first society to exemplify the essential features of.the system, has the historical role of fostering its adoption elsewhere in the world, as well as protecting itself against the efforts of rival nations with competing systems to destroy it. This Soviet self-image is strongly reinforced by the centuries-old Russian concept of Moscow as the "Third Rome" destined to lead humanity into the true Orthodox faith. Thus, both the czarist and the communist rationales combine to sustain the conviction of the Soviet Union's historical destiny to attain its rightful paramount position in the international system through an activist foreign policy employing any means short of a self-destructive nuclear war.

This conception of the Soviet Union's international role does not mean that the Soviet regime has a "blueprint for world conquest," as some observers in the West have maintained, or that it plans the places and times of its foreign-policy moves even in general terms. Since the forces of historical materialism guarantee that its system will sooner or later prevail— just as God's grace guaranteed the ultimate triumph of the Orthodox faith—the Soviet Union can be patient. Above all, it must assure its own security and effectiveness as the "Fatherland of the Socialist Revolution" in the face of the efforts of rival nations, such as the United States, to thwart its historical mission and to try to destroy it. Next, it needs to be ever alert to exploit the inevitable opportunities to fulfill its historical destiny. But, in doing so, it must never, in Lenin's words, "put the Socialist Fatherland to risk," which would violate the overriding self-protective principle of its foreign policy.

Nor does the fulfillment of the Soviet Union's historical destiny mean the eventual establishment of a worldwide Soviet empire—that is, of direct Soviet rule over the nations that will sooner or later adhere to the "Socialist camp." Given the difficulties and costs of managing its existing client states, the Soviet Union is unlikely to extend hegemonic control, let alone direct imperial rule, to ever-increasing numbers of countries, with the exception of those that it believes are essential to its security. Rather, its aim would be to achieve Soviet paramountcy in the international system by assuring the existence in more and more nations of friendly regimes that would willingly follow its leadership in their external affairs and at least make their internal institutions compatible with Soviet needs and conceptions.

In pursuing these objectives, Soviet leaders, including Gorbachev, must operate within the constraints imposed by domestic socioeconomic needs and the political requirements for maintaining themselves at the top of the party and the government. On the one hand, the extent to which they can mitigate the deficiencies and problems of the Soviet economy is in part dependent on reallocating resources from heavy industry and military production to the output of capital and consumer goods and services and on keeping in check the costs of maintaining the Soviet hegemony and achieving other foreign-policy goals. This means that it would be in the interest of both the leadership and the Soviet Union to reach arms-reduction agreements with the United States and avoid conflicts with it that would increase external dangers and thus prevent the internal reallocation of resources. On the other hand, the rivalries among the individuals and cliques comprising the ruling elites and the need to preserve the support of the military and internal-security forces restrain Soviet leaders from forgoing opportunities to advance Soviet interests in the international system and from making the kinds of concessions to the United States that would substantially relax the tensions between the two superpowers.

For these reasons, I believe that the Soviet Union will continue in the foreseeable future to take advantage of situations that arise—usually *not* as the result of its deliberate actions—which would enable it to increase its power and influence in the international system whenever the costs and risks appear to be consistent with its external security and internal constraints. True, Soviet policymakers may sometimes miscalculate the costs, as in Afghanistan, but they have always been cautious about the risks, particularly of a direct confrontation with the United States. In the 1980s, the rebuilding of U.S. nuclear and conventional military capabilities and the hardened attitude of the Reagan administration certainly reinforced Soviet caution. However, the present younger, better-trained, and more skillful Soviet leaders are likely to employ Soviet power and influence more adroitly than did their predecessors in containing the costs and risks of advancing Soviet international objectives.

CHANGES WITHIN CHINA AND IN ITS INTERNATIONAL ROLE

The changes within China since the late 1970s have been more far-reaching and significant than those in the Soviet Union and its East European client states. The failures of a quarter century of efforts to apply Mao Tse-tung's adaptation of Marxist-Leninist doctrines eventuated after his death in the coming to power of more pragmatic leadership under Deng Xiaoping.

The new regime's major economic reforms have included (1) the revival of agriculture by an unprecedented decentralization of production to individual peasant families operating in considerable part under market-type pricing and incentives; (2) the subsequent application of analogous changes to industry, supplemented by permission for cooperatives and small family enterprises to function in the consumer industries and services sector; and (3) the opening of the economy to foreign trade and investment, especially the fostering of manufacturing for export with the help of foreign companies from other East Asian countries and the OECD nations. Enterprises can buy inputs and sell outputs directly from and to one another; they can hire and fire workers, and representatives of the latter can participate in the selection of managers; and they can distribute their after-tax profits between self-financing of capital replacement and expansion and increases in wages and bonuses. In addition, some enterprises have been allowed to raise capital by selling bonds and equities, and secondary markets in these securities have been permitted. In an effort to begin to apply market-type disciplines, a few enterprises have been forced into bankruptcy. Special economic zones and other designated areas have been established in which foreign investors, singly or in joint ventures with Chinese entities, can set up production facilities to supply domestic and foreign markets.

These substantial reforms have resulted in big increases in agricultural production, lesser but still significant growth in some industrial fields, the emergence of a dynamic, quasi-private sector of cooperatives and family enterprises, and impressive improvements in living standards in regions that possess the human and economic resources needed to take advantage of the relaxation of central control. Relative to its previous economic condition and capabilities for growth, China's progress during the 1980s has been much more impressive than that of the Soviet Union and the members of its hegemony.

At the same time, these developments have brought China the same problems of introducing decentralization and market elements into a non-market command economy as those of Hungary and other East European nations. The effects of suppressed inflation have been manifested. Decentralization of decision making to the local and enterprise levels has led to temporary imbalances between and within economic sectors, with consequent shortages of agricultural products, raw materials, and industrial goods in particular regions. The dynamic responses in both the countryside and the cities to the new opportunities for enterprise and family initiatives have resulted not only in raising many nonelite incomes but also in ingenious schemes by mid-level officials to enrich themselves or to advance the interests of their organizations or localities. The inequalities in family and regional incomes are becoming larger and more conspicuous, causing discontent among those who have not so benefited. Growing reliance on imports and exports has generated recurrent foreign-exchange problems, and foreign investors have often been frustrated by the inadequacies of the Chinese legal system and the arbitrariness of Chinese officials. However, the formation of voluntary associations among some enterprises and family-run businesses in the big cities to protect and advance their interests vis-à-vis the central and local authorities has not yet alarmed the latter. In contrast, the regime has sternly suppressed demonstrations by students and others for undefined "democratization."

In addition to the problems generated by the reforms, China faces the fundamental difficulty of keeping economic growth in excess of population growth. The regime has been endeavoring to enforce the policy of single-children families which, to the extent successful, would cut China's birthrate. However, that policy runs counter to the deeply rooted tradition of multiple-children families, especially for sons to perpetuate the lineage, provide manpower for the farm or workshop, and ensure the economic security of aged parents. These incentives for a high birthrate can be weakened only by rising per capita incomes and the availability of and permission to hire nonrelatives for work in family farms and enterprises. Thus, the ability to lower China's birthrate depends on maintaining a high enough rate of economic growth, which is in turn largely dependent on the continued effectiveness of the reforms.

So far, the regime has held steady to the main elements of the reforms while endeavoring to preserve the leading position of the Communist party and its control over the future direction of development. However, its policies are under covert—and sometimes overt—attack by groups within the party leadership and at lower levels that cling to orthodox Maoist principles. The basic questions, therefore, are whether the existing regime can both cope with the difficulties inherent in its reform policies and ensure the succession of a new generation committed to the same general objectives. The longer Deng Xiaoping and his like-minded colleagues remain in control, the more habituated the elites and nonelites generally will be to the benefits and the costs of the far-reaching changes they are introducing into Chinese society, and the more difficult it will be for the remaining Maoists to achieve sufficient power to reverse course. For these reasons, the 1990s will be crucial for the longer-term future of China.

If the orthodox factions in the party become predominant, China would once again enter upon a period of internal disorder, which would probably be more disruptive and bloody than that of the Cultural Revolution in the 1960s and 1970s. In contrast to the earlier period, there would then be large numbers of elites and nonelites who would have benefited from the Dengist reforms and who would undoubtedly resist the suppression of their freedom of action and the resulting loss of their economic gains. In consequence of the disruptions generated by the reimposition of Maoist-type policies and the resistance to them, China's economic growth rate would once again fall and its technological lag would become greater. Preoccupation with such severe domestic problems would probably prevent a new Maoist-type regime from spreading its power and influence in the East Asian region. But, China's internal difficulties and unrest could tempt the Soviet Union to try to regain the influence it exercised over China during the 1950s.

In contrast, if the present leaders ensure the succession of a like-minded regime able to manage a nonmarket economy with a large and dynamic market sector, China would play a more important role in the international system over the foreseeable future. Economically, it would achieve the capabilities and status of an active, self-sustaining participant in the world economy like Japan and the East Asian NICs. Thus, it would gradually acquire the resources not only to raise the living standards of its people but also to extend its political influence in East and South Asia and the Pacific region.

In time, too, it is possible that the regime would increasingly legitimate its rule by a rationale resembling the traditional Confucian justification for paternalistic authoritarian control rather than by communist ideology as such, which is after all an alien set of ideas. As in the great periods of its imperial past, China would become the modern equivalent of the "Middle Kingdom," to which the surrounding nations paid deference and looked for institutional and cultural innovations. We should not forget that, for at least two thousand years, China was the center of one of the planet's greatest civilizations. The motivations and capabilities that made its historical achievements possible could once again revive if and as it makes progress in overcoming its internal problems and divisions. And it is this possibility inherent in China's developmental potential that many Russians fear more than the threat to their security and aspirations to world paramountcy they perceive from the United States.

NOTE

1. Quoted in Marshall I. Goldman, *Gorbachev's Challenge: Economic Reform in the Age of High Technology*, (New York: Norton, 1987) p. 247.

Chapter VII

TRENDS SHAPING THE FUTURE OF THE INTERNATIONAL SYSTEM

This chapter surveys the economic and political trends that are likely to determine both the general direction of change in the international system (outside the Soviet hegemony) over the foreseeable future—the next twenty-five years or so—and the limits within which national policymakers' decisions and actions could influence its development. The next chapter discusses the kinds of policy choices that could be made within these limits and how they could affect the system's future development.

Determinative trends are continuing interactions between the changes, on the one hand, in the structure and functioning of the international system sketched in Chapter III and, on the other hand, in the motivations and capabilities for external action of the different groups of nation-states surveyed in Chapters IV and V. These continuing interactions are identifiable as trends because they retain certain distinguishing characteristics over time. However, it is important to recognize that a societal trend is not like a uniform wave front whose constituent elements are all moving in the same direction at the same rate. Rather, it resembles a broad stream that has a determinate direction of flow but whose waters are moving at different speeds and also contain numerous counter-currents, eddies, and stagnant pools.

THE DETERMINATIVE ECONOMIC TRENDS

I group the major determinative economic trends in the international system under the general term *neomercantilism*. This concept encompasses many other important phenomena in addition to what is conventionally known as "protectionism," that is, the imposition of barriers to prevent or reduce the entry of competing foreign goods and services into a country. By analogy with the mercantilism that shaped the policies of the European states in the 17th and 18th centuries, I define the neomercantilist trend as *the increasing determination of a nation's economic activities, both internal and external, by governmental decisions in accordance with welfare, defense, and other nonefficiency criteria rather than by market forces operating in accordance largely with efficiency criteria.*

Since the end of the postwar period, this shift in the relative scope of the two methods of controlling economic activities has been occurring very gradually, quite markedly in some years and barely perceptibly, even temporarily halted, in others. Over the foreseeable future, the shift is most likely to continue, particularly as it affects the flows of goods, services, and money across national boundaries. Efforts to reverse the neomercantilist trend have a very low probability of being successful because both its international and its national causes are too deeply embedded to be eradicated.

Factors Generating the Neomercantilist Trend

At the international level, the elements that support the neomercantilist trend are the three major modifications in the structure and functioning of the world market economy explained in Chapter III. The first is the change in the international position of the U.S. economy, notably the substantial reduction since the early 1970s in its asymmetrical relationship with the world economy. This has diminished the relative U.S. shares of international trade and investment while making the United States increasingly dependent on imports and exports and substantially more susceptible to the adverse short-term effects of the adjustment process. The second is the corresponding growth in the shares of world trade and investment of the EC, Japan, and the existing and emerging NICs. The third is the more rapid and drastic operation of the adjustment process across national boundaries due to the greater intensity of competition after the unprecedented lowering of barriers to trade and capital movements during the postwar period; the fluctuating exchange-rate system and the free flows of funds between national financial markets; and the faster international dissemination of technological innovations. Thus, the narrowing of disparities and the increasing competition and fluidity characteristic of the highly integrated international economic system that emerged from the postwar period have been among the causes of the neomercantilist trend of the 1970s and 1980s which, in turn, has been eroding the integration of the system.

The factors rooted in the national level that interact with the changes in the international system to produce the neomercantilist trend differ among the various groups of countries surveyed in the preceding chapters.

The transitional nations of Asia and Africa and the modernizing nations of Latin America are by nature neomercantilist; in many ways, their policies and the rationale for them resemble those of the European states during the mercantilist period. Their public-sector economic activities are quite large and their governments exercise extensive control over their private sectors and external economic relations. Even in those nations, as in East Asia, that rely on private enterprise as the main agent for expanding trade and economic growth, governments actively direct and assist their private-sector organizations to export goods and services and limit the import of competing goods and services to a significantly greater extent than do most OECD governments. The persisting debt problems of many Asian, African, and Latin American nations also impel their governments to limit and intervene in the market process. Therefore, although some of them have begun to liberalize their import policies in recent years, the inherent neomercantilist attitudes and practices of Asian, African, and Latin American countries are not likely to diminish significantly in the foreseeable future.

As nonmarket command systems, the economies of the Soviet Union and its client states are also inherently neomercantilist in an even more fundamental sense. Hence, to the extent that they participate in the world market economy, their policies and practices generally reinforce the neomercantilist trend.

Because of their predominant role in international trade and investment, the OECD nations have by far the greatest influence on the present and prospective characteristics of the international economic system. The internal changes responsible for their increasing neomercantilism were explained in Chapter IV, notably (1) the expansion in the scope and cost of the activities of OECD governments and the related emergence of negative-sum welfare/efficiency interactions, (2) the growing constraints on national policymakers' freedom to carry out their responsibilities, (3) other economic and demographic developments that have also contributed to rising factor costs, low economic-growth rates, and high unemployment, especially in Western Europe, and (4) the effects of generational change on the willingness and ability of the OECD countries to cooperate in dealing with their problems.

These internal changes have affected the external policies of the OECD nations in two related ways. First, they have constrained OECD governments to resolve the inherent ambiguity of rational interest, explained in Chapter I, increasingly in favor of avoiding the short-term costs of international integration rather than enduring them so as to obtain the long-term benefits, which have been perceived as more and more uncertain due to the structural changes in the international economic system. Second, the internal factors have impelled national policymakers and opinion leaders toward increasingly particularistic conceptions of how the short-term costs could be avoided and sometimes could be turned into immediate benefits by behaving as free-riders in the world market economy.

Given the persistence of these pressures, the neomercantilist trend at the international level is and will continue to be self-reinforcing. That is, a neomercantilist action by either the United States, the EC, or Japan usually impels the others to react by offsetting or retaliatory measures of their own. Hence, free-rider efforts to avoid and, intentionally or not, to shift to others the costs of the adjustment process are mutually sustaining.

In fact, new or intensified manifestations of neomercantilism have become characteristic of international trade and investment relations during the 1980s, in addition to the restrictive and discriminatory measures noted in Chapter IV. One significant development has been the expansion of "countertrade"—which consists of contemporary versions of the kinds of bilateral barter agreements that flourished during the 1930s and in the immediate postwar years. Taking a variety of direct and indirect forms, countertrade arrangements spread by the late 1970s beyond the COMECON nations—for whose nonmarket economies they are the natural means of trading with one another—to other countries, and current rough estimates of their scope range from 5–10 percent of world trade (OECD, GATT) to 20–30 percent (U.S. Department of Commerce). Another, sometimes related, development has been the proliferation of so-called performance requirements, under which a foreign enterprise is permitted to invest in a country only if it agrees to export much or all of its manufactured output and conform to other conditions that preferentially favor the host country's economy. Countertrade and performance requirements have the effect of substituting essentially nonmarket types of bilateral transactions for those governed predominantly by competitive market forces.

As pointed out at the beginning of this chapter, the elements of which a societal trend is composed do not move uniformly ahead nor do all of them always flow in the same direction. Hitherto, neomercantilism has mainly been manifested in trade relationships, where the high level of integration attained by the end of the postwar period has gradually been eroding. From the early 1970s, in contrast, the direction of development of monetary relations among the OECD nations continued to be toward increasing integration under the system of fluctuating exchange rates and free flows of short- and long-term capital, as explained in Chapter III. However, as international financial integration reached a peak in the 1980s, the international monetary system became more susceptible to unsettling changes in

exchange rates and large speculative, transborder financial flows that aggravate the adverse effects of the adjustment process. This process could sooner
or later impel OECD policymakers toward neomercantilist reactions that
would undermine financial integration and give the international monetary
system the same direction of development as the international trading
system.

Even within the highly integrated EC, the growing neomercantilism of its
members has blocked further economic integration within the existing
common market and has halted the movement toward political and
economic unification. At bottom, this failure to deepen integration reflects
the restoration of the institutions of the nation-state in the course of the
postwar period. The changes of the 1960s and 1970s (sketched in Chapter
IV), which greatly expanded the responsibilities of national govenments and
the resources available to them, have had the effect of reviving their
institutional capabilities and their bureaucrats' sense of importance while
constraining them to act in more nationalistic ways.

Since the end of the postwar period, the EC has been unable to agree on
common policies in taxation, services, and other fields that would equalize
the conditions of competition within the members' economies and prevent
them from taking preferential or discriminatory actions in favor of their own
producers—which they have been doing. National political leaders and EC
officials are always talking about the need for increasing economic integration and proposals for doing so are recurrently considered by heads of
governments and their ministers. But, despite much discussion and numerous reports, no really significant steps beyond the degree of economic
integration achieved by the early 1970s have been approved. The only
notable advance toward further integration has been the establishment of
the European Monetary System; under it, fluctuations in the exchange rates
of members' currencies vis-à-vis one another are held within specified limits
and changes beyond them are made by ageement. However, this arrangement will probably not evolve into a common EC monetary system because
such a development would deprive national governments of control over
their countries' monetary policies and macroeconomic conditions.

Nevertheless, it is unlikely that the neomercantilist trend will be so
strengthened within Western Europe as to lead to the dissolution of the EC.
The integrated system still provides bigger benefits in trade, investment, and
economic aid than the members could obtain in its absence and, within
certain limits, each can on occasion increase its benefits by acting unilaterally
as a free-rider or by threatening to block EC decision making unless it
receives a special subvention or concession. Thus, both the long-term and
the short-term rational interests of the members are likely to keep the EC
more or less in its present state.

Future Changes Affecting the Neomercantilist Trend

The key question, therefore, for the future of the international economic system is: How are prospective changes in the OECD nations and in their interrelations likely to affect the development of the neomercantilist trend over the foreseeable future?

As explained in Chapter IV, the adverse effects of negative-sum welfare/efficiency interactions during the late 1970s and early 1980s halted the previous rapid expansion of national welfare systems and government regulation of economic activities. Nevertheless, it has been politically impossible to reduce by very much the scope and size of these programs. Instead, efforts are being made to improve their efficiency so as to offset at least some of the increase in costs due to indexation and high unemployment. Also, in the United States, some government regulations that have restricted competition in the domestic market have been weakened or abolished. The United Kingdom, France, and other West European countries have sold some state-owned enterprises to private investors. Important as these measures have been in strengthening market forces domestically, their effect on the external economic relations of the OECD nations has not been significant enough to halt, let alone reverse, the trend toward neomercantilist trade and investment practices. The much more drastic and pervasive changes in domestic economic policies that theoretically could do so would not be politically feasible or socially desirable because the period of adjustment would be too long and the adverse transitional effects on employment and incomes too severe.

However, prospective demographic changes are likely to ease the unemployment problem, which has been especially serious in Western Europe, and thus lessen one of the major pressures for neomercantilist actions. During the early 1990s, the levels of structural unemployment will be lowered by the gradual decrease in the annual new entrants into the labor force, the retirement or death of older workers, and the approach to the feasible upper limits of female participation. Nonetheless, persisting immigration of unskilled workers, especially into the United States, and the need to improve international competitiveness by reducing costs and applying technological innovations will undoubtedly partly offset this beneficial effect by continuing to generate some structural unemployment, particularly among unskilled native-born workers. A temporary increase in the numbers of new entrants into the labor force will occur in the second half of the 1990s and the early years of the 21st century due to the "echo" of the postwar baby boom. Thereafter, the decline in the rate of growth of the labor force will resume and probably accelerate as the large postwar baby-boom generation and the earlier immigrants begin to retire. Unemployment should fall substantially, and skilled labor could become relatively scarce by the second or third decade of the new century even though immigration into the United States, and perhaps some of the West European nations, would continue to provide unskilled and semiskilled workers. However, these demographic changes will probably precipitate intergenerational conflicts in the 21st century as the increasing burden of supporting the growing numbers of retired people presses on relatively fewer men and women of working age.

Another set of developments that will importantly affect the neomercantilist trend relates to the real rates of economic growth that the OECD nations could sustain over the foreseeable future. There are three possibilities: (1) that average annual growth rates during the 1990s and beyond will rise to the range of 3.5 to 4.5 percent, that is, substantially higher than the range of 2 to 3 percent of the 1980s; (2) that an international financial crisis and/or a severe recession will depress OECD growth rates even lower than those of the 1980s; and (3) that growth rates will persist within the present range or rise only slightly above it.

The first possibility envisages that the OECD nations will achieve substantially higher average annual rates of economic growth, rates comparable to those of the postwar decades. Such a development would provide the increasing economic resources and employment opportunities needed to meet popular expectations for rising disposable incomes and welfare benefits and to finance other government expenditures without regenerating inflation. Thus, it would significantly relax some of the main pressures generating the neomercantilist trend and help to slow it down. However, the likelihood of changes that could sustain growth rates comparable to those of the postwar period is low due to the same deeply rooted factors that produce neomercantilist actions and to the difficulties lying ahead in the 1990s, which are explained in the next section.

The second possibility for OECD economic-growth rates is that they will be significantly lower than the present range due to the persisting adverse effects of an international financial crisis and/or a severe recession, which may well be presaged by the October 1987 crash in the world economy's stock exchanges. A financial crisis is within the limits of the possible owing to the volatility of the fluctuating exchange-rate system and highly integrated currency and capital markets, the enormous expansion of international credit in the virtually unregulated Euromarkets, and the debt-service problems of the debtor countries. The loss of confidence by international lenders triggered by defaults of major governmental or private-sector borrowers, alarmingly adverse international political developments, or other panic-inducing events could generate a massive contraction of international credit and huge unsettling transborder currency flows that would be beyond the capacity of national monetary authorities in the leading OECD countries to control. As explained in the next section, the failure of the United States to cope effectively with its budgetary and balance-of-payments deficits could also result in a more or less severe U.S. recession that would quickly spread to the rest of the world economy and decisively accelerate the neomercantilist trend.

The third possibility for OECD economic-growth rates is that they would continue within the present range or perhaps rise slightly above it. The latter development would require certain favorable changes in the OECD nations.

On the supply side, somewhat higher economic growth depends critically upon the willingness and ability of the United States and the EC to raise productivity and hence improve their international competitiveness. This means not only applying in all economic sectors the results of the continuing electronic, photonic, and biotechnology revolutions but also making appropriate changes in the organization of the work force, the capabilities and functions of management, and the relations between them. Such tech-nological and managerial innovations, especially those associated with so-called computer-integrated manufacturing systems, would make possible the use of smaller and more flexible production units, the improvement of product quality, and even the lowering of labor costs sufficiently to encour-age some repatriation of manufacturing to these countries. So far, Japan and the United States have taken the lead in developing and applying these innovations; to the extent that the EC continues to lag behind them, it will be constrained to offset its competitive deficiencies by neomercantilist measures.

Moreover, increased public investment in infrastructure would be needed to improve productivity in the private sector. In addition to their current high welfare, defense, and other public-consumption expenditures, many OECD countries, including the United States, have accumulating public-investment requirements for infrastructure and related purposes that will sooner or later have to be filled if economic growth is to continue even at present rates. In the United States, public investment by federal, state, and local governments has dropped steadily from about 2.5 percent of GDP in the 1960s to around 1.3 percent during the first half of the 1980s. These large fiscal claims for public-sector consumption and investment would tend to keep total government spending around existing ratios to GDP and hence are likely in the United States and some other OECD nations to mandate increased taxes or continuing large deficit financing to the extent that higher economic growth does not generate sufficiently bigger revenues.

On the demand side, the market for OECD products in Asia, Africa, and Latin America will probably not increase substantially due to the continuing limited import capabilities of most countries in these regions and the unlikelihood of a large-scale rise in the volume of economic aid and private investment from the United States, the EC, and Japan. The most promising prospect for a sustained expansion of the market would arise in the OECD region itself from (1) the need of producers in all sectors to apply the innovations of the electronic, photonic, and biotechnology revolutions under the spur of domestic and international competition and (2) the attractiveness of the resulting new goods and services to OECD consumers. Undoubtedly, the demand for such high-technology capital and consumer goods and services will increase over the foreseeable future. But, it might not be on the scale required if renewed inflation in the United States and other OECD countries were to raise interest rates and thereby deny the requisite volume of credit to the private sector at low enough cost.

Finally, it must be stressed that future maintenance by the OECD nations of even their current rates of economic growth, let alone the attainment of higher rates, also depends on how the United States deals with its budgetary and balance-of-payments deficits, as explained in the next section.

If they could be sustained, somewhat higher economic-growth rates in the 1990s would certainly help OECD policymakers to resist better the internal pressures generating the neomercantilist trend and hence to slow it down. However, economic growth would not be high enough to produce the substantial relaxation of these pressures that would occur in the much less likely case of rates comparable to those of the postwar period.

Moreover, account needs to be taken of the economic effects of probable political developments in the OECD nations. Domestic interest-group pressures, ideological commitments, or the exigencies of partisan politics could at any time constrain national policymakers in any of these countries to take actions that would revive negative-sum welfare/efficiency interactions, rekindle inflation, provoke recession, or in other ways reinforce the factors that generate the neomercantilist trend.

The Role of the United States in the Prospects for the Neomercantilist Trend

The behavior of the United States will be critical in determining *not* whether the neomercantilist trend will be eliminated but whether it will continue at its present rate of development or can be slowed.

Hitherto, the United States has lagged behind the EC and Japan in restricting imports and subsidizing exports just as, during the postwar period, it was ahead of them in opening its economy to external market forces. True, the United States has induced other countries to accept voluntary export restraints and orderly marketing agreements. It has also unilaterally imposed some import quotas and antidumping prohibitions to restrict the adverse impact of lower-priced imports on its own producers. However, although for particular products (such as steel, automobiles, textiles, clothing, and footwear) these and other restrictions have limited imports substantially, they have applied *in the aggregate* to a smaller percentage of total U.S. tradable goods than have the restrictions of the EC, Japan, and other nations relative to their total tradable goods. On the export side, U.S. actions have so far been limited to subsidizing export credits and some agricultural exports, and these are generally at lower rates than the equivalent subventions of other nations. Nor do its nontariff barriers and other internal regulations constitute obstacles to imports as unsurmountable as those of the EC, Japan, and other countries.

The willingness and ability of the United States to lag behind its trading partners and competitors in the neomercantilist trend mean that it has continued to bear a disproportionate share of the costs of international economic integration. And, this residual manifestation of its postwar hegemonic role has been an essential condition for the existing, still very substantial, degree of integration.

That the United States did not move as far down the neomercantilist road as other countries has been all the more remarkable in view of the considerable increase in the costs of its self-restraint. During the first half of the 1980s, they rose rapidly for two reasons. One was the further decline in the international competitiveness of U.S. manufacturers, workers, and farmers due to the large overvaluation of the dollar. The other was that the greater import restrictions imposed by the EC and other countries effectively diverted some exports from Japan and the old and emerging NICs away from Western Europe to the more open U.S. market. While U.S. consumers benefited from lower-priced goods, severe losses of employment and incomes also resulted from both the rise of competitive imports and the shift of production by U.S. companies to lower-cost countries.

However, although the United States has continued behind the other OECD nations in the neomercantilist trend, a major change in U.S. attitudes and actions has increasingly been manifested during the 1980s. Not only have the pressures from adversely affected producers been intensifying, but also the general perception of rational interest has been shifting from the long term to the short term. That is, despite the short-term costs in higher consumer prices, the short-term benefits to employment and money incomes of restricting imports and subsidizing exports appear to growing numbers of Americans to be larger and definitely more assured than do the increasingly uncertain long-term benefits of refraining from neomercantilist measures while other countries are increasingly resorting to them. Hence, U.S. policymakers are now impelled (1) to prevent such actions by other nations from imposing higher costs on the U.S. economy and (2) to reduce more of the costs that the United States has hitherto borne.

These developments have been undermining the two ways by which the United States helped to maintain the highly integrated international economic system of the postwar period: continued willingness to absorb a disproportionate share of the costs of integration and ability to constrain other nations to abide by the requisite rules of behavior. Since World War II, the predominant view among U.S. policymakers and opinion leaders has been that these two ways are directly related: the willingness of the United States to keep its economy open despite the costs provides it with the influence of precept and example in persuading other countries to refrain from eroding integration. This direct relationship certainly existed during the postwar period but, since the early 1970s, it has become less and less effective. Given their own internal pressures and their weaker commitment to the ideal of unrestricted nondiscriminatory trade and investment (noted in Chapter II), the EC, Japan, and the NICs have naturally been inclined to take advantage of U.S. forbearance and to discount U.S. preaching. Hence, during the 1980s, the actions of U.S. policymakers have been implying a different view. It is that the relationship between the two ways has now become an inverse one: that *the only effective leverage the United States has over the economic behavior of its major trading partners is not precept and example but its power to grant or withhold access to the U.S. market.*

In their negotiations over trade issues, U.S. policymakers have increasingly employed this sanction to induce the EC, Japan, and other countries to rescind or reduce their neomercantilist measures that adversely affect U.S. producers in their own and other markets. To apply the sanction, U.S. policymakers have imposed equivalent restrictions against imports from these nations, which have remained in force whenever the latter were unwilling to grant the requested concessions. More extensive use of this sanction is envisaged in the new trade bills drafted by the Congress in recent years.

However, this shift in tactics has not been accompanied by a corresponding change in the rationale for such actions. U.S. policymakers continue to stress the U.S. commitment to the ideal of unrestricted nondiscriminatory trade and investment. They justify U.S. resort to restrictive and retaliatory measures as designed to induce other countries to abolish their "unfair" practices and thus to make international trade a "level playing field" for U.S. producers.

The way in which the new tactics are being used by the United States also implies that, for many of the products involved, there are minimum levels of domestic production that have to be maintained regardless of whether the output is competitive. This is the contemporary expression of the traditional national-security rationale for protectionism. Today, it reflects the emerging concern that the United States can no longer take for granted assured access to external sources of raw materials and manufactured goods, on which it has become increasingly dependent due to U.S. producers' loss of competitiveness. This concern implies that, for each of these commodities, there is a point at which the higher cost of maintaining minimum levels of domestic productive capacity would be offset by the rising uncertainty of uninterrupted lower-cost supplies from countries that are politically unstable or whose regimes are, or could become, hostile to the United States. Fundamentally, this fear is generated by the declining integration, stability, and calculability of the international system sketched in this chapter.

The serious problems confronting the U.S. economy today and in the years ahead will very likely help to perpetuate the new tactics and will probably sooner or later impel most U.S. policymakers, if not most opinion leaders, to accept explicitly the neomercantilist assumptions that already underlie many of their actions.

True, since the fall of 1985, the substantial decline in the exchange rate of the dollar, especially vis-à-vis the Japanese yen and German mark, has helped to improve the competitive position of U.S. goods and services both abroad and in the domestic market. However, the beneficial effect of this devaluation is limited, because many important trading partners and competitors of the United States, such as Canada, Mexico, the East Asian NICs, and other Asian and Latin American nations, either keep their currencies tied to the dollar or devalue them more than it. Moreover, due to their debt-servicing problems, many Latin American, African, and Asian countries have had to reduce their imports of U.S. goods.

Also, devaluation is at best only a partial and temporary palliative for the loss of international competitiveness. It has to be accompanied by improvements in U.S. productivity through continuing investment in new product and process technologies and marketing strategies and the adoption of new ways of organizing and interrelating management and the work force. Many U.S. manufacturers have lost markets at home and abroad because, even though their prices may be competitive, the design, quality, and servicing of their products have fallen too far behind those of their foreign rivals.

Keeping the exchange rate of the dollar at competitive levels and making the necessary improvements in productivity and product quality are not the only variables involved in reducing substantially the large U.S. budgetary and balance-of-payments deficits, which will be among the most pressing tasks confronting the United States in the years ahead. During the 1980s, U.S. policymakers failed to resolve this very difficult set of interrelated macroeconomic problems due not only to the incompatible policy commitments of the president and the Congress but, more fundamentally, to the constraints imposed by the factors that also generate the neomercantilist trend. They could evade this responsibility because foreign savers were willing to invest unprecedentedly large funds in the United States that helped to finance its deficits and to permit overconsumption in both the public and private sectors.

In effect, during the 1980s, the United States, Western Europe, and Japan had an implicit deal. As explained in Chapter IV, the West European nations and Japan chose to sustain their rates of economic growth mainly by relying on exports, especially to the United States, rather than by stimulating domestic demand. They could do so because they were willing to lend the United States funds with which to cover its deficits. The advantages to the United States of keeping its economy open to their exports and losing markets abroad to them were that the inflows of European and Japanese funds enabled it to finance much higher levels of public and private consumption than would otherwise have been possible and to avoid the painful adjustments necessary to bring its internal and external accounts into balance. However, this implicit agreement cannot continue for much longer because of the consequences for Western Europe, Japan, and the United States not only of a substantial reduction in (let alone the elimination of) the U.S. current-account deficit but also of the steadily mounting U.S. debt-servicing burden.

First, whether through further declines in the dollar exchange rate or improvements in U.S. productivity or both, the current account of the United States will be brought closer to balance by increases in U.S. exports and reductions in U.S. imports of goods and services.[1] For reasons explained in the preceding section, world economic growth rates, including the growth of world trade, are not likely to be high enough to accommodate all or most of this shift in the U.S. trade balance. Hence, as the U.S. current-account deficit shrinks, European and Japanese producers will lose market shares not only in the United States but also within their own economies and in third countries. Given the domestic limitations under which European and Japanese policymakers operate, they will at some point be constrained by falling employment and incomes in the adversely affected industries to check their market losses—by allowing their exchange rates to decline, by restricting their imports and subsidizing their exports, or by some combination of these measures. Thus, the more that the U.S. current-account deficit is reduced, the stronger will be the pressures on its major trading partners and competitors to resist losing market shares by resorting to neomercantilist devices.

Second, the burden on the U.S. economy of servicing its net external debt is already significant and is bound to become heavier in the years ahead at a rate that depends on how fast and how far the U.S. payments imbalance declines. The outpayments on the net external debt of the United States represent a transfer of real resources to Western Europe, Japan, and other assetholders abroad like that which occurred during the 1970s to the surplus OPEC countries. Except in the unlikely event that these or other creditors would be willing indefinitely to go on lending funds to the United States with which to finance such transfers—which would only further increase the U.S. burden—servicing the net external debt means a corresponding reduction in U.S. real national income.

Moreover, since the capacity to reduce the U.S. budgetary deficit by cuts in expenditures is limited, a decline in the inflow of foreign savings to finance the remaining budgetary imbalance would have to be made up by raising interest rates to attract more domestic savings, by increases in taxation, by inflationary deficit financing, or by some combination of these measures. In whatever way it is done, cutting the budgetary deficit means a reduction in the real incomes of businesses and households in the United States. The temptation to resort to inflation would be strong, due not only to domestic political restraints on raising taxes but also to the fact that the external debt of the United States is denominated in dollars and its real burden would be lightened by servicing it in depreciated currency. And, implicit in these difficult choices is the danger of precipitating a severe U.S. recession.

Regardless of which measures are adopted by U.S. policymakers for coping with the painful adjustments involved, the result will be more or less serious conflicts within the United States over how the costs are to be distributed among different groups and institutions in American society. The more difficult these domestic conflicts become, the greater the pressures on U.S. policymakers will be to resort to neomercantilist measures in an attempt to shift as much of the adjustment costs as possible to the trading partners and competitors of the United States.

In sum, the changes in the attitudes of the American people and in the actions of U.S. policymakers, combined with the existing and prospective problems confronting the U.S. economy, mean that the United States in the years ahead will most likely become a more important contributor, directly and indirectly, to the neomercantilist trend than it has been in the past. In all of the OECD countries, resolution of the inherent ambivalence of rational interest has shifted from waiting for the increasingly uncertain long-term benefits to avoiding the short-term costs and, where possible, unilaterally obtaining immediate benefits. Thus, two of the necessary conditions for the maintenance of a high level of international economic integration explained in Chapter I—hegemonic power and long-term rational interest—are becoming too weak to continue for much longer to support such a system.

THE DETERMINATIVE POLITICAL TRENDS

Neomercantilism is the economic dimension of a broader phenomenon: the tensions between obtaining the benefits of international interdependence and preserving those of national freedom of action in both internal and external affairs. These tensions are also manifested in the political dimension of international relations as a *trend toward increasingly nationalistic behavior,* that is, a substantial increase in nations' concern to advance or protect the conceptions of their interests and self-images that predominate within them at the expense of their regard for the interests of other nations and the well-being of the international system as a whole. Since the end of the postwar period, the trend toward more particularistic behavior has gradually become more evident in the external political actions of many nations.

The nationalistic trend has been fostered by the changes in the structure of international power relations surveyed in Chapter III. Most important has been the spreading perception of the declining willingness of the United States to compel and its diminishing ability to persuade other nations to behave in ways that would preserve the high degree of international order and calculability that prevailed during the postwar period. Hence, national governments have felt freer to act unilaterally to advance or protect their conceptions of their interests while at the same time expecting the international system as a whole somehow to maintain its order and security. By so doing, they have increasingly become free-riders in the system.

True, most governments continue to recognize their interest in an international system in which every member acts with at least a minimum degree of self-restraint and conformity with the principles of international law and with the obligations it has assumed in international agreements. Also, international organizations can facilitate the settlement of disputes if the protagonists are willing to accept their mediation or arbitration. However, the classical difficulty still exists: in John Locke's famous formulation, "want of a common judge with authority puts all men in a state of Nature." That is, an international system, unlike a society, contains no central authority with the right and the power to interpret laws and agreements and to enforce its decisions. In these circumstances, it is in the rational interest of a nation to be a free-rider if there are enough other nations willing to exercise self-restraint and conform to international laws and agreements or if the existence of a significant degree of disorder and uncertainty permits it to fish in troubled waters.

In the postwar period, the hegemonic power and influence of the United

States substituted in sufficient measure for the absence of a central authority and offset the effects of the ambivalent rational interest of the members. Just as the growing unwillingness of the United States to bear a disproportionate share of the costs of international economic integration has helped to bring about a gradual decline in the extent of integration, so the decreasing power and influence of the United States since the early 1970s have been essential factors in the parallel decline in the degree of orderliness and calculability of the international political system.

At the national level, the nationalistic trend reflects the changes that have been taking place in the motivations and capabilities of the different types of nation-states sketched in Chapters IV and V.

The Nationalistic Trend in the OECD Nations

Although they have been major contributors to declining economic integration, the OECD nations have by and large continued to support the principles of international law and the preservation of peace and order in the international system. Nonetheless, the divergences in the international political policies and behavior of the OECD nations, especially those between the United States and its NATO allies noted in Chapters III and IV, have indirectly contributed to the decreasing orderliness and calculability of the international system by substantially reducing political coordination among them.

Due to the effects of the institutional and generational changes sketched in Chapter IV, the West Europeans have been increasingly resigned to accepting unfavorable political changes in the international system that do not directly threaten their economic and security interests. And, when these interests are adversely affected, the European inclination is to negotiate the best settlement possible in the circumstances rather than to resort to coercive measures, such as economic sanctions, let alone the threat or use of force.[2] This attitude expresses a realistic understanding of the extent to which many of the profound changes occurring in the different types of nation-states could be prevented or controlled. It reflects the restrictions on European reactions imposed by the European nations' unwillingness to realize the potential military capabilities and hence political power that their immense economic resources could make possible. It is fostered by the belief that the United States will continue to try to maintain the orderliness and calculability of the international system regardless of whether they support its efforts and of the decline in its own power and influence over the behavior of other nations. This attitude also rests on the Europeans' desire to obtain whatever benefits can be derived by dissociating themselves from coercive U.S. actions.

However, when the United States seems inclined to the same conception as the Europeans—as it appeared to be during the late 1970s—they become alarmed that it is not discharging its responsibility to maintain world order. Equally, a more activist assertion by the United States of its remaining capacity to cope with adverse international political developments, as during the 1980s, provokes European criticism that such U.S. behavior increases the threat of war or constitutes unwarranted intervention in the affairs of independent nations.

In the United States, this European attitude tends to be regarded as the contemporary equivalent of the appeasement policy of the 1930s. Moreover, to many Americans, the Europeans appear to be enjoying the benefits of the continuing U.S. effort to preserve international order at too little cost and risk to themselves, as well as the satisfaction of invidiously characterizing U.S. actions as either excessive or inadequate. Yet, as will be explained in Chapter X, majority opinion in the United States is also deeply ambivalent about the U.S. role in maintaining world order. Western Europe's self-imposed dependence on U.S. protection and its consequent limited capacity to influence U.S. actions help to generate resentment against the United States. Similarly, the frustrations and costs for the United States that partly result from the self-imposed limitations on its actions (also explained in Chapter X) contribute to U.S. resentment over the declining support of its allies and their criticisms of its efforts.

The growing divergences in attitudes between the West European nations and the United States can be strikingly illustrated by the results of two recent opinion polls. The first, summarized in *The Economist* (February 21, 1987), found that 49 percent of the British, 55 percent of the French, and 69 percent of the Italians would replace the alliance with the United States by a common European defense or a purely national defense. However, a majority of British and French would not increase their defense spending above present levels, while most Italians and Germans want to cut their defense budgets. Also, 25 percent of the French, 29 percent of the Germans, 35 percent of the British, and 70 percent of the Italians believe that a nonnuclear European army without U.S. support could successfully defend itself against a nuclear-armed Soviet attack! Finally 66 percent of the Germans, 60 percent of the French, and 56 percent of the British want U.S. nuclear weapons removed from Western Europe. In contrast, a poll conducted by the Chicago Council on Foreign Relations, reported in *Foreign Policy* (Spring 1987), showed that, of those polled, 68 percent of the American public and 93 percent of U.S. opinion leaders would still support the use of U.S. troops to defend Western Europe against a Soviet attack.

European doubts about the intentions and capabilities of the Reagan administration certainly played some part in these negative views about the alliance with the United States. Even discounting them, however, the European attitudes revealed in this and other recent polls provide no grounds for assuming either that American attitudes toward European defense will not, sooner or later, be adversely affected by declining European support for NATO or that the alliance will continue indefinitely in its present form.

Thus, the institutional and generational changes occurring on both sides of the Atlantic make it quite unlikely that the United States and the West European nations will reestablish the high degree of political coordination that characterized their postwar relationship. For all the nostalgia of the older generation in the United States and Western Europe for "Atlantic Partnership," it was a goal, not a reality, even in the 1960s, and the chances of achieving it are much less today than they were then. Indeed, a more likely change is that the nationalistic and neomercantilist trends in the OECD nations will reinforce each other. Sooner or later, the nationalistic trend could adversely affect not only, as now, political coordination among the NATO members but military-defense arrangements as well.

During the postwar period, the U.S. commitment to protect Western Europe against the Soviet Union by nuclear means if necessary was credible for two reasons. First, for most of the postwar period, the United States possessed sufficient nuclear superiority over the Soviet Union to convince the latter that, if it invaded Western Europe, it would suffer decisively greater nuclear destruction than would the United States. Second, the political cohesiveness of the NATO alliance was sufficiently strong to make plausible the likelihood that the United States would put its own society at risk of severe nuclear destruction for the sake of its allies. The first basis for credibility disappeared during the 1970s as the Soviet Union achieved nuclear capabilities at least equal to and probably greater than those of the United States. The second basis for the credibility of the U.S. nuclear guarantee has been eroding during the 1980s as the political cohesiveness of the alliance has been loosening. If the divergences in attitudes and interests between the United States and Western Europe continue to increase and the conflicts likely to arise during the 1990s over distribution of the costs of the adjustment process are not satisfactorily resolved, it will become less and less plausible that a U.S. administration would use nuclear means to defend Western Europe at the risk of provoking a Soviet nuclear strike against the United States. The implications for the future of NATO of the declining cohesiveness of the alliance and the policy choices that could be made to cope with the likely consequences are explored in the next chapter.

The Nationalistic Trend in Asian, African, and Latin American Nations

Regardless of how NATO would be affected, the continued weakening of U.S.–West European political coordination would more and more impair the efforts of the OECD nations to try to maintain the orderliness and calculability of the international system. Moreover, the economic difficulties likely to confront them in the years ahead could reduce the economic resources they could allocate for development assistance and other purposes in Asia, Africa, and Latin America and could limit further their willingness to import from these regions manufactured goods and agricultural products that would compete with their own producers.

As explained in Chapter V, the transitional process in Asia and Africa and the modernization process in Latin America make the countries of these regions the major sources of disorder in the international system and incline them to strong assertions of their national freedom of action. Due to their internal processes of change, Asian, African, and Latin American nations are prone in greater or lesser degree to economic crisis, political instability, and social unrest. These internal problems and disorders provide opportunities for other countries to increase their influence over the existing regimes dependent on their help, or to assist dissident groups to establish new regimes, or to obtain other kinds of advantages for themselves. Such interventions are not limited to the two superpowers, the Soviet Union and the United States, acting under the compulsions of their balance-of-power relationship and their world leadership roles. Asian, African, and Latin American nations are often inclined to take advantage of one another to further the ambitions of their own ruling elites or to undermine regimes of which they disapprove for ideological reasons or from whose fall they hope to profit. Some not only cooperate with the Soviet Union and its client states in training guerrillas and supporting their insurgencies but also provide facilities, supplies, and safehavens for terrorists, whose activities have become an increasingly important manifestation of rising disorder and uncertainty in the international system. In these ways, the internal difficulties of troubled Asian, African, and Latin American countries are externalized as issues in world politics, and international issues are in turn internalized and aggravate domestic problems and conflicts.

Asian and African nations in particular are constrained by their basic sociocultural characteristics to nationalism as the means for coping with their problems of societal integration, identity, and legitimation. Many of them, as well as Latin American countries, are basically disaffected from the existing world market system and aspire to a new international economic order (NIEO) in which their governments would exercise determinative power, as explained in Chapter V. And, they have been encouraged toward increasingly nationalistic behavior by their perception of declining U.S. power and influence in the international system and the disinclination of the West Europeans to support U.S. initiatives.

Thus, in varying degree, Asian, African, and Latin American nations feel the least responsibility and have the least capacity for maintaining the orderliness and calculability of the international system. Conversely, they have the strongest internal compulsions for trying to profit from external disorder and uncertainty. It is among these countries that wars are most likely to occur—wars that could involve the superpowers as well. Finally, certain Asian, African, and Latin American nations have already constructed, or are trying to develop or acquire, nuclear weapons and are likely to be the first to use them. In these and other ways, Asia, Africa, and Latin America are and will continue to be the principal sources of instability in the international system.

In sum, the gradually increasing neomercantilist and nationalistic trends and their mutually reinforcing interactions, combined with declining U.S. power and influence, will continue over the foreseeable future to make the international system less integrated, stable, orderly, and calculable than it was in the postwar period. How far this process is likely to go and in what forms it will be manifested depend on the choices that national policymakers and opinion leaders make in the years ahead. These possibilities are analyzed in the next chapter.

NOTES

1. The notion that the United States will become a postindustrial service economy and that its current-account deficit will be eliminated by the growth in its earnings from services has been dispelled by Stephen S. Cohen and John Zysman, *Manufacturing Matters: The Myth of the Post-Industrial Economy* (New York: Basic Books, 1987). Moreover, increasing U.S. earnings from services abroad would at some point be checked by the same countermeasures as would growing goods exports.

2. The major exception has been France, which is still willing to help protect and maintain order in its former African colonies by force, if necessary. The United Kingdom has forcibly defended its remaining possessions, as in the Falklands, but that it would do so for any of the former members of its empire is very doubtful.

Chapter VIII

POLICY CHOICES AND THE FUTURE DEVELOPMENT OF THE INTERNATIONAL SYSTEM

The neomercantilist and nationalistic trends and their interactions are manifestations of the basic tensions between international interdependence and national independence and set the general direction of development of the international system over the foreseeable future, the next twenty-five years or so. This direction of development defines the limits within which the actual course of events will be determined by policymakers in governments and private sectors. Policymakers' decisions and actions are shaped by institutional interests and capabilities, by popular attitudes and expectations, and by their own understanding of the nature of the factors involved and how they could be influenced. Thus, within the general direction, there is a range of possible future courses of international development that expresses the different ways in which policymakers are likely to be willing and able to cope with the tensions, problems, and opportunities generated by the determinative trends. This chapter explains the kinds of actions that policymakers could take and their possible effects on the development of the international system. On this basis, Chapter IX presents a worst-case forecast and some more probable better-case outcomes.

First, however, I want to reiterate that reversing the general direction of development of the international system is not within the limits of the possible. Policymakers cannot bring about the kinds of changes at national and international levels that would be necessary to move the system back to the high degrees of integration, order, and calculability that characterized the postwar period. Neither the establishment of a systemwide supranational authority nor the restoration of the postwar U.S. hegemony is a realistic possibility. What policymakers can do is to accelerate or slow down the determinative trends and to influence the particular forms in which they are manifested.

MANAGING THE NEOMERCANTILIST TREND

The neomercantalist trend is not only self-reinforcing, as explained in the preceding chapter; it is also potentially self-limiting. That is, as the intensity and scope of competition in the world market economy diminish due to the spread of neomercantilist behavior, the pressures to extend measures of these kinds to more and more external economic relations would abate, although they would not disappear. There are two ways by which policy choices in the major trading and investing nations—that is, in the OECD countries and the existing and future NICs—could activate this self-limiting potential.

Allowing a Neomercantilist System to Emerge

The first method would reflect the serious inadequacy of policymakers' efforts to manage the neomercantilist trend. In consequence, the trend would be likely to accelerate and a neomercantilist international economic system—a modern analogue of the 17th- and 18th-century system—would sooner or later emerge. It would be characterized by an extensive network of bilateral agreements between national governments to share trade and investment opportunities in their own and third-country markets and to balance their payments with one another. To implement such agreements, national governments would have to control in greater or lesser degree their countries' imports and exports, inflows and outflows of capital, and currency convertibility. Market forces would continue to operate within these rather narrow limits, and private entrepreneurs would persistently seek—as they have always done in such systems—to evade and erode these restrictions.

In theory, a neomercantilist system would be viable and could be stabilized but at a much lower level of integration than currently exists. National economies and international trade and investment would grow at substantially slower rates than they have been doing in the existing system. Living standards would also rise more slowly, if at all, because the restrictions on competition would prevent consumers from having access to the lowest-cost or best-quality goods and services. Countries that lacked economic, or political/military, bargaining power would have the lowest growth rates and the least gains from trade and would face the greatest difficulties in improving their situations because they would be at a severe disadvantage in trying to realize their potential export capabilities.

As countries increasingly substituted government decision making for market forces, they would be susceptible not only to the problems generated by intensified negative-sum welfare/efficiency interactions but also to those that plague the nonmarket economic systems of the Soviet Union and its client states explained in Chapter VI. Individual and group freedom of action within national societies would be constricted both economically and politically because governments would need to prevent decentralized private initiative and ingenuity from undermining their domestic regulations and international agreements. Thus, the substantial economic and political costs of a neomercantilist international system would far outweigh its benefits.

Existing Efforts to Slow the Neomercantilist Trend

The second method of activating the self-limiting element of the neomercantilist trend would require an effective multilateral approach by policymakers in the OECD nations and the existing and future NICs. This means that the more urgent problems would have to be mitigated through multilateral agreements, changes in international organizations, and other means before they impelled increasing resort to unilateral restrictions and subsidies and discriminatory bilateral arrangements. But isn't this what OECD governments have been trying to do since manifestations of the neomercantilist trend became troublesome? My answer is yes and no: yes in intent and no in terms of their attitude toward and conceptual approach to the issues involved. Hence, the record to date of international negotiation and agreement in checking the self-reinforcing dynamic of the neomercantilist trend has been quite meager.

The frequency of trade disputes among the United States, the EC, Japan, and the NICs—and between them and other Asian, African, and Latin American countries—has increased since the end of the postwar period from one or two a year to one or two a month; the issues have become more difficult to resolve; and, when they can be settled, it is usually on the basis of further trade restrictions. Even when negotiations have led to agreements to reduce neomercantilist measures, they have often been observed only temporarily, or they have been too general to be effective, or the banned practices have soon been replaced by new types of subsidies or restrictions.

For example, the seventh round of GATT negotiations during the 1970s resulted in general codes to govern the use of several important nontariff barriers, such as government-procurement preferences and product-quality standards. However, the codes do not sufficiently specify the permitted and prohibited actions nor do they provide means for ascertaining when violations occur and what should be done about them. Moreover, the GATT members were unable to agree on the crucial "safeguards" code that would spell out the conditions under which countries could restrict the import of competitive products and the measures by which they could do so. Thus, implementation of the codes has not been notably effective. And, unless it can avoid such deficiencies, the eighth GATT round, aimed principally at reducing discriminatory trade practices in agriculture and services, is not likely to be any more successful.

Multilateral coordination of macroeconomic policies has been even less effective than the settlement of trade disputes. Since the introduction of the flexible-rate system and the integration of national financial markets during the 1970s, cooperative efforts among OECD policymakers have been aimed at reducing destabilizing payments imbalances and exchange-rate fluctuations, and moderating the swings of the business cycle. Although "summit" meetings of heads of OECD governments and ministerial conferences during the 1970s and 1980s have recurrently emphasized the need for macromanagement coordination, these declarations have not been translated into effective arrangements for doing so on a continuing basis. Instead, such coordination as has been undertaken has been ad hoc. It has included occasional cooperation by central banks to check speculative transborder currency movements and disruptive short-term capital flows and, most notably since early 1985, the informal agreement to initiate and control a substantial devaluation of the U.S. dollar. The basic reason for the failure to establish effective international arrangements for macrocoordination by mandatory changes in national fiscal and/or monetary policies has been that they would impose another set of external constraints on national policymakers.

The same reason has prevented the adoption of the recurrent proposals for stabilizing exchange rates by reverting to some type of fixed-rate system. This change would not be possible in the absence of a lender of last resort, such as a world central bank or the United States during the postwar period with its then disproportionately large resources and power. National governments are most unlikely to endow an international institution with the power to compel and the resources to assist the member countries to make the sometimes drastic domestic adjustments needed in a fixed-rate system to maintain realistic exchange rates and reasonable balances in their external accounts. A restoration of the postwar U.S. hegemony is equally improbable. Even the more limited suggestions for "target zones" or "reference ranges," within which the OECD countries would undertake to

keep their currencies, have been resisted by national policymakers concerned that this obligation might compel them to take actions that would
adversely affect their domestic employment and incomes. Moreover, as
critics of these proposals have pointed out, their effectiveness would decline
in inverse ratio to the severity of the pressures driving currencies to the top
or bottom of the permitted ranges.

In essence, more effective use of the method of multilateral agreement
requires a change in ways of thinking by the OECD nations, especially the
United States, and the existing and emerging NICs. For, the conceptual
framework that policymakers employ in trying to understand the nature of
problems has to be relevant to the objective situations to which it refers if
their prescriptions for dealing with the difficulties involved are to be effective.

Although U.S. policymakers' actions have been becoming increasingly
neomercantilistic, as explained in Chapter VII, the most prevalent view in
the United States has continued to be that the various manifestations of
neomercantilism at home and abroad are simply temporary aberrations.
They could be eliminated and prevented from recurring if only politicians
and other policymakers in the United States, the EC, Japan, and the NICs
understood the long-term benefits of unimpeded trade and investment and
had the courage to resist the pressures for restrictions on imports and
subsidies for exports. Once policymakers' understanding and resolve were
strengthened, the march toward free trade could be resumed to the benefit
of all. Similarly, inadequate understanding and courage are believed to be
largely responsible for OECD policymakers' refusal to harmonize their
national fiscal and monetary policies so as to moderate payment imbalances
and exchange-rate instability and promote economic growth in the world
economy as a whole.

This way of thinking was relevant to the domestic and international
conditions of the postwar period and, therefore, the prescriptions that
followed from it were realistic goals of policy during those decades. However, to hold to this conceptual approach today means implicitly ignoring the
major changes I have sketched in the structure and functioning of the
international system and in the motivations and capabilities of its members,
including the United States.

At bottom, it is not the ignorance, lack of courage, or irresponsibility of
OECD policymakers that motivates them to choose the more certain
short-term gains from economic integration over its increasingly uncertain
long-term benefits and to pass on its costs to others. Rather, they are
impelled to do so by three developments that have gradually become
apparent since the end of the postwar period. The first is the more drastic and
rapid operation of the adjustment process across national boundaries and
the greater susceptibility of the OECD economies to its adverse short-term

effects. The second results from those institutional and attitudinal changes within the OECD societies that have substantially narrowed policymakers' freedom of action to allocate the costs among their producers and taxpayers. Hence, willingly or perforce, their decisions have to be responsive to the felt needs of the much larger numbers of people and the more numerous and articulate organizations and groups that are now affected by the integration of their national economies into the international system than was the case during the postwar period. The third is the fact that the United States is no longer willing and able to bear a disproportionate share of the costs of the adjustment process, as in the postwar period, nor can it constrain or persuade other nations to abide by the rules of behavior needed for a highly integrated world economy to anywhere near the extent that it could then.

In a remarkable essay in *The Economist* (December 20, 1986), Sir Austin Robinson, "the grand old man of British economics," reminisced about the ways in which both economics and the world economy have changed in the course of his long life. He pointed out that, when Alfred Marshall formulated neoclassical trade theory,

> he was analyzing the workings of the economy of that time—the world of slow change, in which the transfer of technology from country to country was a matter of centuries, in which there was real meaning in the idea that a country possessed and would continue to possess a comparative advantage in a particular industry. . . . And, we were all free-traders, arguing the case on the tacit assumption of full employment of both parties [in international trade], and not asking what happened if either or both had substantial unemployment.
>
> . . . we are only at the beginning of seeing the difficulties of running the multinational world in which the transfer of technology is unbelievably rapid, in which the comparative advantage in shipbuilding shifts in a few years from the Clyde to the Dutch, the Swedes, the Japanese and the Taiwanese; in which the cotton industry has gone from Lancashire, temporarily to Japan and since to India and other developing countries. We now live in a world infinitely different from that assumed in the classical economics in which I was brought up. . . .
>
> Sixty-six years of economics has taught me that there are none so dangerous as those who believe that economics is a set of immutable commandments discovered in the nineteenth century, to be imposed, cost what it may, on the completely different world of the late twentieth century.

A More Effective Multilateral Approach to Slowing the Neomercantilist Trend

Therefore, to cope effectively with the neomercantilist trend, a new way of thinking is needed that is relevant to the realities of the existing and prospective international system. The main features of such a new conceptual framework follow logically from the analysis of the nature of the determinative trends in Chapter VII. The new approach recognizes that the United States can no longer be relied upon to behave in a less neomercantilistic manner than the other OECD nations and the NICs. Hence, if the neomercantilist trend is to be managed effectively, all of these countries have to share equitably in the costs, as well as the benefits, of doing so. In essence, it involves trying to strengthen their rational interest in more responsible behavior as the only substitute for the absence of hegemonic power in slowing the neomercantilist trend and preserving as high a degree of international economic integration as is possible in existing and prospective circumstances.

Due to the institutional and attitudinal changes within nations and the shifts in the structure of the international system since the end of the postwar period, the issue of distributing the costs of the adjustment process among and within the OECD nations and the existing and emerging NICs has already become of central importance and will continue to be so for the foreseeable future, as explained in Chapter VII. Not only must it now be explicitly included in the general task of macroeconomic coordination but the effectiveness of specific efforts to slow down the neomercantilist trend in trade and investment relations also depends on agreement as to how the benefits and costs involved will be distributed. True, the allocation issue has always been basically at stake in disputes among these countries. But, in discussions of macromanagement problems, the assumption has usually been that it need not be specifically taken into account. And, when it has been explicitly considered, as in disputes over restrictions on and subsidies for particular traded commodities, the issue has generally been posed in narrow terms of the relative costs and benefits for the specific producers of these goods in the countries involved. In contrast, the allocation issue needs now to be addressed in its own terms, in the broad national and international contexts, and in a coordinated manner by the OECD nations and the NICs.

At first glance, this prescription appears to be open to the same fatal deficiency that has underlain the failures of the existing approach. Given the domestic and international constraints on their freedom of action, why should national policymakers be any better able to resolve the even more difficult allocation issue than they have been the trade, investment, and macromanagement problems on which they have accumulated so much experience in working together? My answer is that they may not prove capable of dealing with the allocation issue, but it is well worth trying to do so. The new way of thinking is the only alternative to the old approach, which has had so little, if any, success in slowing down the neomercantilist trend. There are reasons, too, for believing that the new approach may enable policymakers to cope more effectively with the distribution problem than initially seems likely.

First, dealing explicitly with the allocation issue means facing squarely the central concern of national policymakers in the present period. Its importance was emphasized in the discussion in Chapter VII of the serious disputes likely to arise during the 1990s among the United States, the other OECD nations, and the NICs over the consequences of substantially reducing, let alone eliminating, the U.S. budgetary and current-account deficits. Continued prevalence of the obsolete notion that the United States will go on bearing a disproportionate (even though declining) share of the cost of these and subsequent operations of the adjustment process would obscure the real difficulties involved and make the outcome of negotiations as unsatisfactory as it has been in the past. In contrast, explicit recognition of the centrality of the distribution issue would improve policymakers' and opinion leaders' understanding of the nature of the problem and of the fact that all participating countries have to contribute to resolving it if the result is to be reasonably equitable tradeoffs among them and sometimes even positive-sum solutions from which all would benefit within a reasonable time.

Second, explicitly facing the allocation issue in the context of present and prospective realities would be conducive to a change in the way in which national policymakers have been resolving the ambivalence of rational interest explained in Chapter I. During the postwar period, the existence of a hegemonic leader willing and able to bear a disproportionate share of the costs of international economic integration and to constrain other nations to the requisite behavior made it credible for the members of the system to accept the short-term costs of the adjustment process so as to enjoy the greater long-term gains from growing international trade and investment. In the 1970s and 1980s, the changes at national and international levels and the declining power and influence of the United States gradually fostered the perception that the short-term adjustment costs were increasing while the long-term benefits were becoming more and more uncertain, thus predisposing resolution of the ambivalence of rational interest in favor of trying unilaterally to pass on to others the short-term costs and to obtain immediate benefits at others' expense. Today and for the foreseeable future, achieving greater international economic integration is no longer a realistic goal; the relevant task now is to slow down the disintegration of the system. In these circumstances, the real tradeoff is between benefits and costs that are both short term, that is, between retaining benefits and minimizing losses that immediately affect employment and incomes positively or negatively. As this latest change in the perception of rational interest spreads, it should increase policymakers' willingness to negotiate the equitable sharing of the short-term benefits and costs involved. For, they would be bargaining with real live birds in the hand and not with illusory birds in the bush.

Third, policymakers and opinion leaders would be able to explain more clearly to their affected interest groups and their people generally the difficulties inherent in these negotiations and the realistic possibilities for coping with them. In turn, this could widen policymakers' freedom to act in accordance with the new perception of rational interest.

However, the conceptual approach sketched here is not a panacea for dealing with the neomercantilist trend. Given the fundamental nature of the changes that have taken place at national and international levels since the early 1970s, rational interest cannot be a sufficient substitute for hegemonic power. At best, therefore, the new conceptual approach could enable policymakers in the OECD nations and the NICs to manage the ongoing neomercantilist trend more effectively than has been possible under the old way of thinking.

This task would be less difficult if the existing intergovernmental institutions were better able to conduct the requisite negotiations and supervise implementation of the agreements. The GATT is not organized to carry out these functions. Its operating principle is to prevent, not coordinate, the use of neomercantilist measures; it allows members with too little at stake to delay or block agreements by those most concerned; and its procedures are too legalistic and time-consuming. However, the GATT could play another important role under the new approach. Implicit in the new approach is the temptation to adapt it to fostering the neomercantilist trend rather than slowing it down. Agreements for equitable sharing of the costs of the adjustment process could be turned into cartel-like arrangements for dividing markets and investment opportunities among groups of exporting countries. With appropriate changes in its functions and staffing, the GATT could serve as a watchdog agency to detect such restrictive efforts and to provide procedures for restraining the would-be monopolists.

Otherwise, the OECD would more readily serve the organizational needs of the new approach. It has long worked on problems of macroeconomic policy in its member countries and the implications for relations among them. It is accustomed to deal with disputes among its members in a flexible ad hoc manner rather than in accordance with detailed rules and precedents, as does the GATT. Under the new approach, the OECD staff (1) would recommend changes in members' fiscal and monetary policies required for equitable sharing of the adjustments needed to reduce excessive deficit and surplus payments imbalances and promote growth, and (2) would mediate members' disputes over allocating the costs of proposed neomercantilist trade and investment measures and would suggest remedial actions for eliminating the need for them. For the OECD to carry out these new functions, however, two institutional changes would be required. First, the staff would need much greater independence than it now has in analyzing members' problems and publicizing its findings. Second, the organization's membership would have to be expanded to include the existing and future NICs.[1]

It is beyond the scope of this book to discuss in any detail the implications of the new way of thinking for dealing with the many existing and prospective international economic problems. All that I can do here is to note briefly the three specific issues that I believe will probably have the most fateful consequences for the future of the international system and which are unlikely to be adequately handled under the old conceptual approach.

The first and most difficult was explained in Chapter VII. It is the need for agreement as to how the costs of reducing the current-account deficit and debt-servicing burden of the United States can be distributed equitably among it and the other OECD nations and NICs involved, especially those that have large trade and/or current-account surpluses. This forthcoming problem can be constructively resolved only by dealing explicitly with the allocation issue, which the new conceptual approach is designed to do.

The second major problem is the need to relieve the debt-servicing burdens of many Latin American, Asian, and African countries. The large commercial banks in the United States, Japan, and Western Europe, which hold most of the debt of these nations not owed to other governments and international institutions, have recognized the limits of the possible. They have substantially increased their reserves for nonperforming loans and have been trying directly and indirectly to convert as much of their holdings as possible into equity securities that can be sold to investors. However, the extent to which these and other actions of the commercial banks can reduce the burden on these countries is quite small. The bulk of the relief will have to be provided by the OECD governments and the international lending organizations under an arrangement for equitably sharing the costs among them. Failure to reduce the debt-servicing burdens of Latin American, Asian, and African nations to manageable proportions would aggravate their propensities to social unrest and political instability and could have seriously disruptive effects on the international economic system.

The third major problem is the significant possibility that an international financial crisis and subsequent world depression would occur. The system is susceptible to such a crisis due to its increasing volatility under the floating exchange-rate regime, the close integration of national financial markets, and the enormous and virtually unregulated expansion of credit in the worldwide Euromarkets. A severe monetary crisis could be precipitated by the failure of the United States to cope adequately with its deficits and debt-servicing burden, or by the refusal to relieve the debt-servicing burdens of Latin American, Asian, and African countries, or by other destabilizing economic or political developments. What is needed is an agreement among the OECD nations to regulate the Euromarkets through (1) imposing common risk-related capital-adequacy standards and liquid-reserve requirements on banks and other financial institutions doing business in them, adequate information-disclosure stipulations for existing and newly issued Eurosecurities, and other appropriate safeguards against unsound credit creation and speculation; and (2) contingency plans for mitigating the severity of an international financial crisis if it should occur. Failure to prevent an international financial crisis would help to trigger a severe and prolonged world depression that would decisively reinforce the neomercantilist trend.

In sum, a new way of thinking and the initiatives that follow from it, along the lines sketched above, would enable the OECD nations and the NICs to slow down and contain the neomercantilist trend. If and as national policymakers and opinion leaders make these changes, the world market economy could eventually be stabilized at a lower level of integration than at present but at one that would still permit significant growth of international trade and investment over time. The costs of this second method of activating the self-limiting element of the neomercantilist trend would certainly be much less, and the benefits greater, than those of the first method—that is, of letting a fully neomercantilist system emerge by default.

COPING WITH THE NATIONALISTIC TREND

The nationalistic trend, too, contains a potentially self-limiting element, which is the rational interest of all members of the international system in maintaining some minimum degree of order and calculability. However, given the ambivalent nature of rational interest, this self-limiting element does not by itself produce a sufficiently high level of political stability and order. The reason is that, in the different types of national societies constituting the international system, the resolution of the ambivalence tends to be markedly particularistic due to the effects of nationalism.

Contemporary nationalism expresses the deepest psychocultural aspects of modern societies' sense of identity and purpose and helps to legitimate their internal distribution of political power, social prestige, and control over economic resources. Both the interests and the emotions of the elites of national societies are heavily engaged in these societal processes. In consequence, policymakers and opinion leaders do not readily submit to restrictions on their nation's freedom of action except under necessity or when desired benefits cannot be obtained in other ways. Moreover, the major sources of instability and disorder in the international system are in Asian, African, and Latin American countries, whose elites are even less willing and able than those of the OECD nations to act with the requisite self-restraint and universalistic concern.

Restructuring the NATO Alliance

Potentially the most serious political danger confronting the United States and Western Europe is the likelihood that the decline in transatlantic political coordination will sooner or later undermine the integrated military-defense arrangements of NATO, which is the principal means for assuring that there will not be a military, and hence political, power vacuum in Western Europe.

Hitherto, efforts to preserve the cohesiveness of NATO have consisted mostly of appeals to common Western values and interests, expressions of nostalgia for an Atlantic Partnership that never existed, and largely futile U.S. exhortations for more equitable sharing of the defense burden between the United States and the West European members. As in the case of neomercantilist conflicts, political disputes between the United States and its NATO allies tend to be regarded as temporary aberrations that would readily be resolved and prevented from recurring if only policymakers on both sides of the Atlantic had the requisite understanding and courage. But, regardless of which policymakers have been in office since the early 1970s, neither the United States nor its European allies have been willing and able to make the kinds of concessions to one another that could restore the cohesion of the postwar period. What is required is not rhetoric but a new way of thinking about the purposes and prospects of NATO that would take account of the basic changes since the early 1970s in the motivations and capabilities of its members, as well as of the Soviet Union.

In the postwar period, the widely prevalent view on both sides of the Atlantic was that the U.S. nuclear guarantee and the stationing of large U.S. conventional forces in Europe were necessitated by (1) the economic weaknesses of the still recovering European economies; (2) the strength of the local communist parties, especially in France and Italy; (3) the seemingly overwhelming Soviet military presence in Eastern Europe; and (4) the fear, engendered by the Greek civil war, the communist coup in Czechoslovakia, and the Berlin Blockade, that a power vacuum in Western Europe would tempt the Soviets to move their armies westward to the Atlantic. Today, in contrast, the EC is an economic, if not a political/military, world power, the West European communist parties are much declined in size and revolutionary zeal, and the Soviet military forces in Eastern Europe are perceived as largely defensive in nature, intended as a counterpoise to NATO and to prevent internal attempts to weaken communist control in the client states. Moreover, the likelihood of a Soviet invasion of Western Europe is quite low: too risky as long as the U.S. commitment to help defend Western Europe is reasonably credible, and unnecessary if it is not because the gradual process of "finlandizing" Western Europe, sketched in the next chapter, would more easily and effectively serve Soviet interests than would military conquest. Thus, the kind of U.S. commitment to Western Europe's defense required now and for the foreseeable future is different from that regarded as necessary during the postwar period.

Never before in the history of mutual-defense alliances have independent nations as populous, rich, technologically competent, and with so strong a sense of their cultural achievements as those of Western Europe allowed themselves to be as dependent for so long on the protection of an ally over whose actions they have so little control. Nor, for its part, did the United States ever expect that it would be maintaining such substantial numbers of troops and such extensive support facilities in Europe at so great a cost to itself for so many years after its European allies had become economically and technologically capable of assuming responsibility for their own defense. In these terms also, NATO in its present form is too much of an anomaly to persist unchanged over the foreseeable future in view of the growing divergences in interests and attitudes between its European members and the United States that reduce the cohesiveness of the alliance and erode the credibility of the U.S. nuclear guarantee.

What is needed is a restructuring of NATO that would preserve its mutual-defense function in ways that are relevant to present and prospective conditions and that would substantially lessen the danger of transatlantic divergences leading to explicit or implicit dissolution of the alliance. Achieving these objectives by eliminating the incompatibilities in interests and attitudes is no longer within the limits of the possible due to the profound changes that have occurred in the motivations and capabilities of the nations concerned. Therefore, the only alternative for slowing down this trend is to reduce the opportunities for the ineradicable divergences to undermine further the cohesiveness of the alliance and hence the credibility of the U.S. commitment to defend Western Europe. This means removing unrealistic expectations regarding the obligations of NATO members and enlarging the scope for independent action by the West European nations, on the one side, and the United States, on the other.

Two expectations that are no longer realistic relate to the functions of the alliance and the allocation of its resource burden. As to the first, the predominant U.S. view has always been that NATO is not simply an alliance for the defense of Western Europe, North America, and their surrounding waters. An equally important function is to protect the interests of its members in other regions and help maintain the stability and orderliness of the international system, which U.S. policymakers generally interpret to mean supporting U.S. efforts to do so. Since the end of the postwar period, the West Europeans—as well as the Canadians—have increasingly rejected this view of NATO's purposes, instead insisting that the alliance covers only the regional function and more and more refusing to support U.S. initiatives in other parts of the world. The United States no longer has the power to constrain or the influence to persuade the West European members to accept its view and, therefore, needs now to reconcile itself to their interpretation of NATO's functions. At the same time, the other NATO members have to accept that they now have the resources to bear all of the costs of their own defense and can no longer expect the United States to continue carrying any substantial portion of them. Removing these two unrealistic expectations and thereby giving each side greater freedom of action would go far in reducing the adverse effects of widening transatlantic divergences on the credibility of the U.S. commitment to help defend Western Europe.

The most desirable way of transforming NATO to achieve these objectives would be for the West European nations to establish a sufficiently large and unified military capability of their own, thereby providing for their own defense and enabling them to play a more independent role in world politics. However, I do not have in mind a revival of the U.S. effort of the postwar period to persuade and assist the West European nations to complete their economic integration and form a political union. Unfortunately, this is not a realistic goal of policy in the present period. Nor is such a high degree of economic integration and political unification in Western Europe required for attaining a credible capacity for self-defense. All that would be needed is for the West European nations to retain among themselves the kind and extent of military integration that has long existed in the NATO alliance. Before outlining one method for fulfilling this requirement, a brief comment on the prospects for any effort to transform NATO is desirable.

Until recently, policymakers on both sides of the Atlantic refused to consider any significant changes in NATO—a result of persistent postwar ways of thinking, as explained above. But, in the course of the 1980s, the realities of the present period have begun to erode these obsolete convictions. In the United States, growing economic constraints and rising irritation over the refusal of its allies to support its policies have stimulated proposals for more or less substantial cuts in U.S. troops and support facilities in Western Europe. In Western Europe, the declining credibility of the U.S. nuclear guarantee and the anxieties provoked by U.S. initiatives have led to the first serious consideration by political leaders of joint measures that might reduce their military dependence on the United States. Thus, a development that until recently was regarded as unthinkable on both sides of the Atlantic is now well within the limits of the possible.

There are various methods for restructuring NATO to accomplish the functions it has to perform today and in the foreseeable future. I believe that the least disruptive and difficult way would be to transform NATO into a conventional mutual-defense alliance between the United States and Western Europe. Under this method, the West Europeans would take over completely the integrated command structure and force arrangements of NATO, to which they would contribute the requisite troops, equipment, and support facilities. In addition, modernized and coordinated—though not necessarily unified—British and French nuclear arsenals would provide the minimum credible nuclear capability. The United States would maintain only a small, token nonnuclear force in Western Europe as earnest that it would come quickly to its ally's aid if the latter were attacked.

Analyzing the many difficulties that would have to be worked out by the Europeans themselves and with the United States is beyond the scope of this book. Suffice it to note here how some of the main problems could be tackled.

The essential organizational change would be gradually to restaff NATO at all levels entirely with Europeans while substantially reducing the number of Americans assigned to it and converting those that remain into liaison officers. As this process progressed, the increasingly Europeanized staff of NATO might be able to bring more effective pressure on European politicians to allocate the bigger resources needed to replace the departing U.S. armed forces and to improve further their countries' conventional and nuclear capabilities. Concurrently, the U.S. troops stationed in Western Europe would be reduced to their eventual token level. The United States would retain rights to use those air and naval bases required for it to maintain surveillance over Soviet activities that could threaten U.S. security or that of its non-European allies.

Reflecting the persistence of postwar ways of thinking, the argument will undoubtedly be made that transforming NATO along the foregoing lines would appear to the West Europeans as "decoupling" the United States from its commitment to help defend them. True, a major danger of trying to restructure NATO would be that the West Europeans' attitudes and anxieties might impel them to take their chances with the Soviet Union rather than incur the risk and expense of greater self-responsibility for their own defense. However, if at any time the process of transforming NATO— or Soviet moves—appeared unduly to alarm the Europeans or to intensify their pacifist and neutralist tendencies (to which institutional and generational changes incline many of them), it could be halted or temporarily reversed until conditions were again conducive to its resumption. In this regard, too, clumsy efforts by U.S. negotiators or thoughtless pronouncements by U.S. politicians would be more likely to help precipitate the West Europeans down the road to pacificism and neutralism—and hence probably to eventual subordination to the Soviet Union, as explained in the next chapter—than to induce them to climb the more difficult path to greater self-reliance and a more independent role in the international system.

It will be objected, too, that such a restructuring of NATO would be perceived by the Soviet Union as de facto abandonment by the United States of its commitment to help defend Western Europe. This is possible but improbable. The credibility of the U.S. commitment does *not* depend on how many or how deeply U.S. armed forces are integrated into the NATO defense structure in Western Europe. Rather, it depends on preventing the divergences in interests and attitudes between the United States and Western Europe from eroding the willingness of a majority of American policymakers, opinion leaders, and people generally to hazard their own safety in helping to defend their European allies. The restructuring of NATO suggested here is designed to reduce substantially the likelihood that such a development would occur. Moreover, the more credible that Western Europe's self-defense capability becomes, the less important the U.S. nuclear guarantee will be in preventing a military/political power vacuum in the region that would tempt the Soviet Union to extend hegemonic control over it.

A restructured NATO would enable the West Europeans to avoid having to establish a new organization for European defense, an effort that would be prolonged, divisive, and unlikely to succeed. Instead, they would gradually come to regard NATO as their own defense organization with which the United States would be allied but which it would no longer dominate. The continuing U.S. military presence in Western Europe would be inconspicuous and nonnuclear yet sufficient to be evidence of the U.S. commitment to help defend its allies. The U.S. relationship to a transformed NATO would resemble in certain respects that which France has had to NATO since Charles de Gaulle removed French forces from the integrated military arrangements in 1966; indeed, France could well be willing to reintegrate its forces into a NATO no longer dominated by the United States. And, most important, the growing divergences in interests and attitudes between the United States and Western Europe would no longer be endangering the region's security. The resulting substantial reduction of their mutual irritations might also make a more self-reliant Western Europe and a less directive United States more inclined to coordinate their political policies for dealing with serious problems in other regions.

Coping with Instability in Asia, Africa, and Latin America

Coordination of policies by the OECD nations would certainly be desirable for coping with the adverse effects on the international system of economic crisis, social unrest, and political instability in Asia, Africa, and Latin America. However, the essential condition for containing the disruptions in the international system generated by the nationalistic trend in these regions is that, at the least, the United States and the other OECD countries do not work at cross-purposes.

The prospects for carrying on this task have been favorably affected during the 1980s by the fact that the OECD aid donors, the international lending institutions, and many of the recipient nations have finally begun to have more realistic conceptions of the complex nature and generational time span of the transitional process in Asia and Africa and the modernization process in Latin America, and have been adjusting their policies and expectations accordingly. Although the ratio of the bilateral and multilateral development assistance provided by the OECD nations to their total GNPs is unlikely to rise above the present aggregate percentage, their aid is being allocated for purposes that contribute more effectively to mitigating the problems of the recipient countries and programmed in ways that are less susceptible to waste and corruption.

Nevertheless, constructive policy choices and coordinated actions by the OECD nations are at best likely to yield modest results in coping with instability and uncertainty in Asia, Africa, and Latin America. Higher and steadier economic growth in the countries of these regions would inhibit, but would certainly not eliminate, their economic inadequacies, social unrest, and political instability. Nor would it substantially reduce their propensity to generate international disorder and conflict that would adversely affect OECD interests and threaten to involve the superpowers. With respect to the future development of Asian, African, and Latin American countries, the major determinative choices are those of their own policymakers, not those of policymakers in the OECD nations.

Within all of the societies of these regions, the crucial element is the willingness and ability of the elite groups to govern their own actions more by universalistic concerns than by particularistic interests, to cooperate more effectively in coping with their countries' internal and external problems, and to acquire the understanding and skills needed to do so. Progress in these respects has been and will continue to be erratic and slow, measured in generations, not decades. True, famines and other natural disasters, the devastations of civil and foreign wars, and too high rates of population growth can make Asian, African, and Latin American countries critically dependent on outside aid. Over the long term, however, the economic resources, technical assistance, and political support that the OECD nations could provide can at best help to encourage and ease the necessary changes in elite attitudes and capabilities; they cannot substitute for them.

The instabilities and uncertainties in these regions will doubtless provide the Soviet Union with opportunities to try to expand the membership of its hegemony or at least its sphere of influence. These efforts will be difficult for the OECD nations to counter given their limited capacity to affect developments in Asia, Africa, and Latin America and the divergences in their interests and attitudes. Nonetheless, the Soviet Union, too, will be confronted with outbreaks of instability and dissension in its Asian, African, and Latin American clients generated by the transitional and modernization processes in these regions. Such developments will provide the OECD nations, and especially the United States, with opportunities to try to wean the affected countries away from Soviet control or influence. Some guidelines for U.S. efforts to deal with these problems and opportunities are suggested in Chapter X.

In sum, coping effectively with the instabilities and uncertainties that are bound to occur in Asia, Africa, and Latin America requires (1) better understanding by the United States and the other OECD nations of the nature and prospects of the processes of change in these regions and (2) willingness, at the least, to refrain from working at cross-purposes and preferably to coordinate their policies to the maximum extent permitted by their own diverging interests and attitudes.

NOTE

1. Hitherto, the NICs have been reluctant to become members of the OECD for fear that they would thereby lose the trade preferences enjoyed by Asian, African, and Latin American countries and would have to reduce their own neomercantilist practices. However, both equity and the effective operation of the new approach require the participation of the NICs, and they would soon recognize that joining the OECD would be the best way to protect access to their principal export markets.

Chapter IX

POSSIBLE FUTURES OF THE INTERNATIONAL SYSTEM

The interactions between the determinative trends and the policy choices of the major nations will determine how the international system will evolve over the foreseeable future. The possible courses of development sketched in this chapter include a worst-case forecast and a range of more likely better-case outcomes. Essentially, the difference between them is that between refusing or failing to manage the determinative trends and being willing and able to do so. Before these forecasts are presented, however, a brief explanation of their nature and limitations is necessary.[1]

Whenever they adopt a course of action to bring about desired developments or to prevent undesired ones, policymakers are making a forecast whether they are aware of doing so or not. That is, they are assuming that they have identified the factors determining the intended outcome and that their actions will be capable of influencing them sufficiently to assure this result. Regardless of whether they are consciously formulated or not, all forecasts are inherently probabilistic. They cannot give certainties but only greater or lesser degrees of probability that the relevant determinative factors and their interactions have been correctly identified and that the actions selected to affect their working out will actually do so in the ways required.

Beyond this dependence on the state of knowledge of the determinative factors, the accuracy of forecasts is also always more or less impaired by two fundamental aspects of the human condition. The first comprises the inherent physiological and psychological limitations of human beings and the distortions built into human perceptions and conceptions by cultural biases and particularistic interests. The second consists of the random elements that continually appear in human affairs due to unpredictable new ideas and capabilities, unforeseeable changes in motivations and behavior, and the intervention of extraneous factors—such as natural disasters, accidents, and psychological aberrations—that cannot be anticipated.

The forecasting of trends is normally less uncertain than the forecasting of specific events. A trend is a more general phenomenon than an event; although it is composed of a sequence of related events, it is not dependent on the nature or timing of any one of them. A trend can be manifested in a variety of possible events; which of them actually occurs is usually determined by the immediately preceding sociocultural factors and policy choices. The worst-case and better-case forecasts presented below are essentially extrapolations of the determinative trends explained in Chapter VII as they are likely to be modified by the different kinds of policy choices discussed in Chapter VIII. The forecasts involve only what can be discerned from the vantage point of the present moment in which they are made. What is least likely to change in forecasts made at future times is the general direction of development of the international system. What will undoubtedly change in future forecasts are the sequences of specific events in which the general direction of development appears to be manifesting itself.

Finally, the inclusion of a worst-case forecast needs to be explained. Americans have generally been conditioned by their culture and life experiences to take an optimistic view of the outcome of their efforts. Such an attitude is often justified. However, in forecasts prepared for policymakers in government and the private sector, too much is usually at stake to risk basing decisions only on those that fulfill the desired outcomes. Policymakers need also to take explicit account of the worst that could happen, however low the probability of its occurrence may be.

A WORST-CASE FORECAST

The worst-case forecast would certainly be for a nuclear war between the United States and the Soviet Union to happen. It is within the limits of the possible but its probability is very low. In my view, there are two plausible ways by which a nuclear war between the superpowers could occur in the foreseeable future.

The first would arise from the coming to power in either of the superpowers of a pathological personality, like Hitler, or of regimes of improbably extreme fanaticism or ineptitude. However, the kinds of regimes most likely to be in office over the foreseeable future in the United States and the Soviet Union would not be sufficiently pathological or fanatical to disregard the very high probability of mutual nuclear destruction if they were to launch such a war. The same is likely to be true of China if it becomes powerful enough to be a rival of the United States and the Soviet Union in regional or world politics.

The second, and somewhat more probable, way would result from miscalculation by one superpower of the capabilities of its first- and second-strike nuclear weapons and its nuclear defensive system relative to those of the other superpower. For, if a superpower were to become convinced that it had a decisive superiority over the other, it might be tempted to take greater risks in exploiting opportunities to advance its power and influence in the international system and be less inclined to refrain from a preemptive first strike or to prevent the resulting conflicts with the other superpower from escalating to the use of nuclear weapons. However, given the constraints of their two-protagonist balance-of-power relationship and their deep mutual distrust, the probability is low that a superpower would be either so imprudent as to allow its nuclear capability to become conspicuously inferior to that of the other or so reckless as to resolve the uncertainties regarding the other's nuclear capability in favor of taking the risk of launching a nuclear attack. For these reasons, the worst-case forecast sketched in this section would not involve a nuclear war between the superpowers and has a higher—though still quite low—probability of occurring.

This forecast originates in the failure of policymakers and opinion leaders in the OECD nations to prevent the neomercantilist and nationalistic trends from mutually reinforcing their disintegrative effects on the international system. Thus, if nationalistic pressures were to intensify the self-reinforcing element of the neomercantilist trend, countries would be impelled to retaliate against one another's restrictions and subsidies by more extreme measures than they would otherwise take. In these circumstances, too, policymakers would be unable to prevent an international financial crisis and ensuing worldwide depression, noted in the preceding chapter. The resulting stagnation of international trade and investment and depressed national economic conditions would further aggravate nationalistic reactions, as they did in the 1930s, intensifying conflicts between nations and further undermining the stability of the international system, especially in Asia, Africa, and Latin America. These increasingly disorderly conditions would provide the Soviet Union with more and better opportunities for expanding the noncontiguous membership of its hegemony and its influence generally in Asia, Africa, and Latin America.

In Western Europe, depression or too low economic growth would intensify the neomercantilist and nationalistic effects of the changes in institutions and generational attitudes sketched in Chapter IV, reinforcing the unwillingness to allocate resources to nuclear and conventional defense and raising neutralist and pacifist attitudes to predominance. Nor would timely efforts be made to ease the tensions between Western Europe and the United States by restructuring NATO, as suggested in Chapter VIII. In consequence, the West European nations would move increasingly toward what they would hope would be a neutral position between the United States and the Soviet Union. Their opposition to developing an adequate defense capability of their own and their more complacent conception of Soviet intentions would induce their governments to seek accommodations with the Soviet Union. For, they would believe that they could resist Soviet pressure on them through their own presumed sociocultural superiority and greater diplomatic skills. At the same time, the West European nations would become increasingly estranged from the United States as conflicts over neomercantilist actions and reactions intensified and their respective conceptions diverged more widely for dealing with the mounting difficulties in Asia, Africa, and Latin America and in relations with the Soviet Union and the members of its hegemony.

This reorientation of Western Europe would accelerate the decline in U.S. willingness and ability to bear a disproportionate share of the costs of the adjustment process and of European defense. Combined with increasing irritation over European neutralist behavior and anti-American sentiments, these developments would revive to predominance the isolationist attitude that characterized the United States for most of its history. And, for its part, the Soviet Union would be adroit enough to encourage the growing tensions between the United States and the West European nations.

As they widened, these divergences would progressively weaken not only, as hitherto, political coordination between the United States and its NATO allies but also the willingness of the United States to risk a nuclear attack for the sake of protecting Western Europe. This process would be aggravated by intensification in Western Europe of the pressure for unilateral nuclear disarmament and the withdrawal of U.S. forces stationed there. Since the West European nations would be unwilling to increase sufficiently their own military capabilities to offset the removal of U.S. armed forces and support facilities, both elite-group and popular opposition would intensify in the United States against continuation of the U.S. pledge to help defend Western Europe. These decisions and the resulting transatlantic recriminations would soon lead to termination of the NATO alliance.

The reorientation of Western Europe, the dissolution of NATO, and the withdrawal of U.S. armed forces would open the way for the gradual "finlandization" of the West European nations. Despite their expectations of being able to manage the Soviets and maintain an independent neutral position, the West Europeans' lack of an effective military capability of their own would make these nations increasingly vulnerable to Soviet pressure once their U.S. defense guarantee was gone. Hence, the Soviet Union would more and more treat the West European countries as it has Finland, allowing them considerable freedom to determine their own political and economic systems but using its power and influence over them to assure that their regimes would be friendly to it and would conduct their external relations in accordance with Soviet conceptions of how they should behave.

For example, as explained in Chapter VI, the Soviet Union has been becoming more dependent on trade with Western Europe and Japan, which are its main sources of the new technology and capital equipment required for modernizing its economy. Given its nonmarket command system, there is a natural tendency for the Soviet Union to use its power and influence to control economic decision making at both ends of its external economic relations so as to assure trade and credit terms favorable to it. Soviet pressure of this kind would constrain the West European and Japanese governments to expand further their regulation of their private sectors so as to assure compliance with trade and financial agreements with the Soviet Union. Thus, the scope for market forces in the internal and external economic activities of the West European nations and Japan would be further reduced and the neomercantilist trend correspondingly reinforced.

In this and other ways, the West European nations would gradually become members of an enlarged and looser Soviet hegemony like that of the United States during the postwar period. Such a development would not necessarily threaten the basic security of the United States. I believe that the isolationist argument is valid—that, even if Western Europe drifted into hegemonic subordination to the Soviet Union, the United States could still maintain military and economic capabilities sufficient to deter the Soviet Union from attempting to establish hegemonic control over it, as well as over nations in the Western Hemisphere and the Pacific that the United States chose to protect and that were willing to be protected. Nor need the economic burden involved be any greater than it is now; indeed, it could well be less.

However, there is another kind of price that Americans would have to pay that would result from the gradual shift of the world economy from a still largely market system to a predominantly nonmarket system as Soviet power and influence spread. In order to maintain access to needed imports, sell the requisite volume of exports, and protect its overseas investments, the United States would itself have to become more neomercantilist, and its economy would in consequence become increasingly nonmarket in character. Such a development would result in lower rates of economic growth and levels of real income. More fundamentally, it would erode the decentraliza-

tion of decision making and initiative in American society that have been
among the essential supports of its democratic freedoms.

Thus, this worst-case forecast envisages the termination of the existing
two-protagonist balance-of-power system through the enlargement of the
Soviet hegemony and sphere of influence to include Western Europe and
additional countries in other regions and the attainment by the Russians of
their long-desired position of world paramountcy. I believe, however, that
its probability is very low because its assumptions are extreme: the total
failure of policymakers in the OECD nations to manage the neomercantilist
and nationalistic trends with even a minimum degree of effectiveness, and
the corresponding absence of serious mistakes and deficiencies on the part
of the Soviet Union.

A MORE PROBABLE BETTER-CASE FORECAST

The range of better-case forecasts would depend on the extent of the
willingness of OECD policymakers to make and their ability to implement
decisions that could effectively manage the neomercantilist trend and cope
with the adverse effects of the nationalistic trend. The more they could do
so, the more favorable the outlook would be although, as explained below,
the best-case outcome does not necessarily have the highest probability.

For better-case forecasts to occur, economic growth rates in the OECD
countries would have to be high enough to prevent their problems of
competitiveness and unemployment from worsening. As explained in Chapter VII, there is a reasonable probability that average growth rates in the
years ahead would at the least be no lower than during the 1980s and possibly
slightly higher. If they are, policymakers in the OECD nations and the NICs
might have the minimum freedom of action needed (1) to agree on mutually
acceptable allocations of the ongoing costs of the adjustment process and (2)
to coordinate and limit their resort to import restrictions, subsidies,
exchange-rate manipulations, and other neomercantilist devices. In this
way, the self-limiting element of the neomercantilist trend could be activated
and the international economic system could be stabilized at a lower level of
integration than now exists but at one that would still help to support
reasonably satisfactory rates of growth of international trade and investment. However, regardless of the extent to which the economic difficulties
of Asian, African, and Latin American countries would be mitigated by
adequate growth rates in and market access to the OECD nations, the
profound processes of societal change occurring in these regions will continue to generate social unrest and political instability.

As in the worst-case forecast, the relations between the United States and the other OECD nations would be a critical determinant not only of the relative favorableness of the better-case forecasts but also of their relative degrees of probability. The maximum extent of coordination between the United States and the other OECD nations does not have the highest probability because of the effects on their behavior of the institutional and generational changes sketched in Chapter IV. They would make it unlikely that these countries could agree on the most constructive resolutions of the very difficult allocation issue and that they could exercise sufficient self-restraint in their use of neomercantilist measures to halt this trend at the present level of international economic integration.

Previous chapters have sketched the very difficult problems that the United States and Western Europe will have to face during the 1990s in coping with their necessary internal and external adjustments. However, Japan's spectacular export performance during the 1970s and 1980s has obscured the fact that its very competence in this respect will intensify its adjustment problems in the years ahead. Japan's unprecedented export surplus has resulted from sales abroad of only a limited range of manufactured goods (mainly steel, motor vehicles, machinery, and electronic components and finished products) on which it is already facing growing competition from the NICs and/or increasing import restrictions in its principal markets in the United States and other OECD nations. Improvements in U.S. and West European competitiveness and substantial reduction of the U.S. balance-of-payments deficit would also adversely affect Japanese export performance. These present and prospective changes and the rising exchange rate of the yen have been impelling Japanese companies to invest abroad in production facilities in the lower-wage NICs and within the economies of its major trading partners. At the same time, generational changes in attitudes and expectations and in the age structure of the population will constrain Japanese policymakers to allocate increasing resources to the improvement of infrastructure and housing and the expansion of the welfare system. Also, political developments in the East Asian and Western Pacific region could compel Japan to upgrade its military-defense capabilities substantially. Thus, in the foreseeable future, Japan will be experiencing growing strains on its resources and difficult problems of internal and external adjustment precisely when it will be under increasing pressure from the United States, the other OECD nations, and the NICs to accept equitable shares of the costs of resolving the recurrent allocation issues.

For these reasons, the best-case forecast would not be the most probable. Instead, the most likely of the better-case outcomes envisages that the spread of more relevant ways of thinking about present and prospective realities in the OECD nations and the NICs would enable their policymakers to cooperate sufficiently in managing the adverse effects of the adjustment process to slow down the neomercantilist trend and stabilize the world market economy at a lower but still beneficial level of integration.

Even if such stabilization could be accomplished, it would probably involve some further development of the trend toward economic-bloc formation that began in the 1970s. The most marked manifestation of this trend would undoubtedly be in the external economic relations of the EC, which would continue to strengthen and expand the formalized preferential trade and financial ties it already enjoys with the African and West Asian nations. The United States would endeavor to restore and maintain its predominant position in the external economic relations of the Western Hemisphere countries, although it would be less likely to do so by means of institutionalized preferential ties like those of the bloc centered on the EC. The possibilities for economic-bloc formation are more limited elsewhere in Asia and in the Pacific region, despite forecasts that Japan would develop a contemporary equivalent of the "Greater East Asia Co-Prosperity Sphere" which it projected during World War II. True, economic relations among the so-called Pacific Rim countries are now more extensive and rapidly growing than those among the nations bordering on the Atlantic Ocean. But, the region does not have—and is unlikely in the foreseeable future to have—a single predominant economy around which a preferential trade and financial bloc could coalesce. Only the countries exporting mainly raw materials are likely to form two-way preferential ties with Japan. The existing and emerging NICs—the fastest growing economies in the region— require markets for their manufactured exports. Even if the pressures, noted above, constrain Japan to increase its manufactured imports significantly, the Japanese economy is not large enough nor is it likely to be sufficiently open to competing capital and consumer goods for it to satisfy the needs of the present and future NICs. Hence, they will continue to rely on the U.S. market, access to which is likely to depend more and more on their willingness to buy U.S. exports. Thus, Japan and the United States would probably be the two competing foci of economic relations in the Pacific Rim region, possibly joined sooner or later in this capacity by China and India.[2]

In the most probable better-case forecast, U.S. and West European policymakers would have the foresight to begin the restructuring of NATO in sufficient time to prevent transatlantic tensions from leading to the dissolution of the alliance. If it continues to exist, therefore, NATO would be most likely to evolve into a conventional type of mutual-defense alliance between the United States and Western Europe, along the lines sketched in Chapter VIII. But, its military capabilities would still be impressive enough and Soviet uncertainties about U.S. intentions sufficiently great to continue to deter the Soviet Union from trying to bring Western Europe under its hegemonic control. Although the Soviet Union would be able in some instances to expand its power and influence in Asia and Africa—perhaps in Latin America as well—it would not achieve a position of world paramountcy in any of the better-case forecasts.

The next section surveys how the better-case developments could eventually transform the international system.

POSSIBLE OUTCOMES OF THE EXISTING TRANSITIONAL INTERNATIONAL SYSTEM

The existing international system is characterized by a basic discontinuity between the structure of its economic dimension, which already has a three-protagonist balance-of-power system (the United States, Japan, and the EC), and the structure of its political dimension, which still has only a two-protagonist balance-of-power system (the United States and the Soviet Union). To use the vaguer conventional term, the international system is becoming economically but not politically multipolar. Another anomaly that differentiates the existing international system from its predecessors is the fact that the protagonists in the economic dimension are different from those in the political dimension, except for the United States. Sooner or later, these discontinuities will be narrowed, probably eliminated. From the vantage point of the present, however, it is possible only to predict the general direction along which such a development is likely to occur and not the specific form it would take. This is why, in Chapter III, I characterized the existing system as transitional.

One way in which the discontinuities could be resolved would be through the emergence of additional superpowers, that is, nations with the economic and technological resources needed to sustain worldwide nuclear and conventional military capabilities on a scale that effectively deters any country other than another superpower from threatening, let alone attacking, them. Thus, the Soviet Union is a superpower despite the fact that its economic role is unimportant outside its own hegemony. In contrast, the EC and Japan are not superpowers because they lack the requisite military capabilities. True, their economic wealth and importance also give them considerable political influence. But, in the absence of an adequate military capability of their own, their political prestige and ability to apply pressure in the international system are limited by the widespread perception of their continued dependence on U.S. protection.

A five-power system like the classical versions that existed among the Italian city-states in the 15th century and the European great powers in the 18th and 19th centuries would be a better-case outcome for the United States. It would give Western Europe, China, and Japan primary responsibility for maintaining security in their regions and would involve them actively in reaching and implementing agreements among the five protagonists for dealing with disorders elsewhere in the international system that threatened to give one or another of them unacceptable advantages. As a result, the United States would be able to reduce substantially both the scope of its primary responsibilities and the scale of its active involvement in the continuing process of maintaining the balance.

However, a worldwide balance-of-power system with five protagonists does not have a high probability of emerging in the foreseeable future. It would require that China make sufficient progress in coping with its internal economic and sociopolitical problems to achieve the requisite political stability, military power, and international economic importance. Western Europe and Japan, too, would have to be willing to convert their economic and technological resources into military power sufficient to give them the worldwide political influence and the freedom of action necessary to play *independent* balancing roles. For reasons already explained, I do not believe that such developments are very likely.

The more probable outcome is that Western Europe, China, and Japan would become regional, rather than worldwide, military and political powers. The transformation of NATO along the lines sketched in Chapter VIII would have this effect for the European region. In the East Asian, Western Pacific, and Indian Ocean region, the principal existing and potential regional powers are China, Japan, and India (perhaps eventually Indonesia), with the Soviet Union and the United States participating actively in maintaining the regional balance of power. China already has a regional nuclear capability and India will probably soon have one, too, and their regional economic importance is likely to increase. Growing concern over its military vulnerability vis-à-vis the Soviet Union and China and declining confidence in the willingness and ability of the United States to protect it, reinforced by generational change, could eventually impel Japan to increase substantially its conventional forces and perhaps to develop at least a regional nuclear capability. To the extent that the regional nuclear powers could counterbalance the Soviet Union, as well as one another, the United States could reduce the degree of its active strategic involvement in this area.

Other regional possibilities are more remote. Brazil has the demographic and economic potentials, the dynamic self-image, and the geopolitical situation for eventually becoming the predominant power in South America, which would constrain the other nations to cooperate in counterbalancing it. Although it is demographically preeminent in sub-Saharan Africa, Nigeria is likely to take even longer than Brazil to achieve the requisite political stability and economic capabilities to become a regional great power. Indeed, a black-ruled South Africa that retained the skills and support of a sufficiently large white minority might be a more likely candidate for regional predominance. Nonetheless, I doubt that these nations would make sufficient progress before the mid-21st century at the earliest to develop the societal coherence, sense of mission, and economic and technological resources that are the prerequisites for attaining regional great-power status.

Also within the limits of the possible are structural changes in the international system that would not involve continuation of some form of balance-of-power relationships. However, I believe that these are the least likely outcomes of the existing transitional system.

One unlikely development would be that envisaged in the worst-case forecast outlined above: an expanded Soviet hegemony and the attainment by the Soviet Union of a position of world paramountcy. Another would be an explicit or tacit agreement by the United States and the Soviet Union to exercise a dual hegemony over the international system. Although possible, such an outcome has a low probability due to the sociocultural incompatibilities and the deep mutual distrust between the two superpowers.

I also regard as quite unlikely the emergence of the kind of system that many people in the OECD nations believe would be the most desirable of all. This would be one in which large and small, powerful and weak nation-states would all be willing and able to respect one anothers' sovereign independence and to settle their conflicts of interest by concession and compromise. And, in the rare instances when a country wasn't willing to do so, the major nations would have enough self-control and desire to cooperate, through a respected and effective international institution, to restrain a would-be aggressor or exploiter from conquering weaker countries or forcing them to comply with its demands. In fact, this is the kind of international system that, during and immediately after World War II, was expected to emerge as the United Nations developed its capabilities and prestige. In 1944, Secretary of State Cordell Hull predicted that, after the postwar establishment of the United Nations organization,

there will no longer be need for spheres of influence, for alliances, for balance of power, or any other of the special arrangements through which, in the unhappy past, the nations strove to safeguard their security or to promote their interests.[3]

However, such an outcome is even less probable now than it was during the postwar period. Today and for the foreseeable future, the incompatibilities in national motivations and the disparities in national capabilities are too great, and the conflicts and instabilities generated by the determinative trends are too frequent and severe, for an international system governed by long-term rational interest and self-restraint to be sufficiently within the limits of the possible.

In sum, the most likely outcome of the existing international system would be continuation of the worldwide balance-of-power relationship between the Soviet Union and the United States and its eventual substantial modification by the emergence of regional balance-of-power systems first in Europe and the East Asian/Western Pacific/Indian Ocean area and much later and more problematically in South America and Africa. Hence, the likelihood is that the United States will be constrained to go on acting in accordance with the demanding behavioral norms of its two-protagonist balance-of-power relationship with the Soviet Union while eventually also participating in one or more multiple-protagonist regional systems that will impose less compulsive and expensive behavioral requirements on their members.

NOTES

1. The explanation here is based on the fuller analysis in my forthcoming book *Country-Outlook Analysis and Political-Risk Assessment: Conceptual Framework and Methodologies.*

2. On the origin and early development of the trend toward economic-bloc formation, see my article, "A World of Trading Blocs?" in the NPA's *Looking Ahead,* April 1971, Vol. 19, No. 3, and the subsequent study by Ernest H. Preeg, *Economic Blocs and U.S. Foreign Policy* (Washington: National Planning Association, 1974).

3. Cordell Hull, "Bases of the Foreign Policy of the United States," *Bulletin* (Washington, D.C.: Department of State, March 25, 1944), p. 276.

Chapter X

COPING WITH THE PERPLEXITIES OF THE INTERNATIONAL ROLE OF THE UNITED STATES

Despite the substantial decline in its relative power and influence, the United States is constrained to persist in trying to maintain world order by two related structural characteristics of the transitional international system. The first is the likely indefinite continuation at the worldwide level of the two-protagonist balance-of-power relationship between the United States and the Soviet Union. The second is the fact that, unless or until the regional balance-of-power systems discussed in the preceding chapter emerge, the United States will remain the only superpower in both the political and the economic dimensions of the international system, and is thus compelled to bear the strains of this structural discontinuity. These requirements define the present and prospective international role of the United States.

This chapter suggests some general guidelines for U.S. actions that could enable U.S. policymakers and opinion leaders to cope more effectively with the perplexities of this international role. It also highlights certain U.S. misconceptions and illusions that breed unrealistic expectations of what the United States could accomplish in the international system over the foreseeable future.

RESPONSIBILITY WITHOUT ENOUGH USABLE POWER

In the contemporary international system, the United States is in a position analogous to that of the United Kingdom and France during the interwar period: constrained to maintain world order but without sufficient power and influence for doing so. The difference is that, while Britain and France lacked the power to preserve the system they had established at the Versailles settlement, the United States has the power to sustain reasonable order and calculability in the international system outside the Soviet hegemony but often cannot apply enough of it to make its actions sufficiently effective. The limitations on the use and effectiveness of U.S. power and influence result from the changes in the motivations and capabilities of the different types of nation-states sketched in previous chapters. In turn, the decline of U.S. power and influence has helped to alter the functional characteristics of the international system, reducing the degrees of integration, stability, and calculability that it can sustain. Nevertheless, for reasons indicated above, the United States is still saddled with quasi-hegemonic responsibilities despite the virtual disintegration of its postwar hegemony.

No other nation outside the Soviet hegemony is as yet able or willing to accept the responsibility for maintaining international peace and realistically sustainable levels of economic integration and political stability. More significant, most countries assume that the United States will continue to discharge it. Whenever any serious economic problem or political crisis arises in the international system that is beyond the capacity of the nations involved to handle, they usually look to the United States to provide ideas and resources for coping with it. Even countries that have provoked and expect to benefit from a problem or crisis and have been emboldened to action by their perception of declining U.S. power nevertheless often anticipate some form of U.S. intervention, whether effective or not. The tendency of friends and opponents alike to blame the United States when anything goes wrong in the international system or even within their own borders attests to their assumption that the United States still has the responsibility for maintaining world order.

Most Americans also continue to expect their country to play the role of world leader by virtue of its obviously immense economic and military capabilities and its sense of moral mission. However, the attitude of the great majority of Americans is ambiguous regarding the application of U.S. power to support or oppose other nations or social groups within them. Most Americans do not object on principle to the use of force in peacetime for these purposes and they do not like to be humiliated by the failure of efforts to apply it, as in the attempt to rescue the embassy hostages in Iran. At the same time, many Americans tend to be morally offended when the United States uses its power to support nations or social groups that they perceive as tyrannical, corrupt, or incompetent or to oppose those they believe are democratically inclined. Nor are they willing to pay the price in American lives and resources for the application of force, especially if the objectives are unclear and the intervention is costly and prolonged. This is why the invasion of Grenada in 1983 was so gratifying to so many Americans. The force employed was small but adequate for a quick and overwhelming success, and the objective was perceived as preventing harm to American lives and U.S. interests "in our own backyard." This is why popular support eroded so rapidly for the so-called peacekeeping mission in Lebanon in 1982. It clearly failed to keep the peace; the cost in American lives was very high relative to the size of the force used; agreement among the Lebanese social groups and interested nations involved seemed ever more elusive; and, hence, the official justification for the mission appeared to be vague, shifting, and less and less credible as its duration looked to be endless.

Attitudes are more complex among American policymakers and opinion leaders involved in international affairs, as well as among the other groups actively concerned about U.S. foreign policy for economic, religious, or other reasons. The majority of them see no alternative to continuing to carry on the task of trying to maintain world order but disagree on the necessity, effectiveness, and morality of the means employed for doing so.

The differing views within these groups can be ranged from the midpoint toward the two opposite ends of a continuum. On one side of the range are those who in greater or lesser degree maintain that U.S. influence exercised through diplomatic activity is likely to be effective to the extent that it is perceived by other nations as backed by U.S. willingness to use its power, which would be credible only if actually employed in appropriate situations. On the other side are those who insist that the use of force in peacetime is rarely, if ever, necessary, effective, or morally justified. Instead, they believe in greater or lesser degree that U.S. prestige and positive induce-ments—as well as such negative sanctions as could be applied without risk of leading to the use of force—would still be great enough to maintain world order provided U.S. actions were clearly perceived by other nations and the American people as motivated and self-restrained by the high moral standards that are the essence of a free and humane society.

I see some truth but also some illusions and wish-fulfillments on both sides of this continuum. The United States is still a superpower; it unquestionably possesses the sheer military power to impose its will on any nation except the Soviet Union. However, enough U.S. power cannot be applied for long enough in peacetime for it to be anywhere near as important a means of foreign policy as it was during the postwar period. The United States is still the most influential nation in the international system, not excepting the Soviet Union. But, its prestige and the positive and negative inducements it can apply have diminished to the point where they are often insufficient to influence the actions of other nations regardless of whether they perceive U.S. policy as moral or immoral. The dilemma of U.S. foreign policy in the late 20th century is that the continuing U.S. effort to maintain world order requires more power than the United States is willing to use in many situations and greater influence than it often can exert. How the constraints of this dilemma might be eased is discussed in the sections that follow.

MORALITY AND FOREIGN POLICY

Americans have never believed that the official actions of their country abroad could be justified by "reasons of state." True, they have always expected that the external actions of their government would necessarily involve a substantial element of national interest. But, they have also wanted the basic values of their society to guide what the United States does or does not do in the international system. Indeed, the question of the morality of both the ends and the means of their foreign policy is as important to most Americans as that of its effectiveness. The problem, however, is that many Americans, including some policymakers and opinion leaders, tend to have two related illusions about the role of moral values in foreign policy. One is that moral behavior is costless and is rewarded in this world. The other is that morality can substitute for power in influencing the behavior of other nations.

For national societies whose moral standards are derived from the Judaeo-Christian religious tradition, guiding foreign policy by them is neither simple nor easy. However absolute they may be in the realm of essence, moral values are often in conflict with one another in the realm of existence. Truth may have to be sacrificed for lovingkindness, freedom may have to be restricted for the sake of equality, mercy may have to be disregarded so that justice may be done—and vice versa. Such choices or compromises between conflicting values often need to be made in the life of societies no less than in that of individuals, which inevitably means that a greater or lesser moral price must be paid.

Moreover, the realization of moral values in actual behavior usually requires that the advancement or protection of self-interest be curtailed in some degree. For example, to refrain for moral reasons from preventing a hostile regime from seizing power in a neighboring country may involve greater risks to national security and bigger offsetting expenditures than would otherwise be the case. Imposing negative sanctions—such as an embargo on grain exports—to express moral disapproval of another country's actions may entail greater economic costs for the United States than for the offending nation. But, many Americans want to have their cake and eat it too. They expect that the more their country's foreign actions conform to their moral standards, the more their national interests will ipso facto be benefited. Thus, doing good would not only be costless but would also be rewarded in the here and now. In reality, however, guiding foreign policy by moral standards means recognizing and accepting the sacrifices of self-interest that it often requires.

One way by which Americans expect to be rewarded for their virtuous conduct is by the greater influence they believe it will give them over the behavior of other nations. In other words, morality is regarded as a *substitute* for power and not only as a complement to it. The perception abroad that U.S. actions are restrained by moral considerations has certainly enhanced the prestige of the United States and hence its international influence. But, this effect depends also on the perception of U.S. power and of U.S. willingness to use it in appropriate situations. Otherwise, the moral rectitude of U.S. actions would give it little more influence in the international system than do the high moral standards that guide the foreign policies of such countries as the Netherlands or Norway. To be efficacious in the relations among nations, morality needs to be bolstered by power, just as power needs to be restrained by morality. They are mutually supporting, not substitutes for each other.

The ability of moral behavior to enhance the prestige of the United States also depends upon the nature of the value systems of the other national societies that it is seeking to influence. This effect is likely to be greatest in societies that share the same values as the United States and in which the predominant policymakers and opinion leaders are strongly enough committed to them to guide their actions by them. In many societies, however, the elites and the people are indifferent toward or even scornful of the morality of U.S. motivations and actions. Their own values may inculcate unqualified respect for the exercise of power, as in many traditional Asian and African societies; or the belief that any means may be used to achieve their ends, as in the Soviet Union; or the conviction that American culture embodies the evils against which they must struggle, as in Iran and the radical Arab states. In such societies, the morality of U.S. motivations and actions does not raise—indeed, it may lower—U.S. prestige in their peoples' eyes. Unfortunately, these are often the countries that the United States is trying most urgently to influence.

A more acute aspect of the issue of morality and foreign policy arises when it is not the conduct of the United States that is in question but that of regimes it supports whose actions fall conspicuously short of Americans' moral standards, such as the Philippines under Marcos, South Africa, Chile, or another Latin American nation under a military dictatorship. If U.S. policymakers are unsuccessful in persuading such a regime to change its reprehensible behavior, they have the alternative of withholding economic and military assistance and political support. In some cases, the cost of doing so to U.S. security or other interests would not be large enough to make a significant difference, although it is by no means always easy to ascertain that before the fact. In many more cases, however, the cost is likely to be significant, which necessitates both a moral choice between the conflicting values involved and the willingness to sustain damage to the national interest. (Other aspects of this issue are discussed in a later section below.)

Morality is concerned with how human beings should behave, but policymakers must also take account of how human beings *actually* behave. Certainly, the record of history indicates that people have inflicted at least as much harm on one another as they have done good to one another. In the last analysis, policymakers are entrusted with the responsibility for their nations' security and well-being. These are not interests in the particularistic sense of the term but are societal values inherent in the nature of independent nation-states. Given the propensity of human beings to do evil and the uncertainties implicit in trying to forecast the consequences of their actions, the more conscientious policymakers are, the more they are constrained not to put national security at too great a risk nor to give an unscrupulous antagonist the benefit of the doubt. Hence, they may often have to decide in favor not of the good but of the lesser evil. Nor can the moral ambiguities within which policymakers must operate be felt in the same degree by opinion leaders and people generally, even though they may have a secondary responsibility in the eventual decision when they exercise their right— indeed, their duty—to voice their opinions on the issue.

Thus, so long as the United States is constrained to try to maintain world order, it will inevitably have to resort to means and to acquiesce in outcomes that fall short of its high moral standards. Indeed, it will sometimes have to do wrong to protect the good. As the existentialists would say, this is one of the tragedies of the human condition. In trying to guide foreign policy by moral standards, the essential requirements are to act with appropriate self-restraint and to strive as hard as possible to avoid self-righteousness or hypocrisy. In the early years of the postwar U.S. hegemony, the theologian Reinhold Niebuhr summed up the basic moral problem confronting Americans in carrying out their world responsibilities and applying their power:

> Our culture knows little of the use and abuse of power; but we have to use power in global terms. Our idealists are divided between those who would renounce the responsibilities of power for the sake of preserving the purity of our soul and those who are ready to cover every ambiguity of good and evil in our actions by the frantic insistence that any measures taken in a good cause must be unequivocally virtuous. We take, and must continue to take, morally hazardous actions to preserve our civilization.

. . . The inadequacy of both types of escape from our moral dilemma proves that there is no purely moral solution for the ultimate moral issues of life; but neither is there a viable solution which disregards the moral factors. Men and nations must use their power with the purpose of making it an instrument of justice and a servant of interests broader than their own. Yet they must be ready to use it though they become aware that the power of a particular nation or individual, even when under strong religious and social sanctions, is never so used that there is a perfect coincidence between the value which justifies it and the interest of the wielder of it.[1]

THE NUCLEAR-ARMS ISSUE AND RELATIONS WITH THE SOVIET UNION

Men and women throughout the world are justifiably concerned at the possibility that a nuclear war between the United States and the Soviet Union would be likely at worst to make the planet uninhabitable and at best to result in the destruction of human lives and means of livelihood on an immense scale. Nor is it reassuring to contemplate the fact that this capability has been developed precisely in the century in which, through wars and fanaticisms, political leaders have already been responsible for perpetrating the greatest deliberate destruction of human beings in history. It is no wonder that movements recurrently arise in the OECD nations seeking the abolition or drastic reduction of nuclear weapons by the two superpowers or unilateral nuclear disarmament by individual West European countries. Understandable as such objectives may be, they nevertheless reflect certain illusions about their probable consequences.

One illusion shared by some of the ardent advocates of the abolition of nuclear weapons is that this development either would assure peace between the superpowers or would at least greatly reduce the tensions that could cause a war between them. Certainly, nuclear weapons are one of the necessary conditions for a nuclear war in the sense that, if they did not exist, there could not be this type of war. However, they are far from being a sufficient condition. Not only are other conditions necessary for producing such an outcome but they are also responsible for the fact that the superpowers continue to maintain and improve their nuclear capabilities. As explained in earlier chapters, these other conditions are (1) the incompatibilities rooted in the societies and cultures of the United States and the Soviet Union and expressed in their conflicting motivations and the compulsive logic of their mutual distrust and (2) the constraints of their roles in the two-protagonist balance-of-power system. These other conditions are generally determinative of whether or not any kind of war breaks out between the superpowers. The existence of nuclear weapons tends to inhibit the outbreak of a nuclear war and is specifically determinative only that a war, if it occurs, would be fought by nuclear means.

Although it would probably be far less destructive than a nuclear war, a conventional war involving the superpowers would still be exceedingly costly in human lives and suffering. In World War II, the firebombing of Dresden and Tokyo killed many more people than the nuclear bombs dropped on Hiroshima and Nagasaki and, since then, the technology of nonnuclear destruction has continued to become more efficiently deadly. Moreover, in the future as in the past, the resort to war by one or the other superpower would be more probable if nuclear weapons did not exist than if they did. True, an initial conventional attack by one superpower directly on the territory of the other would be very difficult and would probably not cripple its capacity to continue the war. Hence, a direct conventional attack would have as low a probability as a nuclear attack. In the absence of nuclear weapons, however, the superpowers would be more likely to take greater risks in exploiting the opportunities to advance their interests in other regions, as well as to intervene to counter the other's efforts to do so. Thus, they could more readily be drawn into wars fought with conventional weapons in Europe, Asia, Africa, or elsewhere. This would tend both to make the international system even more politically unstable than it otherwise would be and to increase the likelihood that such local wars with superpower participation would be expanded to global proportions.

Putting together the already great and growing destructive potential of wars fought with conventional weapons, the substantially higher probability that the superpowers would be drawn into such a war in the absence of nuclear weapons, and the increased instability of the international system prior to its occurrence, I would choose to continue to rely upon the existence of nuclear armaments to help keep the peace between the United States and the Soviet Union so long as their two-protagonist balance-of-power relationship and sociocultural incompatibilities persist.

Others would make the opposite choice. For their decision to be a responsible one, however, they would have to be prepared to accept the consequences likely to follow from it. These would be the greater instability of the international system, the higher probability that it would sooner or later terminate in an unprecedentedly destructive conventional war, and the necessity to maintain more expensive conventional military capabilities, including larger numbers of men under arms, in the United States and abroad. In addition, there would always be the danger that, even after an agreement to abolish nuclear armaments, the superpowers would retain concealed nuclear weapons and means of delivery to use in the event that one or the other of them would be faced with an unacceptable defeat in a conventional war.

Nonetheless, agreements between the United States and the Soviet Union to *reduce* their existing nuclear arsenals would certainly be desirable. Well-designed arrangements to limit the production and deployment of the various types of nuclear weapons and means of delivery would help (1) to preserve the balance between the superpowers by improving retaliatory and defensive capabilities relative to first-strike capabilities, (2) to lower the costs of maintaining mutual nuclear deterrence, and (3) to reduce the danger of nuclear accidents. These benefits are worthwhile and validate continuing efforts to negotiate arms-control arrangements. But, such agreements would not significantly reduce the risk of a nuclear war between the superpowers nor would they, per se, ease the tensions between them. Indeed, the reality is the other way around: mitigating the other factors that generate the tensions between the United States and the Soviet Union is a necessary condition for reaching substantial arms-reduction agreements.

For these reasons, the main emphasis of U.S. policy toward the Soviet Union should be on containing the disputes that will inevitably arise between them so as to try to avert unacceptable advances in Soviet power and influence while preventing escalation of conflicts into a direct superpower confrontation threatening the use of force. Among the prescriptions for how the United States should act toward the Soviet Union are two that embody opposite misconceptions.

The first maintains that, since the overriding concern of the Soviet Union is its national security, the United States must refrain in words and deeds from threatening it. If sufficiently reassured that U.S. intentions and actions do not menace it, the Soviet Union would be able to relax its compulsion to increase its power and influence in the international system and would be willing to settle any disputes that arise with the United States by negotiation and compromise. In its more extreme form, the first view holds that Russian values and norms of behavior are just like those of Americans and, hence, the same kinds of self-restrained and cooperative intergroup relations prevalent in American society could be built between the two superpowers as the most effective means of preserving peace and goodwill between them.

The opposite prescription insists that the difficulties of Soviet society and of its hegemonic control are so great that opportunities are thereby provided for the United States not only to prevent the further expansion of the Soviet sphere of influence but also to push back its existing perimeters. In its more extreme form, the second view contends that the Russians respect only strength and force and, hence, achieving U.S. military superiority over the Soviets and unequivocably demonstrating U.S. willingness to use this power are the most effective means for compelling the Soviets to withdraw their hegemonic control and give up their aspirations to world paramountcy.

Neither of these prescriptions accords closely enough with the real-life possibilities to be a valid guide to U.S. actions toward the Soviet Union. As explained in Chapter VI, national security is the highest priority of Soviet foreign policy in the sense that the pursuit of other objectives must never seriously endanger it. But, the Soviet Union does have other high-priority goals in the international system that adversely affect U.S. interests and that no amount of U.S. reassurance would deter it from seeking to achieve—indeed, might only encourage it to pursue more vigorously, as during the detente of the 1970s. Soviet society is not pluralistic and the only significant intergroup bargaining that exists is among the different factions and cliques within the ruling Communist party. The Soviet Union does face difficult problems, both internally and in maintaining its hegemonic control, that its ruling elites are unlikely to be willing and able to overcome in the foreseeable future. However, these difficulties are not so severe that their adverse effects cannot be endured indefinitely without provoking mass disaffection in the normally passive Russian people or compelling the Soviet leadership to withdraw from its hegemonic responsibilities. Nor would any U.S. administration be likely to obtain the appropriations and have the freedom of action required to attain decisive U.S. military superiority over the Soviet Union and to use its power to hasten the collapse of the Soviet hegemony.

Thus, the United States will have to coexist for the foreseeable future with a superpower whose motivations impel and whose capabilities permit it to pursue objectives that often conflict quite fundamentally with those of the United States. In these circumstances, what would be a set of realistic principles for guiding U.S. behavior toward the Soviet Union?

Before outlining them, the limits of the possible need to be emphasized. Due to the motivations and the economic, political, and military capabilities that make them superpowers, neither the United States nor the Soviet Union has very much leverage over the other's behavior short of the threat to use force. The carrot of positive incentives and the stick of negative sanctions are only marginally effective. This is especially the case with negative sanctions, such as export embargoes or the denial of trade benefits, that could be endured without much cost and to which making the intended response would involve establishing an unacceptable precedent and the loss of national prestige. Thus, in seeking to settle disputes with the Soviet Union, the United States has to assess as objectively as possible the nature of the interests at stake on both sides and whether there would be something on each side that it would be willing to give up to obtain a concession desired from the other. If not, the most that could probably be accomplished would be informal agreement by both superpowers to restrain the pursuit of their interests sufficiently to prevent the escalation of their conflicting efforts toward a resort to force.

As to the general guidelines for U.S. behavior toward the Soviet Union, the first and foremost is that *the United States has to maintain credible nuclear and conventional military capabilities*—or, in the unlikely event of total nuclear disarmament, a conventional capability alone—sufficient for two purposes. One is to deter the Soviet Union from a direct attack on the United States or on the other countries that the United States is willing and able to help defend. The other is to prevent the Soviet Union from using its power to intimidate the United States and these other nations into acceding to Soviet demands.

Second, *the United States needs to have an active diplomacy toward the Soviet Union*, continuously engaging it in discussion of the existing and prospective issues between them. Such contact is an effective way to discover the problems on which an agreement could be reached based on common interests or on an exchange of concessions by the Soviet Union and the United States. Even if disputes cannot be settled, informing the Soviet Union of probable U.S. reactions to Soviet initiatives could significantly reduce the likelihood that the disagreements between them would be aggravated to levels of unmanageable intensity.

Third, *firmness and patience are the watchwords in all negotiations with the Soviet Union*. Soviet negotiating tactics are generally designed to try to wear down the other party with prolonged discussions in the expectation that its desire for an agreement will induce it to make greater concessions.

Fourth, while Soviet violations of international law and agreements and of human rights certainly need to be publicly denounced for what they are, *the United States should otherwise refrain from using insulting or provocative language in addressing or referring to the Soviet Union*. The Soviet leaders and people, despite their nation's superpower status, still have feelings of inferiority toward the West in general and the United States in particular. U.S. verbal restraint might not make the Soviet Union much more amenable to granting concessions but it might ease somewhat the difficult negotiating process.

RELATIONS WITH ASIAN, AFRICAN, AND LATIN AMERICAN NATIONS

The main trends in the relations between the United States and the other OECD nations and policy choices for dealing with them were analyzed in

Chapter VIII and need not be recounted here. Coping with the instabilities in Asian, African, and Latin American countries poses more perplexing problems for U.S. policymakers than do U.S. relations with Western Europe and Japan or even with the Soviet Union. Three of these difficulties are discussed here because they often involve misconceptions and unrealistic .expectations of what the United States could and should accomplish.

Instability and Soviet Intervention

The first set of misconceptions relates to the fact that economic crisis, social unrest and political instability in these regions are generally not due to the machinations of the Soviet Union but to the fundamental processes of societal transformation and modernization that their societies are experiencing, as explained in Chapter V. These processes generate opportunities for the Soviet Union or others to intervene, openly or clandestinely, to advance their interests in the troubled country. In the great majority of cases, such interventions take the form of assistance to indigenous groups that are attempting to seize power or to a regime trying to maintain itself in power. Thus, an Asian, African, or Latin American nation must be *internally susceptible* to outside intervention for such an action to have sufficient chance of success to make it worthwhile. Nor does the Soviet Union always exploit opportunities when they arise. Whether it provides help or not depends (1) upon its assessment of the difficulties involved and of the likely responses of the United States and other nations that might try to counter its efforts and (2) upon the other claims, internal and external, on its attention and resources at the time and the state of opinion within the Soviet leadership.

Nevertheless, there have always been U.S. policymakers and opinion leaders who persist in attributing outbreaks of social unrest and political instability in Asia, Africa, and Latin America solely or mainly to Soviet intervention directly or via one of its client states. This is a dangerous misconception that, if it becomes predominant among U.S. policymakers, would lead to mistaken diagnosis of the factors involved and ineffective prescriptions for dealing with them.

At the same time, however, some policymakers and opinion leaders who recognize the relationship between indigenous susceptibilities and possible' Soviet intervention have misconceptions of their own. They maintain that the United States should focus its efforts on removing the basic causes of economic crisis, social unrest, and political instability in Asia, Africa, and Latin America and thereby prevent opportunities for Soviet intervention from arising. Such advice assumes that the United States has the ability to accelerate and guide the fundamental processes of societal transformation in these regions—a capability which it lacked even when its hegemony was at its height. This is not to say that U.S. development assistance is ineffective or unneeded. Useful as it may be, however, U.S. aid is not a panacea that can overcome economic difficulties and prevent social unrest and political instability, thereby eliminating the opportunities for Soviet intervention.

Just as the transitional and modernization processes in Asia, Africa, and Latin America generate opportunities for Soviet intervention, so too do they make Soviet client states and dependent nations in these regions susceptible to efforts by the United States and other OECD countries to aid dissatisfied regimes or dissident groups within them. Examples are the defections from Soviet dependence of Egypt and Somalia in the 1970s and the Afghan resistance to Soviet control in the 1980s. However, the capacity of the United States to take advantage of such opportunities is more limited than that of the Soviet Union, granted that both superpowers are equally restrained by the need to avoid direct confrontations between them that might escalate to the use of force. First, Soviet control and vigilance over the noncontiguous members of its hegemony or its sphere of influence are usually much greater than those that the United States is able and willing to exercise over nations that it is trying to support. Second, the institutional and attitudinal changes in the United States impose fairly narrow self-restraints on the means that U.S. policymakers can use to help dissident regimes and groups in Soviet client and dependent states. Nonetheless, it is important to recognize that the inherent instabilities of Asian, African, and Latin American nations do not operate one-sidedly in favor of the Soviet Union.

What Regimes Should the United States Support?

The second perplexing problem is that of defining the criteria for distinguishing the kinds of regimes in Asia, Africa, and Latin America that merit U.S. support from those that do not.

One criterion usually proposed is whether the country concerned is vital to the national security of the United States. The difficulty here is that the two ways of defining the importance of any nation to the security of the United States are not conclusive.

The first way is to define national security in an absolute sense, dividing countries into two groups: those that are essential to U.S. security and those that are not. The first group would be very small, probably consisting of no more than Canada and Mexico. The second comprises all the other nations not essential to U.S. security in an absolute sense. This definition implies that the United States has the human resources and the economic and technological capabilities to defend itself against hostile nations elsewhere in the world—although the closer and more powerful they are, the higher the costs of nuclear and conventional deterrence would be.

The second way is in relative terms and relates to the structural constraints in a two-protagonist system to maintain the balance of power between them. Under this definition, the threat to U.S. security is the expansion of Soviet power and influence over time and not necessarily the accession to the Soviet hegemony of any particular nation at any particular time. Some argue that there are two kinds of exceptions to this generalization: (1) the countries of North America and northern South America that are contiguous to the United States or could be used as forward bases for attacks on it and the access routes to it; and (2) the nations of Western Europe and Japan, whose manpower and economic and technological capabilities under hostile control might give an opponent a decisive advantage. However, even these exceptions must be qualified. Although Cuba and Nicaragua have communist regimes, predominant U.S. opinion has refused to recognize them as sufficient threats to U.S. security to warrant using U.S. military power to eliminate them despite their proximity to the United States. As to Soviet domination of Western Europe, Chapter IX has explained that even this development would not produce an irresistible menace to U.S. security so long as the United States maintained a credible nuclear deterrent.

As noted in Chapter II, the United States has long-standing treaty obligations to help defend certain nations that it was convinced were vital to its security. Once made, such commitments cannot be abandoned without better reason than doubts as to whether the countries involved are in fact essential to U.S. security. Beyond these existing obligations, however, the question of whether Soviet domination of any other nation would be an unacceptable threat to the United States would depend on the strategic situation at the time: that is, on what other countries and regions were already under Soviet control or influence and how the addition to them of the nation in question would be likely to affect the balance between the superpowers—the "correlation of forces," to use the Soviet phrase.

Thus, U.S. policymakers are in an ambiguous position. They cannot undertake in advance to try to defend every nation—a commitment that would be much too costly and would not be supported by the Congress and, the American people. At the same time, however, they cannot specify in advance which countries they would or would not try to defend. This refusal irks some U.S. opinion leaders, who claim that, by leaving the Soviet Union and other possible aggressors in doubt about U.S. intentions, they are encouraged to attempt to expand their power and influence into areas in which they would otherwise not move. In my view, this uncertainty about what the United States might do is more of a deterrent to aggression than an encouragement of it provided the United States is clearly seen as possessing and being willing to use the requisite power. Nonetheless, the uncertainty does increase the difficulty that U.S. policymakers face at home in justifying their actions or inaction.

A second criterion, noted earlier in this chapter, relates to whether the United States should support regimes in Asian, African, and Latin American nations that fall substantially short of its standard of morality and effectiveness. In fact, most of them do, but their deficiencies have not prevented the United States from providing many of them with economic and military assistance and political support. It has done so in part to maintain the balance of power with the Soviet Union and in part to express its own sense of mission to encourage and help other nations to progress toward the goals of economic welfare, social justice, and political democracy that embody the basic values of American society. Therefore, these goals usually serve as a standard by which to judge the performance of regimes in Asia, Africa, and Latin America.

Among them, political democracy has usually been the one most heavily emphasized. The concept of democrary has historically been defined by reference to the political institutions of Western Europe and North America—that is, systems in which two or more parties periodically compete for office through free elections whose results they accept, and in which the civil rights of citizens are protected in practice as well as in law. After World War II, the meaning of the term was corrupted by the Soviet Union and its client states when they called their communist dictatorships "people's democracies." More recently, it has become fashionable in the OECD nations to regard any restoration of more or less free elections in Asian, African, and Latin American countries as the triumph of democracy regardless of whether the universalistic values, self-restraining norms of behavior, and pluralistic institutional relationships required for its continued existence have been sufficiently developed. In the great majority of cases, such restorations have been temporary. As explained in Chapter V, the transitional and modernizing societies of these regions sooner or later revert to authoritarian political systems that are consistent with their still predominant particularism and personalism and their limited institutional efficiency. Thus, the concept of democracy either in its original meaning or in its current vague sense is not a realistic standard by which to judge the performance of regimes in Asia, Africa, and Latin America.

In contrast, progress toward the goals of economic welfare and social justice would be a standard more relevant to the aspirations and capabilities of these societies, as well as to the values of American society. I would judge the performance of any regime, regardless of how authoritarian it may be, by three criteria. The first is the extent to which the policies and actions of the regime respect the basic civil rights of the people and foster their efforts to improve their economic welfare. The second is the extent to which the regime and the elite groups supporting it can restrain the pursuit of their own particularistic interests so as to reduce corruption and favoritism, minimize capital flight, and prevent the disparities in income between themselves and the people from becoming ever larger. The third is the extent to which the external policies and actions of the regime are in accordance with international law and agreements and are conducive to maintaining the order and calculability of the international system.

A standard of this kind would avoid the problem raised by a simple distinction between authoritarian regimes that are totalitarian—that is, communist—and those that are not. Many U.S. policymakers and opinion leaders would accept this distinction as far as it goes, but they also want to distinguish between nontotalitarian regimes that merit U.S. support and those that are too repressive, rapacious, or internationally disruptive to do so.

The application to other societies of performance criteria that reflect the values of American society has sometimes been called "cultural imperialism." In a way, it is: every society should be free to define for itself the values that it seeks to realize provided they do not seriously infringe on the right of other societies to do so. But, every society also has the right to decide for itself the conditions under which it would be willing to use its resources and power to assist another society, which implies the right to withhold its aid from those whose values or behavior are repugnant to it. In practice, however, these rights are rarely regarded as absolute and nations have been willing to qualify their exercise of them to obtain important benefits that otherwise would not be available. Moreover, values are generalized concepts that can be realized in a variety of particular forms.

In these circumstances, the use of American values in U.S. performance criteria is justified if they are applied pragmatically by (1) seeking to ascertain the extent of common values, or at least of those that are not incompatible, between the United States and the recipient country, (2) recognizing the differences in the possible institutional and behavioral manifestations of these values, and (3) taking account of the effects on the ability to make progress toward realizing them of existing institutional capabilities and inherited norms of behavior. Economic welfare comes closest to meeting this test as it is the goal most widely professed by Asian, African, and Latin American societies; social justice is next; and political democracy is considerably behind, for the reasons explained above.

How much influence does the United States have in trying to induce Asian African, and Latin American regimes to make progress toward its performance criteria?

Countries with large populations and natural resources or that are relatively self-sufficient may be only marginally dependent, if at all, on U.S. economic and military aid. Hence, their regimes can ignore U.S. pressure for changes in their internal or external behavior. Even in the absence of such assets, the elites may be willing to forgo the economic and other benefits that the United States could provide for the sake of their national freedom of action and the protection of their privileges. Also, U.S. policymakers often overlook incompatibilities between American values and those of recipient nations because they are convinced that U.S. security or ability to maintain the balance with the Soviet Union would otherwise be adversely affected.

Nonetheless, there are countries in Asia, Africa, and Latin America that are sufficiently dependent upon U.S. assistance and political support to make their regimes susceptible to U.S. influence. Even in these cases, however, the threat to reduce or withhold U.S. aid may be insufficient to affect the performance of authoritarian regimes that are becoming increasingly repressive, corrupt, or incompetent, as in the Philippines under Marcos. For this reason, it is important for U.S. representatives always to make clear from the beginning of any new regime that U.S. assistance and support are never unconditional. To emphasize this point, contact should be maintained with noncommunist opposition leaders and groups—both within the country and abroad—so that, whenever necessary, either additional pressure for reform can be put on the incumbent regime or, if that is ineffective, the opposition elements can be encouraged to unite and assisted to replace it.

The Use of U.S. Military Power

The third perplexing problem is whether and in what circumstances the United States would be justified in directly using its military power in Asia, Africa, and Latin America.

Given the conditions for maintaining world order under which the United States continues to act, it cannot renounce completely the use of its military power in peacetime. However, for the application of U.S. military power to be effective and morally valid, three interrelated requirements have to be met: (1) the nature of the problem must make it unlikely to be acceptably solved by nonforcible means and susceptible to a reasonably satisfactory resolution by force; (2) the application of force has to have a high enough probability of being successful within the restrictions imposed by the institutional and attitudinal constraints of American society; and (3) the amount and kind of force applied have to be proportionate to the goal to be achieved.

The first requirement implies that the outcome of directly using U.S. military power is likely, in terms of both U.S. interests and those of the people on whose behalf the United States intervenes, to be significantly more favorable or less unfavorable than that which would result from employing nonforcible means or from doing nothing. For example, by this test, U.S. armed involvement in Vietnam, *had it succeeded*, would have been appropriate and morally valid because the U.S. strategic position in Southeast Asia and the conditions of life of the people of South Vietnam would both be much better than they are today. However, given the misconceptions of Vietnamese capabilities—those of the South as well as of the North—and the self-imposed limitations on and mistakes in the application of U.S. military power, the probability of success was too low and, hence, the costs in lives and resources were not justified either operationally or morally.

The second and third requirements mean that the objectives of any proposed use of military power have to be perceived by opinion leaders and the American people as desirable and clearly attainable, and the means employed have to be adequate for achieving those goals as quickly as possible while minimizing military and civilian casualties and suffering. These are difficult tests for any proposed application of U.S. military power in peacetime to meet. Nonetheless, the effective use of U.S. military power in accordance with these requirements would ipso facto increase the deterrent effect of the implied or overt threat to resort to it in subsequent situations. Effective use of military power would tend both to reduce the frequency with which conditions likely to provoke the employment of force would arise and to slow down the decline in U.S. ability to deal with problems by nonforcible means.

KNOWLEDGE AND POWER

Since the end of the postwar period, the changes within the different groups of nation-states and in the structure of the international system surveyed in earlier chapters have been steadily reducing the effectiveness of the various positive incentives and negative sanctions by which the United States has been endeavoring to maintain world order. At the same time, changes within the United States have been further limiting the freedom of action of U.S. policymakers to use these means of influence and to resort to the application of U.S. military power. Therefore, *the less influence and power U.S. policymakers can exercise in the international system, the more important it is for them to use their remaining capabilities effectively.* This means that they need constantly to improve their understanding of (1) the nature of the ongoing changes at both national and international levels and (2) the extent to which and the ways by which the future courses of national and international development could be affected by policy choices and actions. The old adage "knowledge is power" is especially relevant to the predicament of U.S. policymakers in coping with the disintegrative and disruptive manifestations of the determinative trends in the international system. Nothing illustrates more strikingly the disastrous consequences of insufficient knowledge and understanding than the ill-conceived actions vis-à-vis Iran of both the Carter and the Reagan administrations.

The purpose of this book has been to contribute to such improved understanding. It has analyzed the factors that were mainly responsible for the high degrees of international integration, order, and calculability achieved under the postwar U.S. hegemony and for the changes at national and international levels that, since the early 1970s, have been steadily eroding these features of the international system. Based on this analysis, the trends shaping the system's future direction of development were identified and new ways of thinking relevant to these present and prospective realities were suggested to increase the effectiveness of policymakers' efforts to cope with the difficult problems that lie ahead.

The analysis of the basic determinative trends and the policy guidelines that logically follow from it will be unwelcome to those U.S. policymakers and opinion leaders who consciously or unconsciously assume that the postwar U.S. hegemony is still intact. Nonetheless, such hegemonic functions as the United States now carries on are very much reduced in scope and effectiveness, and their decline means that the international system is today and will in the future be less integrated, orderly, and calculable than it was in the postwar period. Nor will the somber panorama ahead that I have sketched be satisfying to many Americans accustomed to believing that all problems can be readily solved if only enough goodwill and resources are applied to them. Unfortunately, there are no panaceas for harmoniously resolving the conflicts and mutual suspicions between the Soviet Union and the United States, for reconciling the growing divergences in interests and attitudes between the United States and Western Europe, for reversing the trend toward neomercantilism in the relations among the OECD nations and the NICs, and for overcoming the sociocultural obstacles that impede the transitional and modernization processes in Asia, Africa, and Latin America.

Many of the problems and dangers generated by these ineradicable characteristics of the international system in the current period can be mitigated and controlled by relevant ways of thinking and realistic policies, such as those suggested in this book. Where they cannot, they must simply be endured with as little damage as possible to U.S. interests and world order. Knowledge, steadfastness, and self-restraint provide the best assurances that, despite immense difficulties and dangers, U.S. actions will be equal to the requirements of its international role. If they are, the international system has a better chance of completing its transformation in the 21st century in a way conducive to the peace, freedom, and creativity of the many different societies on the planet.

NOTE

1. Reinhold Niebuhr, *The Irony of American History* (New York: Charles Scribner's Sons, 1952), pp. 5, 40–41.

TECHNICAL APPENDIX

DEFINITIONS OF KEY TERMS

A valid analysis requires that the basic concepts in its underlying conceptual framework be clearly defined and consistently used in these senses. The key terms in this book are defined as follows:

A *system* is a set of continuing interactions among the constituent elements that is to a significant degree self-determining (i.e., autonomous) and retains certain distinguishing characteristics over significant periods of time. I prefer this general definition to the more usual one involving the concept of equilibrium, or homeostatic (self-correcting) balance, which restricts the members of the class to those sets of interactions that are wholly or largely self-determining. This definition has limited applicability to societal and intersocietal phenomena, which are less self-determining than most physical systems, and it implies an actual or ideal "steady state" toward which the pattern of interactions always returns, which complicates the task of accounting for systemic change.

A *society* is a macro social system embracing a territorially defined, self-perpetuating, and largely self-determining collectivity of human beings, more or less tightly integrated into continuing relationships (i.e., micro social systems) interacting cooperatively and competitively in accordance with the values and norms of behavior characteristic of its culture, and with a widely shared sense of its unique identity and common destiny vis-à-vis other societies. Micro social systems range from loosely structured *groups*, identified by a specific common set of cultural characteristics, functional interests, and/or physical traits, to more tightly integrated *organizations*, such as families, schools, business firms, and government agencies. In turn, organizations may be integrated into *institutional systems* based on their interrelated functional interests, such as the political/administrative system, the economic system, and the educational system.

170

By the *culture* is meant every society's distinctive modes of feeling, seeing, believing, reasoning, and valuing, as well as its resulting aesthetic and intellectual creations and material artifacts and the techniques by which they are produced. For our purposes, four important components of any culture are its *value commitments* (its notions of good and bad, proper and improper, desirable and undesirable); its *norms of behavior* (the specific rules, procedures, and prohibitions that are internalized by the members of the society and guide their actions); its *knowledge and understanding* of the nature and determinative factors of its own society, of other societies, and of the international system and its *technological capabilities* for affecting them; and its *dramatic design* (the set of self-images and explanatory rationales by which every society justifies to its members—and to outsiders—its reason for being, its unique identity, its aspirations, and its claim for its members' loyalty).

A *nation-state* is a politically independent society with a strong sense of identity and dramatic design and a highly developed, pervasive, and impersonal political/administrative system that exercises sovereign power and is legitimated and made effective by universalistic values and behavioral norms which stress the overriding importance of the nation as a unifying symbol and thereby help to restrain and orient toward common goals the particularism of the society's constituent individuals, groups, and organizations.

An *international system* is a set of interactions among nation-states that is sufficiently self-determining to have a significant effect on the present condition and future development both of the system per se and of its constituent nation-states. The differences between an international system and its constituent national societies, and the nature of the relationships between them, are discussed below. The more general term for a system of interactions among all types of independent societies is *intersocietal system*.

An *hegemony* is an intersocietal system in which the dominant member, the *hegemon*, possesses the motivation and the capabilities for controlling the external policies and actions of the other members (the client states) so as to maintain the structural form and functional relationships of the system in accordance with its own conception of the needs and purposes of the system. Hegemons may exercise a minimum degree of control over the client states, as did the United States during the postwar period, or a maximum degree, as did and still does the Soviet Union, whose control sometimes verges on that characteristic of an imperial system. In an *imperial system,* or *empire*, the imperial power possesses the motivation and the capabilities for controlling both the internal and the external policies and actions of the subordinated societies, usually be exercising direct rule over them. Strictly speaking, the Soviet Union is itself an empire in that the dominant Russian society rules over numerous non-Russian societies in the Baltic, Caucasus, and central Asian regions; and its relationship with the East European and other client states is hegemonic, since its control over their internal affairs does not involve continuous direct rule.

A *market economy or sector* is an economic system in which most goods and services are produced in accordance predominantly with efficiency criteria for sale at competitive prices that fluctuate mainly in accordance with supply and demand, which in turn vary as prices rise and fall. A predominantly market economic system is sufficiently autonomous of the other institutional systems of the society to be more or less self-equilibrating through the continuous integration of the decisions of producers and consumers, savers and investors by means of fluctuating prices, including the price of money (interest).

A *nonmarket economy or sector* is an economic system in which the production of most goods and services is governed by criteria among which efficiency is generally subordinated to other considerations (e.g., political, social, moral, familial, and other noneconomic criteria) and in which the resulting output is either for use by the producing organizations or for distribution to other organizations in accordance with equivalents (in the case of exchanges) or of amounts (in the case of transfers) that are fixed by custom and /or by command decisions. Thus, a predominantly nonmarket economy is usually not sufficiently autonomous of the other institutional systems of the society to be substantially self-equilibrating.

By *power* is meant the ability—though not necessarily the right—to use force or the explicit or implicit threat of force to compel or constrain others to do something they do not want to do or to refrain from doing something they want to do. By *influence* is meant the possession of sufficient prestige and/or positive and negative inducements to be able to persuade others to do something they otherwise would not do or to refrain from doing something they want to do.

Integration means that some or all of the continuing interactions between two or more macro or micro social systems are among the necessary factors that account—qualitatively and/or quantitatively—for their internal conditions and development over time. By *coordination* is meant the alignment of the policies and actions of two or more macro or micro social systems such that their behavior is mutually supporting or complementary.

An international system can be *integrated* in some or all of its sets of functional relationships. One of the most important forms of international integration is economic: countries open their economies so that goods, services, and money can flow in and out, and their patterns of production and levels of employment and income become more or less dependent on these movements. Political integration may take a variety of forms, such as the military arrangements of the North Atlantic Treaty Organization (NATO) or the control over the political systems of its client states exercised by the Soviet Union. Cultural integration involves the dependence of countries on the transborder flows among them of scientific knowledge and technologies, political and philosophical ideas, literary and artistic expressions, and other elements of life-styles.

RELATIONS BETWEEN AN INTERSOCIETAL SYSTEM
AND ITS CONSTITUENT SOCIETIES

International-relations theorists have long debated the nature and significance of the relationships between the international system and its constituent national societies, or—put another way—the kind and degree of
self-determinacy of the international system. References to some recent
publications on this question are given in the bibliography to Chapter I. My
own conceptual approach to this problem can be sketched as follows.

Any independent society that is significantly and continuously affected by
its external relationships is ipso facto a member of an intersocietal system.
Conversely, an intersocietal system is by its nature composed of societies
whose internal processes of change continuously affect the development of
the system as a whole in greater or lesser degree. Also, the ways in which the
intersocietal and the societal levels interact change as modifications occur at
each level. Each level has its own determinative factors in addition to those
operating on it from the other.

The determinative factors inherent at the intersocietal level are functions
of its structural form. Thus, for example, the formation and persistence of a
hegemonic system depend on the hegemon taking the kinds of actions
needed to maintain its control over the client states or the system will
disintegrate or be overthrown. A balance-of-power system requires that
the protagonists act in various ways (including by war, if necessary) to
prevent any one of them from achieving a position of dominance over the
others. This requirement is usually more constraining in two-protagonist
systems than in multiple-protagonist systems like those of the 18th and 19th
centuries.

To construct models of intersocietal systems that define the principles
governing their operation, theorists have to focus on the structural determinants inherent in the intersocietal level and assume that those factors
affecting them from the societal level are uniform and unchanging and hence
can be disregarded. However, the nature of an intersocietal system is never
the sole determinant of its *history*—of whether it exists, how its functional
requirements are met, how its structure changes over time, and when and
how it ends. To understand any real-life intersocietal system, it is necessary
also to include in the analysis the political, economic, other social-institu-
tional, and psychocultural characteristics and development of its constituent
societies, especially of its more powerful and influential members. In turn,
the changes in the sociocultural characteristics of the constituent societies
and in their resulting motivations and capabilities for external action are
significantly affected by the nature and development of the intersocietal
system of which they are members.

This mutually determinative relationship between an intersocietal system and its members is usually asymmetrical. That is, by their nature societies tend to have a substantially higher degree of autonomy, or self-determinacy, than do the intersocietal systems of which they are members. Indeed, by their nature, intersocietal systems are *not* societies precisely because their degree of self-determinacy is too low, which in turn reflects their much lower level of social integration and cultural homogeneity. For this reason, I believe that the concept of "international society" used by some theorists is invalid and misleading.

BIBLIOGRAPHICAL APPENDIX

As stated in the preface, the purpose of this bibliography is to provide readers with a short list of books that either elaborate on or present some differing views concerning subjects discussed in each chapter. It is not intended as a guide to the immense body of theoretical and empirical literature on the political and economic development of the international system and its constituent nation-states since World War II. Except for the early chapters, the materials selected are for the most part recently published policy-oriented books and reports.

Journal articles have been omitted from the bibliography but readers can refer to *Foreign Affairs, Foreign Policy,* and *The National Interest* for current policy-oriented materials, and to *World Politics, International Organization,* and the regional-studies journals for more theoretical and empirical analyses. *The Economist* is invaluable for keeping abreast of economic and political developments in the international system.

Many of the key interpretations in this book are further developments of ideas first expressed in my earlier publications. The analysis in Chapter V of the transitional process in Asia and Africa and the modernization process in Latin America is based on my *The Conflicted Relationship: The West and the Transformation of Asia, Africa and Latin America*, (New York: McGraw-Hill for the Council on Foreign Relations, 1967) and subsequent monographs on the development problems and prospects of nations in these regions. The interrelations between the growth of the welfare state and the rise of neomercantilism were first outlined in a paper read at a State Department Conference at Airlie House, Warrenton, Virginia, on May 1, 1975, published in the National Planning Association's *Looking Ahead*, July 1975, Vol. 1, No. 5, and later analyzed in detail in my *Welfare and Efficiency: Their Interactions in Western Europe and Implications for International*

Economic Relations, (Washington, D.C.: National Planning Association, 1978, paperback edition; London: Macmillan, 1979, hardback edition). The nature of the postwar U.S. hegemony, the reasons for its disintegration, and the consequences for the international economic and political system were broadly sketched in a presentation to the British–North American Committee at its meeting in June 1982 at Torquay, England, and published in NPA's *Looking Ahead*, December 1982, Vol. 7, No. 1.

CHAPTER I

The main theoretical approaches to explicating the nature of the international system are surveyed and appraised in Robert O. Keohane, ed., *Neorealism and Its Critics* (New York: Columbia University Press, 1986); see also the study that stimulated the papers in that volume: Kenneth N. Waltz, *Theory of International Politics* (Reading, Mass.: Addison-Wesley, 1979).

The "classic" economic analysis of the benefits and costs of international integration is Richard N. Cooper, *The Economics of Interdependence* (New York: McGraw-Hill for the Council on Foreign Relations, 1968), and the parallel political analysis is Robert O. Keohane and Joseph S. Nye, *Power and Interdependence: World Politics in Transition* (Boston: Little, Brown, 1977). On the "free-rider" and related problems, see Mancur Olson, *The Logic of Collective Action: Public Goods and the Theory of Groups* (Cambridge, Mass.: Harvard University Press, 1971), and Douglass C. North, *Structure and Change in Economic History* (New York: W. W. Norton, 1981), Part 1; for a clear analysis in terms of game theory, see Robert O. Keohane, *After Hegemony: Cooperation and Discord in the World Political Economy* (Princeton, N.J.: Princeton University Press, 1984), Chapter 2.

On market and nonmarket economies in the contemporary international system, see Charles E. Lindblom, *Politics and Markets: The World's Political-Economic Systems* (New York: Basic Books, 1977); my essay "Using the Market/Nonmarket Distinction" in *New International Realities,* October 1976, Vol. 2, No. 1 (Washington, D.C.: National Planning Association); and my *Welfare and Efficiency* (cited), Chapter 1.

The importance of an hegemonic leader in maintaining the economic integration of an international system was first stressed in Charles P. Kindelberger, *The World in Depression, 1929–1939* (Berkeley: University of California Press, 1973, rev. ed. 1986), Chapter 14. This concept has subsequently been applied by several political scientists concerned with the international system, notably in Keohane and Nye, *Power and Interdependence* (cited); the papers in William P. Avery and David P. Rapkin, eds., *America in a Changing World Political Economy* (New York: Longman, 1982); and Keohane, *After Hegemony* (cited). Most recently, the fruitful use of this concept has been demonstrated in great detail in Robert Gilpin, with the assistance of Jean M. Gilpin, *The Political Economy of International Relations* (Princeton, N.J.: Princeton University Press, 1987). I obtained a copy of this scholarly treatise only after the final draft of my book had been sent to the publisher and am pleased to see that many of its interpretations are similar to my own, particularly that the hegemonic role of the United States was a necessary condition for the postwar attainment of a high level of international economic integration, which has been eroding as relative U.S. international power and influence have been declining. Like Gilpin, I believe that Keohane and other scholars overestimate the extent to which "international regimes"—that is, the institutionalized rules and norms of behavior followed voluntaristically by nation-states—can maintain a high level of international integration, order, and calculability in the absence of hegemonic power. On international regimes, see Stephen D. Krasner, ed., *International Regimes* (Ithaca, N.Y.: Cornell University Press, 1983).

CHAPTERS II AND III

A leading standard history of the international system since World War II is Peter Calvocoressi, *World Politics Since 1945* (New York: Longman, rev. ed. 1986); for a stimulating popularly written account, see Paul Johnson, *Modern Times: The World from the Twenties to the Eighties* (New York: Harper and Row, 1983). The economic development of the international system is surveyed in W. M. Scammell, *The International Economy Since 1945* (New York: St. Martin's Press, rev. ed. 1984).

Books that analyze the ways of thinking that motivated the postwar reconstruction of the international system and the organization of the U.S. and Soviet hegemonies include my *The Fortunes of the West* (Bloomington: Indiana University Press, 1973); Stanley Hoffmann, *Gulliver's Troubles, or the Setting of American Foreign Policy* (New York: McGraw-Hill for the Council on Foreign Relations, 1968); Richard N. Gardner, *In Pursuit of World Order: U.S. Foreign Policy and International Organization* (New York: Praeger, rev. ed. 1966); and Zbigniew Brzezinski, *The Soviet*

Bloc: Unity and Conflict (Cambridge, Mass.: Harvard University Press, 1969).

For a variety of views on relations between the U.S. and Soviet hegemonies during the postwar period, see Louis J. Halle, *The Cold War as History* (New York: Harper and Row, 1967); André Fontaine, *History of the Cold War, 1917–1969,* Vol. 1 (New York: Pantheon, 1968) and Vol. 2 (New York: Vintage, 1970); Walter LaFeber, *America, Russia and the Cold War* (New York: Knopf, rev. ed. 1984); Adam B. Ulam, *The Rivals: America and Russia Since World War II* (New York: Viking, 1971); and John Lewis Gaddis, *Russia, the Soviet Union and the United States: An Interpretive History* (New York: Wiley, 1978).

Statistical sources for these chapters include the Economic Reports of the President (Council of Economic Advisers); Statistical Abstracts of the United States; OECD Annual Reports; IMF International Financial Statistics and Balance of Payments Yearbooks; UN Statistical Yearbooks; GATT Statistical Yearbooks; and Japanese Statistical Yearbooks.

CHAPTER IV

On institutional changes within the OECD nations, see my *Welfare and Efficiency* (cited); Andrew Shonfield, *In Defense of the Mixed Economy,* ed. Zuzanna Shonfield (New York: Oxford University Press, 1984); Mancur Olson, *The Rise and Decline of Nations: Economic Growth, Stagflation and Social Rigidities* (New Haven, Conn.: Yale University Press, 1982); Corelli Barnett, *The Pride and the Fall: The Dream and Illusion of Britain as a Great Nation* (New York: The Free Press, 1987); Fritz Stern, *Dreams and Delusions: The Drama of German History* (New York: Knopf, 1987); Jacques Pelkmans, *Market Integration in the European Community* (The Hague: Martinus Nijhoff, 1984); and David B. H. Denoon, ed., *Constraints on Strategy: The Economics of Western Security* (Elmsford, N.Y.: Pergamon, 1986).

On generational change and attitudes in the OECD nations, see Walter Laqueur, *A Continent Astray* (New York: Oxford University Press, 1979); Stephen F. Szabo, *The Successor Generation: International Perspectives of Postwar Europeans* (Woburn, Mass.: Butterworths, 1983); Ole R. Holsti and James N. Rosenau, *American Leadership in World Affairs: Vietnam and the Breakdown of Consensus* (Winchester, Mass.: Allen & Unwin, 1984); Sanford J. Unger, ed., *Estrangement: America and the World* (New York: Oxford University Press, 1985); Yasusuke Murakami and Yutaka Kosai, eds., *Japan in the Global Community: Its Role and Contribution on the Eve of the 21st Century* (Tokyo: University of Tokyo Press, 1986); and Kozo Yamamura and Yasukichi Yasuba, eds., *The Political Economy of Japan, Vol. 1, The Domestic Transition* (Stanford, Calif.: Stanford University Press, 1987).

Opinion polls on attitudes toward external relations are published periodically by the European Community in Brussels, the Atlantic Institute in Paris, the Chicago Council on Foreign Relations, and commercial polling organizations in Western Europe and the United States.

CHAPTER V

The literature on social change and economic development in Asia, Africa, and Latin America has grown enormously since these processes became of major interest to policymakers and opinion leaders in the early postwar years. Hence, only a few of the latest survey publications for each region are noted here.

My own views on these complex subjects were presented in book form in my *The Conflicted Relationship* (cited) and in numerous monographs and articles on individual Asian, African, and Latin American countries.

Two recent collections of papers review economic-development theory generally: Gerald M. Meier and Dudley Seers, eds., *Pioneers in Development* (New York: Oxford University Press for the World Bank, 1984); and John P. Lewis and Valleriana Kallab, eds., *Development Strategies Reconsidered* (Washington D.C.: Overseas Development Council, 1986). A parallel assessment of political development is Myron Weiner and Samuel P. Huntington, eds., *Understanding Political Development* (Boston: Little, Brown, 1987).

For recent surveys of Asian nations, see Robert A. Scalapino, Seizaburo Sato, and Jusuf Wanandi, eds., *Asian Political Institutionalization* (Berkeley: University of California Press, 1986) and *Asian Economic Development—Present and Future* (Berkeley: University of California Press, 1985); see also Lucian W. Pye with Mary W. Pye, *Asian Power and Politics: The Cultural Dimensions of Authority* (Cambridge, Mass.: Harvard University Press, 1985).

On African nations, recent surveys include Robert J. Berg and Jennifer Seymour Whitaker, eds., *Strategies for African Development* (Berkeley: University of California Press, 1986); Richard Sandbrook, *The Politics of Africa's Economic Stagnation* (Cambridge: Cambridge University Press,

1986); Carol Lancaster and John Williamson, eds., *African Debt and Financing* (Washington, D.C.: Institute for International Economics, 1986); Gwendolen M. Carter and Patrick O'Meara, eds., *African Independence: The First Twenty-Five Years* (Bloomington: Indiana University Press, 1986); Goran Hyden, *No Shortcuts to Progress: African Development Management in Perspective* (Berkeley: University of California Press, 1983); Robert H. Bates, *Essays on the Political Economy of Rural Africa* (Berkeley: University of California Press, 1987); and, for a popularly written account, Sanford J. Unger, *The People and Politics of an Emerging Continent* (New York: Simon and Schuster, 1985).

On Latin American nations, recent surveys include Bela Balassa et al., *Toward Renewed Growth in Latin America* (Washington, D.C.: Institute for International Economics, 1986); Jonathan Hartlyn and Samuel A. Morley, eds., *Latin American Political Economy: Financial Crisis and Political Change* (Boulder, Colo.: Westview Press, 1986); Howard J. Wiarda and Harvey Kline, eds., *Latin American Politics and Development* (Boulder, Colo.: Westview Press, rev. ed. 1985); and Lawrence E. Harrison, *Underdevelopment Is a State of Mind: The Latin American Case* (Washington, D.C.: University Press of America, 1985). Works that have helped to shape my own interpretation of Latin America's sociocultural development, current problems, and future prospects are Americo Castro, *The Spaniards: An Introduction to Their History* (Berkeley: University of California Press, 1971); Richard M. Morse, "The Heritage of Latin America," reprinted in Howard J. Wiarda, ed., *Politics and Social Change in Latin America: The Distinct Tradition* (Amherst: University of Massachusetts Press, 1974); Howard J. Wiarda, *Corporatism and National Development in Latin America* (Boulder, Colo.: Westview Press, 1981); Claudio Veliz, *The Centralist Tradition in Latin America* (Princeton, N.J.: Princeton University Press, 1980); and James M. Malloy, ed., *Authoritarianism and Corporatism in Latin America* (Pittsburgh: University of Pittsburgh Press, 1977).

On attitudes and relations between the OECD nations and the Third World countries, see Richard L. Jackson, *The Non-Aligned, the UN and the Superpowers* (New York: Praeger, 1983); Stephen D. Krasner, *Structural Conflict: The Third World Against Global Liberalism* (Berkeley: University of California Press, 1985); C. Rangeel, *Third World Ideology and Western Reality* (New Brunswick, N.J.: Transaction Books, 1985); Pascal Bruckner, *The Tears of the White Man: Compassion as Contempt* (New York: The Free Press, 1986); Kevin J. Middlebrook and Carlos Rico, *The United States and Latin America in the 1980s* (Pittsburgh: University of Pittsburgh Press, 1986); and Abraham F. Lowenthal, *Partners in Conflict: The United States and Latin America* (Baltimore: Johns Hopkins University Press, 1987).

CHAPTER VI

Recent analyses of the Soviet Union's problems and prospects include Marshall I. Goldman, *Gorbachev's Challenge: Economic Reform in the Age of High Technology* (New York: W. W. Norton, 1987); Seweryn Bialer, *The Soviet Paradox: External Expansion, Internal Decline* (New York: Knopf, 1986); Timothy J. Colton, *The Dilemma of Reform in the Soviet Union* (New York: Council on Foreign Relations, 1986); Alec Nove, *The Soviet Economic System* (Winchester, Mass.: Allen & Unwin, rev. ed. 1986); Abram Bergson and Herbert S. Levine, *The Soviet Economy: Toward the Year 2000* (Winchester, Mass.: Allen & Unwin, 1983); Horst Herlemann, ed., *Quality of Life in the Soviet Union* (Boulder, Colo.: Westview Press, 1987); Robert C. Tucker, *Political Culture and Leadership in Soviet Russia: From Lenin to Gorbachev* (Brighton: Wheatsheaf Books, 1987); and the periodic reports of the Joint Economic Committee of the U.S. Congress.

On the current problems and future prospects of the Soviet hegemony and its client states, see Sarah Meiklejohn Terry, ed., *Soviet Policy in Eastern Europe* (New Haven, Conn.: Yale University Press for the Council on Foreign Relations, 1984); David Holloway and Jane M. O. Sharp, eds., *The Warsaw Pact: Alliance in Transition?* (Ithaca, N.Y.: Cornell University Press, 1984); and Henry S. Rowen and Charles Wolf, Jr., eds., *The Future of the Soviet Empire* (San Francisco: Institute for Contemporary Studies Press, 1986). The foreign policies and likely future international behavior of the Soviet Union and its relations with the United States are appraised in Adam B. Ulam, *Dangerous Relations: The Soviet Union in World Politics, 1970–1982* (New York: Oxford University Press, 1983); Jonathan Steele, *Soviet Power: The Kremlin's Foreign Policy* (New York: Simon and Schuster, 1983); Edward N. Luttwak, *The Grand Strategy of the Soviet Union* (New York: St. Martin's Press, 1983); Raymond L. Garthoff, *Detente and Confrontation: American-Soviet Relations from Nixon to Reagan* (Washington, D.C.: Brookings, 1985); Zbigniew Brzezinski, *Game Plan: How to Conduct the U.S.-Soviet Contest* (Boston: Atlantic Monthly Press, 1986); Arnold J. Horelick, ed., *U.S.-Soviet Relations: The Next Phase* (Ithaca, N.Y.: Cornell University Press, 1987); and William G. Hyland, *Mortal Rivals: Superpower Relations from Nixon to Reagan* (New York: Random House, 1987); as well as the Bialer book cited in the preceding paragraph.

China's internal problems and prospects are analyzed in John King Fairbank, *The Great Chinese Revolution 1800–1985* (New York: Harper and Row, 1986); World Bank Country Economic Report, *China: Long-Term Development Issues and Options* (Baltimore: Johns Hopkins University Press, 1985); and A. Doak Barnett and Ralph N. Clough, eds., *Modernizing*

China: Post-Mao Reform and Development (Boulder, Colo.: Westview Press, 1986). China's foreign policy and likely future international behavior are appraised in Harry Harding, ed., *China's Foreign Relations in the 1980s* (New Haven, Conn.: Yale University Press, 1984); Robert G. Sutter, *Chinese Foreign Policy: Developments After Mao* (New York: Praeger, 1986); and along with those of other Pacific powers in Robert A. Scalapino, *Major Power Relations in Northeast Asia* (Washington, D.C.: University Press of America, 1987).

Statistical sources for this chapter include UN Statistical Yearbooks; CIA Handbooks of Economic Statistics; and Reports of the Joint Economic Committee of the U.S. Congress.

CHAPTERS VII AND VIII

Recent publications expressing a variety of views on the determinative economic trends and the policy options for coping with them include:

(1) *on OECD capabilities and policies,* Michael Stewart, *The Age of Interdependence: Economic Policy in a Shrinking World* (Boston: MIT Press, 1984); Robert Z. Lawrence, *Can America Compete?* (Washington, D.C.: Brookings, 1984); Stephen S. Cohen and John Zysman, *Manufacturing Matters: The Myth of the Post-Industrial Economy* (New York: Basic Books, 1987); and Andrew J. Pierre, ed., *A High Technology Gap? Europe, America and Japan* (New York: New York University Press for the Council on Foreign Relations, 1987); Paul R. Krugman, ed., *Strategic Trade Policy and the New International Economics* (Boston: MIT Press, 1987), and Paul R. Krugman and George N. Hatsopoulos, "The Problem of U.S. Competitiveness in Manufacturing," in *New England Economic Review* (Federal Reserve Bank of Boston), Jan.–Feb., 1987; and Bruce R. Scott and Paul W. Cherington, *U.S. Competitiveness in the World Economy: An Update* (Cambridge, Mass.: Harvard University Press, 1987);

(2) *on trade problems,* Miriam Camps and William Diebold, Jr., *The New Multilateralism: Can the World Trading System Be Saved?* (New York: Council on Foreign Relations, 1983); Robert E. Baldwin, *The Political Economy of U.S. Import Policy* (Boston: MIT Press, 1985); Raymond Vernon, "Old Rules and New Players: GATT in the World Trading System" in Samuel P. Huntington and Joseph S. Nye, eds., *Global Dilemmas* (Washington, D.C.: University Press of America, 1985); C. Michael Aho and Jonathan David Aronson, *Trade Talks: America Better Listen!* (New York: Council on Foreign Relations, 1985); Robert Z. Lawrence and Robert E. Litan, *Saving Free Trade: A Pragmatic Approach* (Washington,

D.C.: Brookings, 1986); Gary C. Hufbauer and Jeffrey J. Schott, *Trading for Growth: The Next Round of Trade Negotiations* (Washington, D.C.: Institute for International Economics, 1985); Gary C. Hufbauer and Howard F. Rosen, *Trade Policy for Troubled Industries* and *Domestic Adjustment and International Trade* (Washington, D.C.: Institute for International Economics, 1986); I. M. Destler, *American Trade Politics: System Under Stress* (Washington, D.C.: Institute for International Economics, 1986); and Raymond J. Waldmann, *Managed Trade: The New Competition Between Nations* (Cambridge, Mass.: Ballinger, 1986);

(3) *on financial and monetary problems,* Stephen Marris, *Deficits and the Dollar: The World Economy at Risk* (Washington, D.C.: Institute for International Economics, 1985); Miles Kahler, ed., *The Politics of International Debt* (Ithaca, N.Y.: Cornell University Press, 1986); Benjamin J. Cohen, *In Whose Interest? International Banking and American Foreign Policy* (New Haven, Conn.: Yale University Press for the Council on Foreign Relations, 1986); Adrian Hamilton, *The Financial Revolution* (New York: The Free Press, 1986); Susan Strange, *Casino Capitalism* (New York: Basil Blackwell, 1986); Theodore H. Moran et al., *Investing in Development: New Roles for Private Capital?* (New Brunswick, N.J.: Transaction Books for the Overseas Development Council, 1986); Harold Lever and Christopher Huhne, *Debt and Danger: The World Financial Crisis* (Boston: Atlantic Monthly Press, 1986); Peter Nunnenkamp, *The International Debt Crisis of the Third World: Causes and Consequences for the World Economy* (New York: St. Martin's Press, 1986); Gerald Corrigan, *The Longer View* (New York: Federal Reserve Bank, 1987); and Irving S. Friedman, *Toward World Prosperity: Reshaping the Global Money System* (Lexington, Mass.: Lexington Books, 1987).

Recent publications presenting differing views on the determinative political trends and policy options include Walter Laqueur and Robert Hunter, eds., *European Peace Movements and the Future of the Western Alliance* (New Brunswick, N.J.: Transaction Books, 1985); James E. Dougherty and Robert L. Pfaltzgraff, Jr., eds., *Shattering Europe's Defense Alliance: The Antinuclear Protest Movement and the Future of NATO* (Elmsford, N.Y.: Pergamon, 1985); Peter H. Langer, *Transatlantic Discord and NATO's Crisis of Cohesion* (Elmsford, N.Y.: Pergamon, 1986); Geoffrey Lee Williams and Alan Lee Williams, *The European Defense Initiative: Europe's Bid for Equality* (New York: St. Martin's Press, 1986); Stephen J. Flanagan and Fen Osler Hampson, eds., *Securing Europe's Future* (Dover, Mass.: Auburn House, 1986); and Melvyn Krauss, *How NATO Weakens the West* (New York: Simon and Schuster, 1986). On the problems and prospects of political relations between the OECD nations and the Third World countries, see the bibliography for Chapter V.

CHAPTERS IX AND X

A variety of views on the perplexities of U.S. foreign policy and the problems of maintaining world order are presented in Stanley Hoffmann, *Primacy or World Order: American Foreign Policy Since the Cold War* (New York: McGraw-Hill, 1978), *Duties Beyond Borders: On the Limits and Possibilities of Ethical International Politics* (Syracuse, N.Y.: Syracuse University Press, 1981), and *Janus and Minerva: Essays in the Theory and Practice of International Relations* (Boulder, Colo.: Westview Press, 1987); John Lewis Gaddis, *Strategies of Containment: A Critical Appraisal of Postwar National Security Policy* (New York: Oxford University Press, 1982); the papers in Samuel P. Huntington and Joseph S. Nye, eds., *Global Dilemmas* (cited), especially Stanley Hoffmann, "The Future of the International Political System: A Sketch"; and the bibliography for Chapter I. For a theoretical treatment of the problem of world order, see Hedley Bull, *The Anarchical Society: A Study of Order in World Politics* (New York: Columbia University Press, 1977) and *Justice in International Relations* (Waterloo, Ont.: University of Waterloo Press, 1983). See also articles in Robert J. Myers, ed., *Ethics and International Affairs* (New York: Carnegie Council on Ethics and International Affairs, 1987), the first volume of a projected annual publication.

Index